THE DOMINICANS

AND THE POPE

T0311262

MEDIEVAL
INSTITUTE

University of Notre Dame

The Conway Lectures in Medieval Studies

2002

The Medieval Institute gratefully acknowledges the generosity of Robert M. Conway and his support for the lecture series and publications resulting from it.

PREVIOUS TITLES IN THIS SERIES:

Paul Strohm
Politique: Languages of Statecraft between Chaucer and Shakespeare (2005)

The Dominicans and the Pope

Papal Teaching Authority in the Medieval and Early Modern Thomist Tradition

Ulrich Horst, O.P.

Translated by James D. Mixson

Foreword by Thomas Prügl

University of Notre Dame Press

Notre Dame, Indiana

Published in the United States of America

Library of Congress Cataloging in-Publication Data

Horst, Ulrich, 1931–
The Dominicans and the Pope : papal teaching authority in the medieval and early modern
Thomist tradition / Ulrich Horst ; translated by James D. Mixson ; foreword by Thomas Pügl.
p.   cm. — (The Conway lectures in medieval studies)
Includes bibliographical references and index.
ISBN-13: 978-0-268-03077-3 (pbk. : alk. paper)
ISBN-10: 0-268-03077-4 (pbk. : alk. paper)
1. Catholic Church—Teaching office.   2. Popes—Primacy.   3. Dominicans.
4. Thomas, Aquinas, Saint, 1225?–1274.   I. Title.
BX1746.H585   2006
262'.13--dc22

                    2006028850

Contents

Foreword

In 2002 the Medieval Institute at the University of Notre Dame established an annual lecture series honoring university trustee Robert M. Conway, a long-time supporter and generous sponsor of the Medieval Institute. The idea behind the Conway Lectures is to invite distinguished senior scholars from various disciplines within medieval studies to the Notre Dame campus for three lectures on successive days. The speakers are asked to talk about one important topic of their lifelong research in an accessible way to the wider audience of medieval scholars and friends of the Middle Ages, and then turn their lectures into a book. In the fall of 2002, Father Ulrich Horst, a Dominican theologian from Germany, started the series, which since its inception has included Professor Paul Strohm (English), Columbia University (2003); Professor Rosamond McKitterick (history), University of Cambridge (2004); and Professor Calvin Bower (music), University of Notre Dame (2005).[1]

An internationally renowned authority in historical theology, Fr. Ulrich Horst, O.P., has been a luminary in the Department of Theology at the University of Munich from his early days as a doctoral student there, through his return to Munich as a teacher in 1985, and continuing even after his retirement from his formal duties as a senior professor and research institute director in 1999. In Munich, Ulrich Horst directed the Grabmann Institute for the Study of Medieval Theology and Philosophy, a center founded in 1954 and located within the Department of Theology. He himself was a student there in the early 1960s, preparing for his doctorate in theology. After finishing his degree, he started his teaching career at the Dominican study house in Walberberg, a small place between Bonn and Cologne but well known in scholarly circles. Horst was offered his first university-level position in historical theology at the Pädagogische Hochschule in Bonn, where he taught until he returned to Munich to became director of the Grabmann Institute.

Fr. Horst's scholarship and his scholarly interests emerged from the theological tradition of his own religious order. The main focus for Dominicans since their origin has been the study of Scripture and sound theological formation. As followers in the path of Thomas Aquinas, their goal is to be readily equipped for preaching and individual pastoral care. Consequently, Fr. Horst's research topics are grouped around three subject areas: the church, the Dominicans, and Thomas Aquinas. Nonetheless, his scholarship has always been additionally inspired by questions of contemporary theology that he has tried to answer by providing the historical context of doctrinal development.

Fr. Horst's doctoral dissertation focused on Robert of Melun, an interesting figure in the theological landscape of the early twelfth century and a contemporary of Peter Abelard and Peter Lombard. Horst published two books on Robert which investigate, respectively, his doctrine of the Trinity and his idea of salvation history.[2]

After establishing himself as a medievalist, Fr. Horst turned to the other research area that would become his main field of expertise. In preparing for his Habilitation (an advanced degree required for a career at German and Austrian universities), he studied scores of primarily Dominican authors from the sixteenth and seventeenth centuries and their views on the church and the papacy. *Papst, Konzil, Unfehlbarkeit* (Pope, Council, Infallibility), the main title of the resulting publication, was a milestone for early modern theology; it established Horst's reputation as an authority on premodern and modern ecclesiology and as one of the most important scholars of the history of papal infallibility.[3] The major achievement of this book was, first of all, the discovery of a completely new set of theological sources: the numerous commentaries on Thomas Aquinas's *Summa Theologiae*, safely stored for centuries in manuscript libraries all over the world. Horst's research showed that there was a long tradition within the Dominican order of commenting on papal infallibility and the role of conciliar authority, which dated back to controversies on fifteenth-century conciliarism. Through his extended research in Spanish libraries, Fr. Horst also became a highly regarded scholar on the Iberian Peninsula, a region of which he became very fond over the years.

Papst, Konzil, Unfehlbarkeit was a breakthrough for a better understanding of the definition of papal infallibility at the First Vatican Council. This dogma was also the subject of Fr. Horst's next book, to which he gave the title *Unfehlbarkeit und Geschichte* (Infallibility and History) and which examined the teachings of certain Catholic theologians in the eighteenth and nineteenth centuries against Gallicanism.[4] It showed how, from the early nineteenth century on, a new and strong awareness of the role and the importance of the papacy for the church wiped out the dominating influence of Gallicanism and episcopalism present in most textbooks of ecclesiology in the seventeenth and eighteenth centuries. The last chapter of *Unfehlbarkeit und Geschichte* offers a comprehensive survey of the history of papal infallibility, starting with Thomas Aquinas, who provided the key texts and arguments for the development of that doctrine in the early modern period. *Unfehlbarkeit und Geschichte* enhanced Horst's reputation as one of the foremost experts on papal infallibility.

After accepting the chair of medieval theology at the University of Munich, Fr. Horst looked more closely into the medieval doctrines of the papal teaching office and the controversies about conciliarism in the late Middle Ages. Relying primarily on unprinted manuscript sources, he studied several Dominican authors and their writings against the conciliarism promoted by the Council of Basel, further confirming his thesis that fifteenth-century conciliarism has determined the course of Catholic ecclesiology in the modern period much more than the Protestant Reformation.[5] The Council of Basel also played a role in the interest Fr. Horst developed in the definition of the Immaculate Conception of the Blessed Virgin Mary. However, it was not so much the mariological as the methodological side of the dogma that attracted his attention. Besides observing that theologians of the Dominican order, following the teaching of Thomas Aquinas, had opposed this doctrine for centuries, Horst pointed out that the push for this dogma since the late Middle Ages and into the nineteenth century was motivated equally by political and by ecclesiological intentions.[6] The controversy also revealed a profound disagreement about the role of systematic versus positive theology among the parties involved.

In the 1990s, Horst embarked on a completely new area of research. Encouraged and prepared by courses and seminars he taught at the Grabmann Institute, he took a closer look at the controversies about mendicant poverty that erupted in the mid-thirteenth century between the new mendicant orders and the secular masters of the University of Paris. Starting with Thomas Aquinas, Fr. Horst first focused on the Angelic Doctor's understanding of mendicant poverty and his theology of the religious life.[7] He published a second book on the continuation of this controversy into the early fourteenth century, when the debate about "apostolic poverty" erupted and the Franciscan order clashed with Pope John XXII. Horst pointed out that the problem of mendicant or apostolic poverty carried serious ecclesiological implications that forced theologians to reconsider the teaching office and the authority of the pope.[8]

In recent years, Ulrich Horst has returned to work on sixteenth-century Spanish Dominicans. One important figure, the founder of the School of Salamanca, Francisco de Vitoria, caught his particular interest. For the translation of Vitoria's *Relectiones* into German, Horst provided an extended introduction on the life and works of this great theologian.[9] He situated Vitoria's writings and teachings within the historical developments of the time: the discovery of the Americas, the political situation in Spain, the need for church reform in the wake of the Fifth Lateran Council, and the religious upheaval in Germany. Vitoria's endeavor to reconcile the old foes of papalism and conciliarism, however, did not always meet with sympathy from his students, such as Domingo Bañez or Melchior Cano, who put a different emphasis in their teachings on church and papal magisterium.[10]

I do not want to conclude this short introduction to Fr. Horst's scholarship without mentioning his lifelong love and veneration for the theology of Thomas Aquinas. The numerous dissertations he has directed, the courses and seminars he has taught over fifteen years as director of the Grabmann Institute, and the major publications he has written on selected topics of Thomas's theology all testify to his high esteem for Thomas Aquinas. In 2001—just as he began his life as a retired professor—Fr. Horst published a book on the gifts of the Holy Spirit according to Thomas Aquinas.[11] Although he had been interested for a long time in Thomas's idea of the *instinctus spiritus sancti* (the "impulse" of the Holy Spirit), a formula which Thomas brought up in various contexts, including the case of papal magisterium, it appears to me that this became a very personal book for Fr. Horst. He was fascinated by the depth of Thomas's doctrine of the Holy Spirit, who, besides granting grace and virtues, stimulates people's lives by making their minds quick and agile. There could not be a better proof for such intellectual agility than the scholarly career of Fr. Ulrich Horst, who is restless in his intellectual curiosity and desire to learn about new texts and ideas. As a student and colleague of Fr. Horst in Munich, I had the privilege to benefit from his skills as teacher and scholar for years. Avoiding dogmatic narrowness, he has always encouraged his students to follow their scholarly instincts and to explore whatever captures their interests. Perhaps such an approach to the scholarly life, combined with a loyalty to the Catholic tradition, is not so far away from the gifts of the Holy Spirit.

I thank the University of Notre Dame Press and its director, Barbara Hanrahan, for support and fruitful cooperation on this and the other books coming out of the Conway Lectures. I also express my gratitude to Professor James D. Mixson of the University of Alabama, Tuscaloosa, who agreed to translate Fr. Horst's manuscript and who discussed its content with the author intensively. A final thank you is owed to Roberta Baranowski, assistant director of the Medieval Institute, who helped in many ways to make this publication happen.

Thomas Prügl
Acting Director of the Medieval Institute
11 November 2005

Introduction

The early Dominicans, who authored the first constitutions of their young order and whose theologians stood in a long monastic and intellectual tradition, soon modified and expanded that tradition in essential ways. This was true for ecclesiology as well, which the Dominicans made their own, and which they grounded above all in the theory of *plenitudo potestatis* developed by the canonists. Thomas Aquinas presupposed that theory in the controversies surrounding the role of the mendicants in the church, and he, together with the Franciscan Bonaventure, developed it in great detail in favor of the new orders. The application of this doctrine to pastoral care and teaching in the universities soon inspired sharp protest from the secular clergy, but the decisive intervention of the Apostolic See quieted their opposition relatively quickly—a sign that, in principle, not even the secular clergy disputed the fullness of the pope's power.

In his early work *Contra impugnantes*, Thomas's discussion of papal teaching authority is not truly original. But new accents begin to emerge from *Quodlibet* IX.16, where Thomas, in an allusion to the prophecy of the high priest Caiaphas

(John 11:50), seems to explore the idea of a *charisma veritatis* of the pope that guarantees the truth of his judgments. An *instinctus Spiritus Sancti,* argued Thomas, led the pope in matters of faith and guarded him from error. Was it an accident that this early argument no longer played a role in Thomas's later works?

A question often discussed is whether Thomas's *Contra errores Graecorum* also reveals a shift in ecclesiological course. That Thomas found confirmation in apocryphal citations of his teaching on papal primacy is true, but the fact that he later failed to mention those citations precisely where they would have been most useful to him suggests that he viewed them with skepticism, and indeed that in the end his ecclesiology did not need them. In any event, it can be said with certainty that these "Greek fathers" inspired no new model of papal teaching authority. Thomas is far more convinced that his view of papal primacy was grounded in the practice of the ancient councils, as he described in *De potentia* and as his great interest in synodal texts makes impressively clear. The writings of the canonists, for whom there was "no general council without the pope, [but surely] a pope without a general council,"[1] merely strengthened his position. Yet Thomas differed sharply with contemporary canonists in that, while decisively subordinating the bishops' synods to the pope, he nowhere raised the possibility of a conflict between pope and council. This was a possibility taken very seriously in contemporary canonistic literature, but for Thomas it seems not to have existed, even in theory. Nor did Thomas discuss the possibility of a heretical pope, with all of its implications. His silence here had serious consequences. Later theologians writing in the tradition of Thomas Aquinas drew from it the conclusion that by virtue of his apostolic plentitude of power, the pope could overrule any conciliar majority. Thomas surely must have known the intense discussions of his day about the possibility of conflict and heresy, but he ignored them. Was this accident or intention? Thomas's purpose was to stress that the pope had the last word in any controversy because his judgments required agreement "with unshakable faith" (*inconcussa fide*). Yet Thomas did not say whether or how such papal judgments might be bound by conditions—for example, concerning a necessary cooperation between the pope and the cardinals and theologians. May one conclude from this silence (*Summa Theologiae* II-II, article 10 of q. 1) that Thomas did not want to give or could not give a clear answer to such questions?

Surprisingly, in the decades after Thomas, the Dominican theologians neither took up nor commented on this article of the *Summa.* A Carmelite, Guido Terreni, was the first to do so. In their controversies with the Franciscans at the beginning of the fourteenth century, the Dominicans turned instead to canon law to refute arguments grounded in the bull *Exiit*. Essential conciliar elements are also to be found in the ecclesiology of John Torquemada, who made it a requirement of a binding final judgment that the pope cooperate with the College of Cardinals and with synods. Torquemada anchored the leadership and teaching of the church's highest authority in the *sedes apostolica*, which he regarded as much more than the occupant of that office alone. Among the Dominican theologians, Thomas de Vio Cajetan was the first to break with such ecclesiological principles. For him, the Apostolic See consisted of the pope alone and no one else. This marked a turning point in the Dominican order. Cajetan taught a strictly personal papal infallibility, one that admitted of no kind of limitation or condition.

Francisco de Vitoria, founder of the School of Salamanca, did not follow this quasi-official line, which his Master General outlined at the beginning of the sixteenth century. He developed instead a doctrine of the highest teaching authority that allowed for an essential cooperation of the pope with theologians and, in especially difficult situations, with councils. He also respected the universal jurisdiction of the Roman pope, although in certain cases he defended the superiority of councils in matters of faith. Vitoria's students, however, Melchior Cano above all, decidedly distanced themselves from this position, though Juan de la Peña remains a notable exception. Nevertheless, without exception these theologians strongly defended the idea that proper preparation was essential to any definition of faith, just as they considered papal heresy, with all of its consequences, a self-evident possibility.

It was the theologians of the Jesuit order who finally discarded these "relics" of a long tradition that had fused the authority and binding force of papal teaching with broader ecclesiological concerns. The intervention in the First Vatican Council of the Dominican cardinal Filippo Maria Guidi, who criticized a papal infallibility without certain conditions, was the last attempt to orient the discussion to the late medieval and early modern theologians of the cardinal's order. The rejection of his proposal by the majority of the fathers and pope Pius IX showed that a long and complex history of papal teaching authority had come definitely to an end.

In September 2002 I had the great honor of inaugurating the Conway lectures at the University of Notre Dame, and I am now delighted to publish them here. For the invitation to give the lectures and for the generous hospitality he extended to me, I sincerely thank Professor Thomas F. X. Noble, Robert M. Conway

Director of the Medieval Institute at the University of Notre Dame. I also thank
the Department of Theology at Notre Dame, as well as the community of the Congregation of the Holy Cross at Corby Hall. For the preparation and organization of
my visit to the beautiful campus at Notre Dame, I am indebted to Ms. Dianne
Phillips. In the library of the Medieval Institute, Ms. Marina Smyth was always
ready to assist me. James D. Mixson, now assistant professor of history at the University of Alabama, took on with patience and great knowledge of my subject
matter the task of preparing the final version of the lectures. I thank him also for
his many criticisms and insights, all of which have made for a clearer text. And
with Thomas Prügl of the University of Notre Dame, I have discussed the problems treated here across many years. To all of these colleagues I remain as grate-
ful as I am indebted. Finally, I feel obligated to express my special gratitude to
Rebecca DeBoer of the University of Notre Dame Press for her meticulous copy-
editing of my book.

ONE

Thomas Aquinas
on Papal Teaching Authority

THE CANONIZATION OF ST. THOMAS

The Dominican Petrus Guidonis tells us that soon after his election, Pope John XXII expressed to Berengar of Landora (Dominican Master General, 1312–17) his desire to canonize a Dominican in order to bring honor to the Order of the Preachers. The pope himself thought of Martin Donadieu of Carcassonne, about whom we know little today.[1] The Dominican's answer is as noteworthy as the pope's request. Berengar acknowledged that Martin's sanctity was beyond question. Nevertheless, the people of his region did not deserve the favor of his canonization.[2] Their veneration was insufficient, and they had rebelled against the Order of Preachers and the Inquisition.

But there remained compelling long-term strategic reasons for canonizing a Dominican from crisis-ridden southern France, especially in light of the imminent clashes with the Franciscan Spirituals of that region. Berengar thus directed the pope's attention to Thomas Aquinas, and it surely took little to convince John that canonizing Thomas could accomplish many things. The pope was, after all, intimately familiar with this theologian. Between 1316 and 1324 he had the works of Thomas Aquinas copied out in fourteen volumes, which he himself glossed.[3] The pope knew, moreover, that in Franciscan Spiritual circles Thomas was regarded as a figure symbolic of the fight against John Peter Olivi and his followers, and that the reference to the current controversies was self-evident. As William of Tocco attests, the order sought to be in accord with the stance of the pope and the curia in the controversy. In the twenty-first chapter of his *History of St. Thomas*, William represents Thomas as the theologian who refuted the erroneous teachings of the "brethren of the poor life" (*fraterculi de vita paupere*),[4] as well as the notion from Olivi's commentary on the *Apocalypse* that the pope was the leader of the "carnal church."[5] The pope and Thomas, as William saw it, were unified in the struggle against such heresies, past and present. Yet William did not concern himself merely with the problem of poverty in the narrow sense. Rather, he spoke in general terms of the theology of history that Joachim of Fiore had begun and that Olivi had propagated (though the latter is not mentioned by name). Clearly, the struggle with the Franciscan Spirituals was an important impetus for Thomas Aquinas's canonization. Thomas's role as leading theologian of the Order of Preachers was the genesis of the honor. But in light of the difficult challenges that stood before the pope and the Avignonese church, the Dominican conception of poverty and the theology of the evangelical counsels as Thomas had developed them offered themselves as welcome allies.

The canonization itself (July 18, 1323) yields notable if indirect evidence of John XXII's aims.[6] In a sermon in the apostolic palace preached on the occasion of the public consistory, the pope said Thomas had led an "apostolic life" in the Order of Preachers, a life whose qualities he described by saying that the brothers "had nothing of their own, even if they had, like the apostles, *some things in common*."[7] A crucial distinction had emerged—the Dominican order held property in the form of common ownership, while individual religious had nothing *in speciali*. The Preachers stood in succession to the apostles, who, so the pope's listeners were to conclude, similarly shared a common purse. With these sentiments, John had clearly drawn a firm line in the controversy with the Minorites.

It was the pope's intention to have Thomas's authority on his side. Even if from very early on—at least, when writing the second part of his *Summa*—Thomas was conscious of the profound differences between Bonaventure's conception of mendicant poverty and his own, he of course had no idea that his doctrine of the evangelical counsels would play such an important role half a century later. Since this doctrine is of great importance for understanding the later controversies, a brief survey of the arguments is necessary here.[8]

Perfection in the religious life (*perfectio*), Thomas argues, consists not essentially in poverty, but in following Christ (*in Christi sequela*). Like the two other vows, poverty is merely an instrument for reaching that perfection. And because it is only a means, it must conform to the end that it serves.[9] Also, because the orders have various aims—for example, contemplation, care for the sick, pastoral care, and preaching—the practice of poverty must therefore have different "gradations."[10] For the Order of Preachers, Thomas explains, this means a life as free as possible from the cares associated with property. Its members are to be "content with little."[11] A further conclusion, one we have already heard in the sermon of John XXII on the occasion of Thomas Aquinas's canonization, concerns whether common property diminished religious perfection: common property, Aquinas argues, is for every order, from the monastery to the mendicant convent. It is the roof, so to speak, under which all are to live, however graduated their various observances.[12]

Noteworthy here is that Thomas does not mention the ideal of poverty among the Franciscans, who wanted to abandon even common property. For a Franciscan reader of the *Summa Theologiae* this must have been a provocative omission. Among all of the possible forms of poverty practiced by the various orders, the Franciscan conception apparently had no place. True, Thomas does not say why he did not mention it. Did it have, in his eyes, no theological foundation? More important for Thomas, in any case, especially in light of later controversies, was the Christological foundation. For Thomas, Christ taught "common ownership" (*habere in communi*) because he shared with his apostles a "purse" (*loculi*) of money.[13] Christ's example thus legitimated the enjoyment of money among the orders. The Franciscans must have felt that this, too, was a sharp provocation.

CONTRA IMPUGNANTES DEI CULTUM ET RELIGIONEM

These considerations make clear the stakes of the canonization of Thomas in 1322, but in raising them we have anticipated future developments. No conflict existed as yet between competing Dominican and Franciscan conceptions of poverty. In 1256, Bonaventure and Thomas had fought shoulder to shoulder defending the mendicant orders against the secular masters of the University of

Paris. Yet despite their common ground they differed on important points. To see these, we must turn to Thomas as a young professor in Paris. The fact that the conflict between the mendicants and the *magistri* of the University of Paris was essentially a controversy about the rights of the papal primate needs no emphasis—this we know from a famous article of Yves Congar.[14] The clergy and the bishops of France reacted, as far as their traditional rights were concerned, with greater sensitivity than in other parts of the church against the interference, real or imagined, from the pope and his representatives, the friars.[15] At the heart of the conflict in 1256, when Thomas published his work *Contra impugnantes Dei cultum et religionem*,[16] was his response to the tract *De periculis novissimorum temporum* (published at Easter, 1256) of William of Saint-Amour, spokesman of the university masters.[17] William's argument, in brief, was that within the structure of the early and high medieval church there was no place for monks with ambitions for pastoral care, and even less for monks seeking teaching positions at the university.[18] As an old expression put it, the monk's task was to grieve, not to teach or to preach (*monachi non est docendi* [*et praedicandi*], *sed plangentis officium*).[19] Yet the Dominicans and the Minorites were becoming recognized preachers, and they were now poised both to take over chairs at the university and to attract students in droves.[20]

That the mendicants' sucesses inspired growing disgust and envy in secular clergy such as William of Saint-Amour explains much, but not all, of their hostility. There were also serious jurisdictional issues. Parishes and dioceses had boundaries within which priests carried out their pastoral duties. The new orders, by contrast, were associations of those not bound permanently to one place, as monks were traditionally believed to be.[21] The mendicants made their living neither from landed property, nor foundations, nor manual work, but from "begging," that is to say, from the money and the gifts they were given in return for preaching and hearing confessions.[22] The secular clergy thus perceived the mendicants as outsiders and intruders, unwelcome guests whose novel ways unsettled traditional life in the towns and the universities.[23]

Thomas answered such attacks with a variety of arguments.[24] Most need not be surveyed here. It suffices to note their general thrust: the new orders were especially well suited to carry out pastoral activities.[25] But one argument is particularly worthy of mention, because it is closely related to an idea we will soon discuss: that because they are obliged to practice meditation, professed religious in general—and not merely mendicants—are particularly suited to teaching.[26] Moreover, for Thomas the task of teaching is especially enjoined upon those who observe poverty, for it assists in gaining "knowledge of Scripture."[27] It was thus sensible, he argued, that orders be established to devote themselves to that task.

I will concentrate more fully here, however, on Thomas's attempts to ensure mendicant preaching and teaching a legitimate place in the structure of the church, because it is here that arguments about the pope and his jurisdiction come fully into play.

No representatives of the secular clergy, of course, denied the authority of the pope. The doctrine of the "fullness of power" (*plenitudo potestatis*) was a well-established one and not an invention of the friars.[28] In his confrontation with Thomas of York, even the Parisian master Gerard of Abbeville regarded the pope as the summit and culmination of the church hierarchy.[29] The Parisian professors, however, were not willing to accept the consequences this position entailed. Thomas argued that if the welfare of the church so required, the pope, who bore responsibility for the whole church, could confirm new orders to preach and carry out pastoral duties along with the bishops and parish priests. The pope had the right, moreover, to entrust those orders with missions that encompassed whole territories and even encompassed pastoral care within dioceses, all without consulting the bishops.

Against this view, others raised primarily these objections: It was against the intention of the Apostle Paul that the pope should give license to these "foreign preachers"—the new orders—to preach before the "foreign" faithful—those who did not belong to the flock of the mendicant preachers. Here the rights of the pope met their limits.[30] For him to make laws that stood in contradiction to doctrine and the apostles was to abuse his office and to teach error.[31] And for him to concede license for pastoral care to a new order was to destroy the traditional structures of the church.

How did Thomas answer such arguments? Although the pope could not alter divine law (*ius divinum*), Thomas responded, he could alter positive law (*ius positivum*)—the laws that provincial and universal synods had passed over time. This was especially true if the laws promoted the common good of the church (*utilitas ecclesiae*).[32] Just as the papal legates could preach without hindrance in all those places to which they are sent, so could the mendicants. They, too, were messengers of the Holy See.[33] What the mendicants could not do by their own right, they could do by virtue of papal order and commission.[34]

Mendicant teaching, too, had a particular significance. The Dominican order from its beginnings, of course, had made study a prerequisite for preaching and pastoral care. St. Dominic himself had emphasized the close relationship between study and preaching, while the oldest Dominican constitutions stated that no convent could be established "without a doctor."[35] A good example of St. Dominic's emphasis on the close relationship between study and preaching is that he sent the first friars to Paris and Bologna.[36] Two of them soon succeeded in winning chairs at the University of Paris (Roland of Cremona and Hugh of St. Cher), a right the secular clergy disputed until Alexander IV intervened in the mendicants' favor with the bull *Quasi lignum vitae* (April 14, 1255).[37] The Parisian professors' attempt to limit the jurisdiction of the pope by forbidding the mendicants to engage in academic pursuits thus had important consequences, in Thomas's eyes, for the highest teaching authority in the church.

The Parisian masters knew that the universities owed a great deal to the papacy, and that the popes had supported the foundation and development of the universities by granting them privileges.[38] Gregory IX had granted a very important and much-coveted privilege to the university of Toulouse in 1233 by stating that any *magister* who graduated from there had the right to teach *in qualibet facultate et ubique*—the origin of the famous *licentia ubique docendi*.[39] Yet the Parisian professors were reluctant to give mendicants—and religious in general—teaching positions in the university. Even papal authority could not compel them to yield, they argued, since according to civil law every corporation is grounded in its own rights and free to choose its members without the interference of outside parties.[40]

For Thomas, this was a rejection of papal authority. The regulation of study, he writes in the *Contra impugnantes*, lies with the one who bears the responsibility for the whole, and this can be no other than the pope, who as universal pastor is endowed with the appropriate rights and obligations. Moreover, because of the close relationship between jurisdiction and teaching authority, the Parisian professors were guilty of heresy if they excluded the mendicants from the teaching chairs. For according to canon law, the pope enjoyed an authority in matters of doctrine because the Roman church is the "mother of faith."[41] The Roman church and the pope within her are the guarantees of proper belief. Christ gave the church this privilege "so that all would obey her like Christ."[42] The practical consequence was that the University of Paris could not exclude the mendicants from its teaching positions.

To ground this line of argument, Thomas quoted a significant, if problematic, patristic text, a citation of Pseudo-Cyrill (though Thomas could not have known it was of dubious origin). The text can be reduced to a few essential points: we remain in unity with the Apostolic See only when we ask this Apostolic Throne what we must believe and observe; it alone can give orders, bind, and loose; and all bow their heads to it and obey its commands as those of Christ himself.[43] Thomas did not discuss the exact meaning of the phrase "to ask in Rome about the faith," but he considered the quotation alone sufficient to silence the opponents. Noteworthy here is the variation in terminology. Thomas speaks alternately of the "Roman church" and the "Apostolic Throne," without distinguishing between the "seat" (*sedes*) and the "office-holder" (*sedens*). And, tellingly for future developments, he nowhere discusses precisely how the highest teaching authority expresses itself, or under what conditions. The first practical consequence of this argument was that the University of Paris could not exclude the mendicants from holding teaching chairs.[44]

THOMAS AND BONAVENTURE

Before we continue our analysis of Thomas's works, it might be helpful to compare his arguments with those of his contemporary, Bonaventure. We have mentioned already that they shared an intention to defend the mendicants. Yet owing to the divergent histories of their respective orders, the two friars also had remarkable differences. In *Contra impugnantes* Thomas mentioned neither St. Dominic, nor his canonization, nor the approbation of his order or any detail, and he mentioned St. Dominic together with St. Francis only once in one of his sermons—and there, only in passing.[45] The historical events surrounding the foundation of his own order seem to have been of no importance for Thomas's ecclesiological ideas. Thomas sought instead to generalize the problem facing him and to find solutions that would be applicable not only to the mendicants but to all orders.[46]

Bonaventure's enthusiasm for Francis stands in striking contrast to Thomas's silence on Dominic. St. Francis, for Bonaventure and his theology, had a meaning that went far beyond the mendicant controversies.[47] Unlike Thomas, Bonaventure, as General Minister, had to take positions on difficult and ongoing controversies within his order.[48] He therefore had to present St. Francis as an ideal that could secure the unity of an order whose members had sharply divided opinions on crucial points. A special opportunity to do so came from the

General Chapter of Narbonne (1260), which commissioned Bonaventure to compose an official biography of St. Francis in order to put an end to the contradictory interpretations of his life and work. The result of the commission was the *Legenda maior sancti Francisci*.[49] The General Chapter of Paris (1263) approved the text and demanded its exclusive use in the order. All other versions of Francis's life then in circulation were to be destroyed in order to stave off any possible dissent.[50]

What St. Francis and the papal approval of his order meant to Bonaventure became clear in the first pronouncements in defense of the mendicants on the occasion of the disputation *De perfectione evangelica* of 1256–57. The argumentation here differs strongly from *Contra impugnantes*. To the objection that the church could approve no form of life based on begging, Bonaventure answers that the Apostolic See has confirmed the orders of the Minorites and Preachers.[51] The special poor form of life is included in the approval of the *Rule* of St. Francis by Honorius III (1223), and it enjoys the same legitimacy as the *Rule* itself.[52] Moreover, since it is clear that the universal church accepts both orders, were the pope to have erred in his approval, this would have dire consequences. But it would be "most horrible and most unbelievable" that God would have allowed "all of his holy people" and "so many wise men" to fall into error.[53] In light of these facts, who would dare presume to judge the Apostolic See, which is subject only to the judgment of God?[54]

From this line of argument two ideas emerge: The pope is, in certain articulations of his teaching authority, free from error. But the church is also free from error if it accepts the decision. The leading role in any case falls to the pope, whom the church must follow—though it also seems that the church's acceptance gives the ultimate judgment greater certainty. The result of Bonaventure's argument is clear. The approval of the two mendicant orders is not one mere legal act among others, but an act of supreme teaching authority not subject to revision. The Franciscan way of life is irrevocable and can never be changed.[55]

For Thomas, too, there is a close connection between the mission of the mendicants and papal teaching authority, although it was much looser than for Bonaventure. Thomas did not say a word about the confirmation of the Dominican way of life, the *Rule* of St. Augustine, or the conception of poverty, for the simple reason that the friars never asked for papal approbation of their constitutions. As the Dominicans understood themselves, they were a self-governing corporation who approved their way of life and their constitutions independently.

They thereby spared themselves serious conflicts, both with the papacy and within their own ranks.

Even more significant for Bonaventure's view of the Franciscan order is a text from his *Apologia pauperum*, which he wrote in 1269 in the second phase of the mendicant controversy. Why, he asked, did St. Francis warn so intensely against the handling of money?[56] The answer was that true holiness not only guarded against but also actively shunned any possible occasion of committing sin. In the mouth of a saint, such words were far more than pious advice. For Bonaventure, they were spoken by the *imitator praecipuus Christi*, a man who was not simply one among others but a unique imitator of Christ, the only person in history to bear the *stigmata* of our Lord, and thus one with a unique authority among all saints and a special position in the church. For Bonaventure, Francis's sanctity and privileges had no parallel in the history of the monastic orders. He therefore concluded that all who argued that the founder of the Franciscan order had erred attacked not only an exemplary saint but the whole church. Indeed, he put it in even stronger language—this was blasphemy against Christ, the "the master of truth" (*magister veritatis*), as well as blasphemy against the doctrine and life of his apostles.[57]

In making such claims, the gift of the stigmata was obviously of greatest theological importance for Bonaventure. The gift was not only a personal privilege of St. Francis, but also a sign that the highest authority legitimated the *Rule* of the order and its special form of life, to such an extent that any opposition to the *Rule* was an attack against Christ, the giver of the gift of the stigmata.[58] The order thus enjoyed the blessings of the highest authority.

Bonaventure also passionately invoked the Roman church as the defender of truth and of morals. If one ascribed an error to the Franciscan order, he argued, one also ascribed error to the church, which had confirmed Francis's rule. The church itself, heretofore upheld, like Christ, as the "master of truth," would thereby be accused of having left the path of truth.[59]

The arguments in the *Apologia* were carefully chosen, the language highly emotional. For Bonaventure the controversy about poverty was not one issue among others. It was an attack against his order and against a Roman church that had not only recognized but fully identified with the Franciscans. St. Francis was to be worshiped as a saint, the *imitator praecipuus* who surpassed all others in the imitation of our Lord. And his work lived on in his order, which was to be revered as the most authentic embodiment of the poverty of Christ and his apostles. Thus, those who disputed the essential rights granted to the order of-fended against the gospel that had found its purest realization in St. Francis's *Rule*, and against the Roman church. By canonizing Francis and approving his *Rule*, the Roman church agreed to protect and guarantee the inviolability of the Franciscan way of life—and should the Roman church renounce that protec-tion and guarantee, it would commit a grave dogmatic error and lose its authority forever.

These were strong words, unique in the history of the monastic orders. Never before had an order claimed such things for itself. For Bonaventure, the Franciscan order and the Roman church had become intertwined in a way that neither could escape. It was a view that would make Bonaventure a key figure in the subsequent conflicts. His contemporaries may have seen his arguments as hardly more than pious rhetoric, but these arguments needed only to be intensi-fied by Ockham and others in days to come, as factions within the order recovered Bonaventure's program to confront new papal decisions.

QUODLIBET IX.16

A digression through another sector of the Parisian battlefield both pro-vides a better understanding of Thomas Aquinas's ideas of the papal teaching office and prepares the way for our next discusion. In a *quodlibet* (IX.16) disputed shortly after *Contra impugnantes* (Christmas, 1257), Thomas addressed the ques-tion "whether all saints canonized by the church are in heaven, or whether some are in hell."[60] Since at that time canonization belonged firmly to the privileges of the pope, the question had a direct bearing on papal teaching authority.[61] At issue was how a judgment could have absolute certainty if it was based on human testimony obtained from witnesses and therefore potentially subject to error. Thomas answered that although the pope as a private person could err, the sol-emn pronouncement of a candidate's sanctity enjoyed certainty because the Holy Spirit guided the church in such matters and preserved it from error.[62] Thomas did not speak of the church merely in general terms (*ecclesia universalis*), how-ever. For him the church was represented in the person of the pope, whose pro-nouncement was therefore to be respected more than the opinion of learned theologians.[63] Thomas demonstrated this through a revealing comparison. Just as Caiaphas—despite his wickedness—unwittingly prophesied in his capacity as high priest (*pontifex*) that Christ would die for the people (John 11:51), so on the occasion of a canonization the pope pronounces his sentence in this same prophetic spirit.[64]

In other words, when judging as pope, the pope enjoys a *charisma veritatis*, a kind of inspiration to speak the truth. Here is an idea that is of obvious and great importance in tracing the history of papal teaching authority—yet strangely enough, Thomas never repeated it again.

Confronted with the particular problem that canonization depends on the testimony of potentially fallible witnesses, Thomas concludes that we can have no absolute certainty but rather only moral certainty concerning the process (*pie credendum est*), a moral certainty derived from miracles and the inspiration of the Holy Spirit (*per instinctum Spiritus Sancti*).[65] And yet again, though the *instinctus* through which God urges mankind to right action plays an important role in Thomas's theology, he never again mentions it in reference to the teaching authority of the pope.[66]

CATENA AUREA

The "Golden Chain" (*Catena aurea*) is a commentary on the four Gospels composed almost exclusively of quotations of Greek and Latin church fathers strung together like a chain. Thomas composed the work in Orvieto on the request of Urban IV and finished it before 1264.[67] The work lacks originality, but it thrust Thomas into an inspiring confrontation with the patristic texts from which the *Catena* was drawn. Relevant to our discussion are his interpretations of Matthew 16 and Luke 22:32.[68] Here we again come across a quotation from Pseudo-Cyrill. In the negotiations about the union with the Greek church held at the papal court in Orvieto, this quotation was a text with a special resonance. According to the Lord's prophecy, it said, the gates of hell would not prevail against the church; the "apostolic church of Peter" (*ecclesia apostolica Petri*) remained free from deception and seduction by heresy; the church always remained in full faith and in the authority of the first of the apostles; it stood above all bishops and primates; though other churches were to feel ashamed because of their errors, the church of Peter alone remained unshaken and firm; it imposed silence on heretics; and it has at all times been an example of truth and loyalty to the apostolic tradition.[69]

Only one thing need be said of these claims: the text from Pseudo-Cyrill does not speak directly of a personal privilege of truth given to St. Peter's successor. Christ's prophecy refers to the church of St. Peter, not explicitly to the holder of the office. Moreover, the distinction, often used by the canonists, between the *sedes*, the see, and the *episcopus Romanus*, the Roman pontiff, should not be overemphasized. Though we will come across it at a later time, it plays no role in Thomas's works.

Luke 22:32 was even more important than Matthew 16 for the papal teaching authority in the Middle Ages. It speaks of Satan's temptation of Peter, who succumbed when he denied our Lord (Luke 22:55–62). Peter's faith was weak, when the devil "sifted him as wheat," but the Lord promised him that he would pray for him "so that his faith would not fail." A converted Peter would then strengthen his brethren. After his denial, some time then passed in which Peter's faith failed. Consequently, he was no longer a "rock." Like numerous theologians before and after him, Albert the Great had understood the text in the sense that Peter professed the true faith only "toward the end" (*finaliter*). So, Christ's prayer preserved him neither absolutely nor always from error, but only "toward the end," after a certain period of weakness and faltering.[70]

Yet nowhere did Thomas draw such a conclusion. He never mentioned the possibility of a papal heresy. But he, too, conceded that Peter had yielded to Satan's temptation. Using the words of the Byzantine theologian Theophylactus († 1125), Thomas wrote that even if Christ allowed Peter to be "sifted for a short while," he still held the "hidden seed of faith." Peter denied the Lord, but after some time (*aliquando*) he was converted, and he strengthened his brethren. Together with his Lord he thus remains the strength and the rock of the church.[71]

CONTRA ERRORES GRAECORUM

In the *Catena aurea* papal teaching authority is treated only indirectly, through quotations from the church fathers. Thomas employed this same method in another work, one that attracted far more attention even in contemporary ecclesiological disputes. This was the *Contra errores Graecorum*, which Thomas composed in 1263–64, also in Orvieto, where pope Urban IV and the curia had their residence.[72] Requested amid discussions between the Greek and Latin churches over certain controversial questions, *Against the Errors of the Greeks* is an expert opinion on a collection of quotations from Greek church fathers. Pope Urban IV asked Aquinas to examine this collection, perhaps because the curia already had doubts about its origins. (Today we know that large parts of the collection are forgeries that do not represent the Greek theological tradition. This is especially true for the ecclesiological texts.) Thomas had no principal doubts about the authenticity of the texts, although in the prologue he apparently has some reservations, and others seem to have dawned on him later.

To Pseudo-Cyrill can now be added another quotation from a letter of Maximus: "Everywhere in the world catholics look up to the Roman Church as to the sun and to receive from it the light of the catholic and apostolic faith."[73] It goes without saying that a Latin theologian who knew the deep rift between East and West would have been just as delighted about this sentence as about that of Pseudo-Cyrill paraphrased above. Here was patristic confirmation of the primacy of the Roman church. Yet what does it mean that Thomas and so many other theologians, down to the First Vatican Council and beyond, fell into the trap of forgery concerning papal authority? Does that mean that the Thomas's edifice of thought on papal primacy and teaching authority was built on sand? Franz H. Reusch and Ignaz Döllinger, experts in their day on medieval forgeries, were convinced of this, and Hans Küng uncritically adopted their views.[74] We have now become more cautious with such judgments, however, especially thanks to Horst Fuhrmann's research on the forgeries of Isidorus Mercator.[75]

No scholar now pretends that the decretals of Pseudo-Isidore changed the constitution of the church. The Middle Ages rarely invented through forgery a new reality, new facts, and new rights. Medieval forgers looked instead for documents or quotations of renowned authors that clothed already existing rights or facts with written authority, thus inventing not so much the right or fact as simply a written record.

Analogously, we have to ponder the conclusions and consequences arising from the forgeries with which Thomas found himself confronted here, and on which he had to comment. The Greek texts did not inspire him to write about the papal teaching authority, still less to invent it. He was familiar with it through a long-held tradition. The fact that even a Greek church father was also a witness of that tradition proved in his eyes a great help for the discussions concerning the union with the Greeks. Let me also add one note: it is most probable that Thomas soon harbored doubts about the authenticity of these texts, because he never quoted them again, not even in instances where they might have served his purpose very well—and yet he never saw a reason to alter his doctrine.

THE *LECTURA* ON THE GOSPEL OF ST. MATTHEW

In this context, Thomas's *Lectura* on the Gospel of St. Matthew, a classroom lecture from Thomas's second stay in Paris, offers some interesting details.[76] Here Thomas no longer quoted Pseudo-Cyrill, but rather attended directly to the Latin-Greek controversies. He argued that although heresies existed in other churches—Constantinople was the typical example—through the centuries the Church of Rome alone had kept its faith whole. In it, Christ's prayer (Luke 22:32) is fulfilled, and from it the true faith has spread to the entire Western church. Yet here there is an important additional claim: that the faith remained whole was due not only to the Roman church, but also to the faith of St. Peter.[77]

SUMMA THEOLOGIAE II-II, Q. 1, ART. 10

The culmination and the conclusion of our survey of St. Thomas on papal teaching authority is the famous article 10 of the first question of the *Secunda Secundae*. It became the *locus classicus* for the dogmatic treatise *De Romano pontifice et de conciliis* from the sixteenth century on.[78] The article addresses the question: Who has the right to promulgate a new creed? Since in order to set aside heretical errors it is necessary from time to time to promulgate a new creed (*symbolum*), Thomas argues, the content of any controversial article of faith must be explicated, and it is the task of a general council to formulate the creed anew.[79] Thomas intentionally says "in a council" (*in concilio*), not "by a council" (*a concilio*), to make clear that it is not a council alone that decides, but a council in concert with the pope. Here he certainly had in mind the Fourth Lateran Council. This was the greatest congregation of bishops in the Middle Ages,[80] and for Thomas and his contemporaries it had been the model of a general council. It had passed the creed *Firmiter*, on which Thomas commented (after 1261) in his short exposition *Super primam decretalem*, together with a short commentary on *Damnamus*.[81]

After emphasizing the role of councils in the *sed contra* of article 10, Thomas, astonishingly, never again mentions the importance of councils. How are we to explain this? The fact is surprising indeed, because we know that Thomas was the first medieval theologian highly interested in the texts of the classical councils—especially Chalcedon, of which he made abundant use.[82] But why does he not take the role of councils into consideration here? Perhaps a passage from *De potentia* provides an explanation. There, the question at issue was why the church introduced the *filioque* into the creed, although the councils of Nicea and Chalcedon had forbidden all further revisions. Thomas answered this objection with the argument that although in the creed of Nicea the Catholic faith had been handed down in a sufficent form, later heresies had made further explication necessary.[83] The procession of the Holy Spirit from the Son is contained implicitly in the creed of Constantinople. But as errors began to circulate, it was fitting that the *filioque* be formulated explicitly in a creed. From these historical facts Thomas draws a general conclusion: just as a later synod has the authority to interpret an earlier one, so the Roman pontiff also has the power to make such an interpretation, since he alone can call a council and confirm its decrees. All of this is clear, as Thomas says, from the acts of the Council of Chalcedon.[84] Thomas is convinced that his teaching of the primacy of St. Peter rests on this council. The theology is therefore not dependent on the forgeries of the *Liber de fide trinitatis* or other dubious texts. It was without doubt that the pope had the rights and powers in question, such that councils were not absolutely necessary—for as Thomas pointed out, it was sometimes (*quandoque*) impossible (in the case of a war, for example) for the fathers to come together in a given place. In such a situation, the pope can and must make decisions alone in order to protect the church from error. He thus fulfills a function that under normal circumstances a council would fill.[85]

Let us now turn to the details of Thomas's argumentation in the *Summa*. Thomas argues that the promulgation of a new *symbolum* belongs to a general council, but the right to convoke a council lies with the pope alone. The implication here is that he who summons a synod also has the authority to confirm its decrees.[86] The precise relationship between council and pope is not conceived as a problem, however. There is no hint of any rivalry, and Thomas never mentions any potential for tension and conflict between pope and council.[87] The responsibility of promulgating a new formulation of the creed lies with the person who is empowered to determine matters of faith *finaliter*.[88]

It is noteworthy to point out that in order to describe the papal *magisterium*, Thomas uses the scholastic terminology that was common in disputations at the university, where a *magister* proposed a thesis to be discussed and a *baccalaureus* had to argue in favor of the thesis while an *opponens* tried to refute it. During the first stage of the disputation, when the assistants and doctoral students collected arguments and counterarguments, the *magister* did not interfere. Only on the following day did the *magister* play an active role, by giving a final answer (*determinat magistraliter*) and summarizing the arguments *pro* and *contra* in his *determinatio*.[89]

Which elements from the scholastic disputation are to be applied to the papal *determinatio* of our issue? Must it be preceded by a disputation among the theologians?[90] Besides the terminology, Thomas gives no further explanation. Decades and centuries later, Thomist theologians would say that discussions with cardinals and theologians are an indispensable condition for a definition. The master put an end to the disputation, but that did not mean that the answer had to be final. The subject could be reconsidered at another occasion. The pope's *determinatio*, in contrast, had to be accepted with "unshakable faith" (*inconcussa fide*). That expression, found in a text of the Council of Chalcedon and quoted already by Thomas in *De potentia*, is quite strong, admitting of neither divergence nor contradiction.[91] Nowhere did Thomas use a more unambiguous expression—one that resonated with the words of the Council of Chalcedon itself—to characterize papal teaching authority.

What are the subjects to be brought before the pope for his *determinatio*? According to Gratian's *Decretum*, the so-called *maiores causae*, "the more important and more difficult questions," were to be brought before the Apostolic See, especially all controversies concerning the faith.[92] Luke 22:32 ("I have prayed for you that your faith shall not fail . . .") offers the biblical justification, in which Christ promised to Peter that he would pray for him to be able to strengthen his brethren.[93] Only in this way could the unity of faith and the unity of the church be guaranteed. Just as the sentence of a supreme court is universally binding, the *sententia* of the pope must be observed and upheld by all. There is no possibility of further appeal to the higher authority of a council.

Two matters reveal an important shift of emphasis here. Thomas takes Christ's prayer (Luke 22:32) to have been directed at Peter, and thereby diverges sharply from the interpretation that influential canonists had given the passage. Huguccio, for example, said that Christ had prayed for Peter *in figura ecclesiae*.[94] More commonly, this had been interpreted as a prayer addressed through Peter to all Christ's followers for final perseverance in the faith.[95] All of the canonists and many later theologians, in any case, taught of the possibility that a pope could fall into heresy. Notably, however, Thomas (along with Bonaventure) never mentions such a possibility. There is no need to emphasize that this would have serious consequences for the doctrine of papal teaching authority.[96]

Finally, it should be noted that Thomas never used the term *infallibilis, infallibilitas* with regard to the person of the pope or his judgments. That term was reserved for characterizing the certainty of Scripture and the rule of faith (*regula fidei*). Nor did he say anywhere that the pope could not err (*papa non potest errare*).[97] Thomas spoke not of a pope who could not err, but of a church—and he did so frequently. The term *inconcussa fide*, which describes the disposition by which the church has to comply with the *determinatio summi pontificis*, is the sole equivalent for Thomas—and at the same time the most important one—to the papal privilege expressed in the formula *papa non potest errare*.

—We have come to the end of our consideration of Thomas's view of papal teaching authority. Complicated arguments and difficult solutions arise from the very nature of this subject, one in which so many historical and theological problems converge. Why did Thomas leave so many questions unanswered? The reason is simple: our questions and categories were not his own. Nevertheless, the answers he did give considerably influenced later discussions. This leads to a final question, which will receive some clarification in the following chapters. Is Thomas a direct witness to, or an immediate forerunner of, the dogma of infallibility? At the First Vatican Council the minds of the bishops were divided.[98] As we shall see, even among the Thomists the journey to that council made its way not along a straight path, but along a very winding road.

TWO

The Medieval Thomist Discussion

THE ROAD TO CONFLICT UNDER POPE JOHN XXII

The ideal of poverty among the early Franciscans provides perhaps the most famous example of a theme central to the religious history of the High Middle Ages: that of charismatic personalities who attracted more and more followers to their religious ideals, and the communities that emerged to face the inevitable difficulties of institutionalization. Francis's simple message of poverty almost immediately inspired a whole set of difficult institutional questions: What counts as "poverty" in a given circumstance? Where is the line between poverty and wealth? Who owns the buildings and churches of the Franciscan order? Can a Franciscan be considered poor while dwelling with a privileged community in a sumptuous convent? Already in the thirteenth century, commentaries on the *Rule* of St. Francis appeared in which these questions of poverty and institutions played a central role.[1]

Yet the leaders of the Franciscan order found themselves incapable of re-
solving those questions in a way that could satisfy all who had a stake in the answers. Their only recourse, therefore, was to turn to the pope for a decision. It was
a recourse which St. Francis's last will had strictly prohibited. In his *Testament*
Francis had forbidden his brethren to ask for any "letter" from the Roman curia
out of fear that this might require modifications of their observance of poverty.
For the same reason, Francis insisted on a literal observance of his rule and prohibited any comment or interpretation.[2] Yet a rapidly expanding order, under-
standably, could not maintain such prohibitions without compromise. Prompted
by the General Chapter, the Franciscan General Minister thus turned to Pope
Gregory IX, requesting that he interpret the *Rule* (*pro interpretatione regulae*).[3] The
General Minister's request, quite apart from the pope's response, was of great
significance. The order had made the pope its judge and the guarantor of the
proper interpretation of the *Rule*. But the pope's response was of equal significance. According to a foundational principle of canon law, "an equal has no jurisdiction over an equal" (*par in parem non habet imperium*). Hence not even the
founder of an order could bind his successor to observe the founder's rulings.
The pope thus decreed in the bull *Quo elongati* of September 28, 1230, that St.
Francis's *Testament* had no legal force.[4] Gregory then declared that the friars
were allowed to own neither individual nor common property, but that they were
allowed to "use" the objects placed at their disposal.[5] The decision found broad
acceptance among the Minorites.

But the pope had avoided the thorny question of ownership, and it soon became clear that his decision would not be the last. Papal intervention was soon
necessary again because the Franciscan superiors were unable to settle the dissension. In the bull *Ordinem vestrum*, Pope Innocent IV decreed in 1245 that ownership (*proprietas, dominium*) of all Franciscan property was to be passed to the
pope and the Holy See.[6] The Friars were to retain only the "use" (*usus*) of goods.
Setting aside the question of whether this was a legal fiction, it is clear that from
this moment on the Franciscans considered legitimate their claim to be the only
order to observe the highest degree of poverty (*altissima paupertas*) in relation to
the Dominicans, Augustinians, and Carmelites, who owned common property
(*proprietas communis*), and whom the Franciscans deemed to be in a lesser state of
perfection.[7]

Without question, *Ordinem vestrum* was a turning point. From that moment,
the papacy began a close relationship with the Franciscans and their ideology, a

relationship that had no parallel in church history. The bull's solution seemed to offer advantages to both sides, but it also sowed the seeds of new conflicts. Should the papacy one day abandon its alliance with the order, a fierce theological debate would be unavoidable. Another of Innocent IV's bulls, *Quanto studiosus* of 1254, offered a foretaste of just such conflicts. The bull, which gave the Franciscan order greater freedom in financial matters,[8] met with great resistance. The General Chapters of Metz (1254) and Narbonne (1260)—whose acts Bonaventure approved as General Minister—claimed that the order could make no use of the privilege, and that Innocent IV's declaration indeed was to be suspended.[9]

A dilemma had emerged that would haunt the Franciscan order from then on. On the one hand, when it found itself in situations that it could not manage on its own, the order sought the help of the papacy. Yet should the highest authority of the church not be prepared to affirm their particular vision of the order, certain groups stood ready to voice their opposition. Those who know the story will already have noticed that behind these tensions over details of observance, profound ecclesiological questions awaited answers.

Bonaventure was the key figure in the elaboration of the theoretical foundations for "highest poverty."[10] Among the many components of his theological program, I want to recall only one argument which would later have considerable impact: that Christ only had the "simple use" of things and lacked any legal ownership. This, for Bonaventure, was the way of life of the apostles,[11] whom he saw, consequently, as the "first Franciscans." Though bolstered with series of citations from patristic texts that gave it the appearance of a commonly accepted tradition, this was a new approach to the problem of evangelical poverty. Bonaventure rejected the argument, introduced by Thomas Aquinas, among others, that Judas was the "bursar" of the apostles (John 12:6; 13:29), and that Jesus therefore did not live in "highest poverty" but had even disposed of money. According to Bonaventure, Jesus for various reasons had only tolerated the existence of a "money box," both because he wanted to give comfort to the weak who could not renounce money entirely, and because he wanted to rebuke those heretics who considered money intrinsically evil. The "money box," moreover, was intended as a warning for the greedy, who were to consider that the man who administered the money was the traitor Judas. And lastly, Christ wanted to give an example to other non-Franciscan orders, that they should renounce personal goods. In sum, Christ's "money box" was both a concession to and an expression of compassion for the weak, but it was in no way a diminution of absolute apostolic poverty.[12]

Bonaventure's arguments imply that the Franciscan order is unique, because its members alone observe poverty as Christ and the apostles had. The Franciscans therefore have, according to Bonaventure, a privileged position in the church that cannot be revoked. And as a consequence, any who would attempt to deny them that privileged position would offend against the gospel and the Roman church.

As long as Bonaventure's arguments remained theological and ascetical, they were harmless. But the situation soon changed, and the arguments became the cause of controversy both within and beyond the Franciscan order. In the years after Bonaventure's death the Franciscans became sharply conscious that their conception of poverty diverged fundamentally from that of the Dominicans. John Pecham at first argued that the two orders observed the highest form of poverty equally, but he then had to admit that on this point Thomas Aquinas was of a different opinion.[13] It appears that the doctrinal rivalries between the Preachers and the Minorites first broke out in England—as Pecham's *Tractatus contra Culvardem* suggests. The interpretation of Judas's "money box" plays an important role in the polemic. The conclusion that Pecham draws from Robert Kilwardby's theses is interesting: the preachers are not mendicants; rather, they are much more like a monastic order.[14] And it is especially worthy of note that only a few years after Thomas Aquinas's death, Peter John Olivi in his commentary on the Gospel of Matthew (1279–80) recognized this crucial issue and launched a polemic against Thomas.[15]

The Franciscan criticisms of Thomas, as articulated in William de la Mare's *Correctorium Fratris Thome*, led to a long controversy between the two orders. An important consequence of the struggle was the gradual emergence of two theological schools that squared off with increasing intellectual animosity. Already in 1282 the Franciscan General Chapter had decreed that Thomas Aquinas's *Summa Theologiae* could be read only by experienced professors.[16] The tensions between the two orders in Provence was so great that the Dominican Master General John of Vercelli and the Franciscan General Minister Hieronimus of Ascoli saw the need to compose a letter together to call their followers to peace.[17]

Under the pressure of both internal opposition and external enemies, the Franciscan order once again found itself in the position of having to seek the support of the Apostolic See. The General Minister Bonagrazia went to the pope requesting that he make a final, universally valid decision in matters of poverty, one that eliminated the possibility of any further objection or ambiguity.[18] After thorough consultation, Pope Nicholas III, a friend of the order, issued the bull

Exiit qui seminat on August 14, 1279. The document adopted some of Bonaventure's central arguments and combined them with the practical solutions that were indispensable in large cities driven by all manner of financial transactions.[19] The pope again confirmed that the order had transferred ownership of all of its property to the Apostolic See. The bull established further that Christ had abandoned both common and individual property, and that he had taught the apostles this way of life, the "money box" notwithstanding.[20]

The form of the bull was as striking as its doctrine. Because the pope wanted the document to be an authoritative statement whose binding force could not be violated, and because he wanted to protect it from controversial debate, he allowed only a grammatical explanation of its text. Any interpretation or use of glosses in the schools was prohibited.[21] Nicholas III considered *Exiit* a final settlement of all disputes about Franciscan poverty, but he reasoned that any future doubts would be resolved by the popes.[22] The numerous threats of sanctions at the end of the text are a clear indication that not even the Roman curia was fully convinced that *Exiit* would prevent future controversies. As the immediate reactions show, outside the mendicant orders the bull found little acceptance, and theologians did not regard it as an irreversible decision. Franciscan theologians, however, thenceforth attributed great dogmatic import to the document.

The controversies that soon arose within the Franciscan order are of little interest in this context, and in any case they have recently received magisterial treatment in the hands of David Burr.[23] Our concern here is with those witnesses from southern France who have a direct relevance to our theme. Bernard Gui reports, for example, that radical Franciscans in the territory where he was inquisitor defended the thesis that their order represented the most perfect estate in the church and not the bishops, as was the universal teaching.[24] They also argued that the pope could not change the *Rule* of St. Francis, since the gospel and the *Rule* were in a certain sense identical.[25] And they taught that in their day the true church and the faith of Christ existed only in certain circles of Beguines—a view that is witnessed in various formulations among the Spirituals. These groups considered Thomas Aquinas the primary opponent of the strict Franciscan position.[26] Especially interesting is a comment that Prous Boneta made in 1325 before the Inquisition in Carcassonne. In her eyes, because he had spiritually murdered his brother Olivi, Thomas was compared to Cain.[27]

These circles of Spirituals in Southern France based their views on the bull *Exiit*, which they understood as the irrevocable and unchangeable teaching of the church. This claim and other heretical doctrines made Pope John XXII

suspicious—he was an experienced jurist, and he quickly realized their ecclesiological implications.[28] In order to examine the extent of the authority of *Exiit*
it was necessary, however, to lift the bull's strict ban prohibiting discussion and
commentary concerning its text. This was accomplished by the bull *Quia nonnumquam* in 1322, which freed theologians and canonists to interpret the document according to commonly accepted rules.[29] The bull declared that the pope, as
legislator, is obliged to revise his laws and those of his predecessors, if necessary,
or to suspend them in order to respond to new circumstances.[30] John's intention
was clear: on some decisive points, the authority of *Exiit* had to be limited.

The Franciscans realized the implications of John's intention, and they reacted fiercely. To open *Exiit* to discussion and competing interpretations was
to endanger the order's exceptional status. The General Chapter at Perugia in
1322 therefore aired a public letter of protest addressed to the whole Christian
world and warning against a papal decision that, in the Franciscan view, put
even the gospel at risk. The letter's central argument was that the sentence "Christ
owned no property" was not heretical. On the contrary, it was an expression of
Catholic faith, because the church has declared it to be so in *Exiit*. Consequently
the heretics were not the Franciscans, but rather the pope who was about to offend against the doctrine of his predecessor.[31] The central point was this: what
the pope had defined in *Exiit* was not reversible, because it had become part of
the faith of the church.

Hidden in a doctrine of poverty that had at first glance seemed so harmlessly
pious was an explosive question of faith and authority, which has justifiably captured the attention of historians down to our own day.

After Pope John acted, events moved quickly. In December 1322 he published the bull *Ad conditorem canonum*, by which he returned to the Franciscan order full ownership of all of its goods.[32] With this act, the Franciscans' claim
that they alone lived without ownership was rendered invalid. From that moment
on, the Minorites were no poorer than the Dominicans, the Augustinians, or the
Carmelites. Meanwhile, the pope carefully prepared a final, decisive step. He commanded theologians of all parties in the dispute to compose position papers on
the issue. Among the Dominicans, the notable responses were those of Hervaeus
Natalis and Durandus de S. Porciano,[33] and on the Franciscan side, the tract of
Bonagratia of Bergamo.[34] In a consistory (January 14, 1323), Bonagratia also had
occasion to present a hidden appeal to the Roman church in a *libellus* (a formal
statement or petition), but John XXII immediately rejected it.[35]

Relying on the teachings of Thomas Aquinas (who in the midst of all the arguments was canonized on July 18, 1323) and on the authority of his consultation with theologians, John next published on November 12, 1323, the bull *Cum inter nonnullos.*[36] This decree asserted that though there were deep divisions among scholastic theologians about apostolic poverty, the dispute was now to be ended once and for all. Scripture taught in many places that Christ and the apostles not only had possessed "certain things" (*nonnulla*), but also had the right to give away and to sell things. Therefore, the thesis that Christ and the apostles did not own anything, either as individuals or as a community, was now to be judged as "erroneous and heretical."[37]

The Minorites reacted to this decision with every means at their disposal. Not without historical irony, an order that had wanted to live in the greatest humility, renouncing any right to ownership, now sought an alliance with the powerful Emperor Lewis of Bavaria, who was eager to use the Franciscans as propagandists in his struggles with the pope. An important result of their alliance was the *Appeal of Sachsenhausen* (1324)—or more precisely, the Franciscan "insertion" (*excursus*) in the *Appeal* that astonishingly mounted political arguments against papal teaching authority. The relevant passage reads as follows:

> What the Roman Pontiffs have once defined in faith and morals through the key of knowledge is immutable, because the Roman church is unerring. . . . what is once defined through the key of knowledge by the supreme pontiffs, the vicars of God, to be the truth of faith cannot be called into doubt by any successor, nor can the contrary to what is defined be affirmed without the one doing this being manifestly judged a heretic. . . . what is once defined in faith and morals is true for all eternity and unchangeable by anyone. It is otherwise in things that are established with the key of power. For often what is fitting to do at one time, it is fitting to prohibit at another time.[38]

It has not been possible to identify the author or authors of this *excursus*, though Brian Tierney thought it to have been Bonagratia of Bergamo.[39] All that is for certain is that the *excursus* cites texts from Olivi's *Question on Evangelical Perfection* (q. 8).[40]

The *Sachsenhausen Appeal* is of great significance, and its text has rightly been judged an important step in the development of the doctrine of papal infallibility. It allowed John XXII to be declared a heretic and allowed the Minorites to reclaim their privileged position in the observance of poverty. The intention of the document is relatively easy to discern. Since *Ad conditorem canonum* it had been clear that John wanted to revise certain passages of the bull *Exiit.* This was possible, in his opinion, because the document was of a merely disciplinary and not a dogmatic nature. The Franciscans therefore had to show that the decisions in *Exiit* directly concerned the beliefs of the church. But because (as all conceded) an individual pope could be declared a heretic, it was also necessary to prove that in this case there had been continuity in the doctrine under discussion, and that many popes had shared the same teaching—hence the tract's insistence that "what the Roman Pontiffs have once defined in faith and morals . . . is immutable, because the Roman church is unerring."

Two aspects of this passage are important. First, it speaks not of a single pope but of many, implying that a series of popes have taught successively, consistently, and therefore irrevocably about the same issue. The document does not use the singular (*per Romanum pontificem*), even though it concerns the decision of a single pope, Nicholas III in *Exiit.* Rather, the author of the *Sachsenhausen Appeal* uses the plural (*per Romanos pontifices*) to argue that the irrevocability of *Exiit* rests not on Nicholas III alone, but on a tradition sanctioned by its reception among the pope's successors. John's bull *Cum inter nonnullos* was scandalous precisely for this reason, because it implied a break with the tradition of the Roman church.[41]

The *Declaratio* of the General Chapter of Perugia (1322) asserted that this was a matter not of the judgment of an individual pope, but of a tradition approved by the Roman church. *Exiit*, these Franciscans argued, had been taken up into church law, approved through the decretal *Exivi de paradiso* of the Council of Vienne, and renewed yet again in John XXII's bull *Quorundam exigit.*[42] From these successive approvals it followed that what made a judgment irrevocable was not an individual pope, but an overall pattern of reception. This meant, further, that in the case of a conflict with the head of the church over doctrine, the solution of the dissent is to be sought in an even higher authority, the Roman church as guarantor of tradition. The church alone is the ultimate arbiter in matters of faith. There could thus be no question at all of infallibility in the sense of a personal privilege of the pope.

—From the poverty controversies in the Franciscan order we turn now to the Dominican theologians. The Dominicans produced a relatively small number of treatises on the problem of poverty, compared to those composed by the Minorites.[43] But several works are of particular importance in the history of the dispute. Both the treatise *De paupertate Christi et apostolorum* (1322) by the Dominican Master General Hervaeus Natalis and the report of Durandus de S. Porciano dealt with papal teaching authority indirectly.[44] In these works Hervaeus Natalis and Durandus treated problems regarding Christ's poverty and, in general, the juridical meaning of property, but not the ecclesiological issues in which I am most interested here. More important in our context are an earlier work of Hervaeus Natalis, *De potestate papae*, and the treatises *Quaestio de paupertate* of John of Naples and *De paupertate Christi et apostolorum* of Peter de Palude. Though it has been hardly noticed in recent research, this last work (1329) offers, in a certain sense, a review of the discussion.

HERVAEUS NATALIS

Before the outbreak of crisis, Hervaeus Natalis had articulated in his *De potestate papae* (1317–18) representative Dominican arguments that would provide important material for later discussions.[45] Hervaeus's question was this: How should the church handle differing opinions on difficult questions of faith and doctrine? He reasoned that she might seek the answer either by rational inquiry and arguments that have no binding force, or by authoritative and binding decree.[46] The authority to issue a binding decree, however, lies solely and absolutely with the pope, who has such authority because the church must have a leader to make decisions whenever doubts arise in matters of faith. Only this can guarantee the unity of the church.[47] Yet the pope is also an individual (*persona particularis*) who can sin and err—if his actions follow from personal convictions, for example, or if he acts from his own impetus (*proprio motu agens*). Obviously the distinction between the pope as a "private" and a "public" person is therefore crucial. A legendary example illustrates the distinction: at a synod, Pope Leo (confused in some sources with pope Liberius) consented to the Arian heresy as a private person, until bishop Hilarius opposed him and finally unmasked him as a heretic. Hervaeus Natalis concludes that if the pope seeks advice and assistance from the universal church, according to God's will he cannot err, and it is impossible that the church would accept any erroneous decision as truth.[48]

Yet although Hervaeus argued that a pope's dogmatic determination is binding only if certain conditions are fulfilled, he did not specify how the pope was to seek advice, or from whom, or what was to count as "assistance" from the universal church. Is a council the appropriate means? Hervaeus does not say. Nevertheless, the formula he used was to have a noteworthy fate: St. Antoninus of Florence quoted it in his *Summa Theologiae*,[49] and from this monumental work the idea was in turn recovered by a minority of theologians and bishops at the First Vatican Council, who used it as an argument in their favor.[50]

JOHN OF NAPLES

During these critical years, John of Naples was at the papal court in Avignon to promote the canonization of Thomas Aquinas. His *Quaestio de paupertate* therefore merits careful attention as a witness to the poverty controversy in its papal context.[51] He cites the text of the *Sachsenhausen Appeal* concerning papal teaching authority and the Minorites' accusation that in revoking *Exiit*, John XXII had become a heretic. How does John of Naples answer that charge? He raises the possibility that the binding character of *Exiit* had merely been suspended, and that the decree therefore had had no authority during its suspension, even if the matter itself had not been decided. John did not pursue this line of argument, however, and in his eyes this was clearly no solution. Far more penetrating for him was the argument that in reality there was no opposition between *Exiit* and *Cum inter nonnullos*, and that the Franciscan assertion of a contradiction between two popes was therefore a fiction.[52] John does not directly address the question of why John XXII suspended the bull *Exiit* in the bull *Quia nonnumquam*, and he does not discuss the deep dissension the pope had clearly faced. He simply discerns for himself a continuity in the teaching of the two decrees and concludes that they could be reconciled.

John formulates this position with a notable qualification, however: his view, he notes, is merely more "fitting" and "reasonable" than the position, taken by certain theologians, that one or the other bull is heretical. Under this cautious qualification, for John the two bulls have the same dogmatic authority—with the result that the dispute between the Franciscans and the pope has no theological foundation. And the fact that John did not pronounce definitively on the matter makes it clear that he anticipated opposition.

Finally, on the question, known to us since Thomas Aquinas, of whether the pope can err with regard to canonization, John of Naples answered in a *quodli-*

bet with a distinction: if one sees the pope and the cardinals as "private" persons, they can indeed err. In light of divine providence as embodied in the pope's official function, however, one must believe that the pope (with the cardinals) cannot err.[53]

PETER DE PALUDE

The most important Dominican contribution to our subject comes from Peter de Palude. He, too, had taken up a position on the problem of the teaching authority of the pope well before the outbreak of the poverty controversy, on the occasion of the conflict between the mendicants and the secular clergy.[54] In 1304 Benedict XI had published the constitution *Inter cunctas*, in which he returned to the mendicants the privileges concerning the pulpit and the confessional that Boniface VIII's *Super cathedram* had taken from them in 1300.[55] In the bull *Dudum*, Benedict's successor Clement V then pressed for a return to *Super cathedram*.[56] But Clement wanted theologians to have thoroughly discussed his constitution before its approval by the Council of Vienne. Because the pope died before those discussions took place, it remained uncertain whether the document was binding. Especially controversial was the question whether someone who had confessed to a friar should repeat that confession to his pastor. Peter de Palude denied this.[57] Although Peter did not think of it, the most simple thing to do would have been to declare *Inter cunctas* irrevocable, as the author of the *Sachsenhausen Appeal* and other Franciscans would do later for *Exiit*. Instead, Peter found the solution in the distinction between a doctrine of belief—which is unchangeable and in which the Roman church could never err—and disciplinary precepts adaptable to circumstance.[58] The rule of faith is the Roman church, and the pope cannot err as long as he relies, as Benedict XI did with *Inter cunctas*, on the "counsel of all his brothers," that is, the College of Cardinals.[59] But even this is valid only with the important qualification that the last court of appeal is not the pope and the Roman church, but a council.[60]

The result of our overview of the Dominican teaching up to this point is notable in several ways. In the years that were of such great importance for the refinement of papal teaching authority, leading Dominicans and canonists had articulated a theory that bound the judgments of the pope to certain conditions, thereby foreclosing the possibility of personal infallibility. It is also interesting that the famous article of the *Summa Theologiae* of Thomas Aquinas (II-II, q. 1, art. 10) played no role in the first decades of the fourteenth century. Finally, the example of John of Naples shows that there was a plurality of opinions within the Dominican order.

How did Peter de Palude respond to the Minorites' view that *Exiit* was an irrevocable document that contained an article of faith? He gave the answer in his treatise *De paupertate Christi et apostolorum*, written in the first months of 1329.[61] A variety of solutions presented themselves in the eyes of Peter. It was possible, for instance, that the bull contained nothing false, if one interpreted it properly. But even if there were errors to be found in it, that did not mean the church had taught error. In this case she would have tolerated the error with patience but would not have approved it. Soon, however, the situation changed because the church accepted the decisions of the present pope after long discussions and consultations.[62] The interpretation of the prayer of Christ for Peter (Luke 22:32) is interesting in this context. The words were directed not to the person of Peter, who had erred, but to the universal church, who is instructed in the truth through the Holy Spirit. The Roman church also remains in truth, which is embodied not only in a pope who might "for a certain time" fall into error, but in the head of the church together with the cardinals and prelates.[63]

As these and the following texts show, Peter de Palude represents the classical teaching of the canonists, who placed the highest teaching authority in the College of Cardinals of the Roman church together with the pope, thus giving it the broadest possible base. This alone guaranteed the security all desired. In the case of papal error, the council is the final authority. If the pope remains obstinate, cardinals and bishops can advocate the calling of a synod.[64]

Next, Peter summarized his reflections and applied them to contemporary controversies. In the case of Franciscan poverty, it had never been established that a pope working with both cardinals and prelates had decreed anything that contradicted the teaching of the church. For it would then follow that the Roman church had, "for a certain time," fallen into error.[65] Moreover, it is not only possible, but in several cases historically witnessed, that individual popes had erred, though their errors were private and were not to be ascribed to the Roman church.[66] The distinction between an official and a private function proved helpful in light of *Exiit*, because this bull had been issued at the private initiative of Nicholas III. The cardinals and the curia were not involved in its promulgation. The constitutions of John XXII, however, were quite another matter. These were issued with the consent of all, including professors of canon law and theology.[67]

This cooperation between pope and prelates guaranteed continuity of teaching, and their concord is the condition of infallibility. In Peter's eyes, teaching authority conceived as cooperation between pope and prelates was the best answer to the Franciscan attack, because it was bound up with conditions that one could test. Moreover, apart from this, it rested on a broad foundation and made reaching a consensus much easier. It grew out of principles that Peter had already articulated in his *Quodlibet* of 1314 and in his *Tractatus de potestate pape*.[68]

It is also notable that Peter ignored Thomas Aquinas's arguments concerning the teaching office of the pope, although he surely knew them. How can this be explained? Should one assume that the problem of a heretical pope made it impossible for Peter to answer in the spirit of *Summa Theologiae* II-II, q. 1, art. 10? As we have seen, Thomas said nothing about the possibility of a heretical pope and therefore had no need to provide a solution for the resulting difficulties. It was otherwise with the canonists and the Dominicans in the fourteenth century. For them, it was firmly established that in the course of its history the Roman church had remained free from error, although individual popes had not, and that only the alliance of Roman church and pope guaranteed dogmatic security. Nevertheless, problems remained even for Peter de Palude, such that he allowed for a council as the last court of appeal in extreme situations. Finally, who was to say in difficult cases whether the pope had in fact made a decision "with the counsel of the brothers"? This could always be disputed. Clearly, even in this conception of cooperative authority there was no absolute certainty.

Guido Terreni

Just when the conditions established among the Dominican theologians seemed to allow no way out of their dilemma—for them, the lack of absolute certainty—the Carmelite Guido Terreni, who was at the papal court in Avignon at the time the problems were under discussion, made a radical new suggestion.[69] Guido, too, allowed for the possibility of a heretical pope. But he was convinced that God would never allow a pope to assert heresy definitively, because the error would remain a private matter that would not be expressed in public form.[70] God's care for the church, and the prayer of Christ that the "prayer of Peter on the Apostolic chair" would not waver, remained as guarantees.

Guido illustrated his case with biblical examples: just as God prevented the "bad prophet" Balaam from deserting the people He had blessed (Numbers 22),

He would never allow a pope to teach a heresy.[71] God might prevent this in various ways. He might allow the pope to die before the final determination, or he might instruct him through inspiration to decide rightly, though against his original intention. Another example is Caiaphas—an especially compelling one with a long exegetical tradition that is also cited by Aquinas—who prophesied in his capacity as high priest. Although he was inwardly evil, by virtue of his office Caiaphas predicted that Christ would die for the people.[72] Applied to the pope, this meant that, like the biblical authors, he was inspired such that in his official capacity he could never err.[73] When did a pope make a determination as pope and not as a private person? An exact terminology, such as would later be captured in the concept *ex cathedra*, was not yet to hand. But Guido was precise in the matter: the pope must have the intention to determine a truth that concerned all of the faithful and the entire church.[74] This is the only criterion. Such inspiration rendered superfluous—although it did not exclude—the cooperation of cardinals, the Roman curia, and the theologians.

With this line of reasoning Guido Terreni had turned the discussion in a fundamentally new direction, leaving behind him the last remnants of the ecclesiology of the canonists. As far as we are able to tell, this was also the first time a theologian invoked Thomas Aquinas both in subject matter and terminology, even though the Carmelite's *Quaestio* is not simply a commentary on Thomas's article (*STh* II-II, q. 1, art. 10), but rather the product of a broader discussion. Yet Thomas's arguments, though original and well suited to be a weapon in the hands of the papal party, exerted influence neither on his contemporaries nor on the coming generation. Article 10 was a text whose hour would come only much later. The Dominican theologians of our period shared different traditions and views, and among these Thomas's arguments, especially those of the *Summa*, seem strikingly to have played no role at all.

JOHN TORQUEMADA

In the last part of this survey, I want to turn our attention to one of the most important and influential Dominicans of the late Middle Ages, Cardinal John Torquemada, who died in 1468. His *Summa de Ecclesia*, completed in 1453, became the most important manual of ecclesiology until the Council of Trent, and generations of theologians who came after him drew arguments and citations from that work.[75] He was without doubt one of the leading protagonists of the papal primacy of jurisdiction, though the oft-repeated assertion that he was also a resolute supporter of papal infallibility has no justification.

Torquemada was quite familiar with the teaching of papal primacy as Thomas Aquinas had elaborated it. Unlike the Dominicans before him, he both knew and cited all of the relevant texts. For Julian Cesarini, president of the Council of Basel, he pulled together a collection of 73 *sententiae* from Thomas's works.[76] He was, moreover, an excellent canonist, trained at Paris, who had authored an exposition on Gratian's *Decretum*.

The first articulation of papal teaching authority relevant for our purposes is found in a speech that Torquemada delivered before a diet in Mainz in early 1439.[77] He wanted to convince the princes that the translation of the council from Basel to Ferrara and from Ferrara to Florence had been legitimate. To ground his argument he referred to the fact that the "apostolic throne" is in truth so established that its judgment in matters of faith could not be in error. It is therefore fitting that this "seat," which through divine providence has become teacher of the faith and leader of all churches, has in matters of faith been blessed by God with the gift of infallible judgment.[78] The fact that Torquemada here uses the concept of *infallibilitas*, which in the Middle Ages was reserved for God or Holy Scripture, may be surprising, and it has given the impression that this was a discussion of the personal infallibility of the pope. One must not, however, overlook the fact that in this passage, as elsewhere, Torquemada speaks of a privilege of the "Apostolic See," and not simply of the highest pontiff. A careful attention to the terminology recalls the old distinction between the "See" (*sedes*) and the "occupant of the See" (*sedens*). In the Apostolic See alone is the faith preserved "unscathed" in the course of time. The "See" is more than the individual pope.[79] The fact that there have been a few popes who have fallen into heresy compels Torquemada to make a distinction that, as we already know, has important implications. The privilege of making judgments in matters of faith is not proper to the pope but to his office, and it is articulated in a public judgment that the pope makes "on the Roman seat," that is, in his official function.[80] What precisely was the difference between a private and an official decision is not discussed, but it was presumed to be known. Doubtless presumed as well were the conditions that a pope would have to meet before issuing his judgment. Such a definition, according to what has been said, must come from the heart of the Roman church.

Torquemada's understanding of the highest teaching authority was complex, and there is grave danger in reading it through a modern lens. This is made all too clear given the question of what should happen in the case of a dissension between the cardinals and the pope. Torquemada answers with a distinction. If a point of controversy has already been decided by the Apostolic See, one must stand firm on the side of the pope, whatever the objections of the bishops and cardinals. If the issue has not yet been decided, however, this is reversed: one is then instead obligated (*magis regulariter*) to follow the judgment of the bishops and cardinals. In support of his view Torquemada invokes a gloss of canon law, in which it is said that in matters of belief the pope must consult a council. In these cases the judgment of the bishops rather than the pope must be followed, even in matters of faith. Here Torquemada cites the rule that "the synod carries more weight than the pope," at least in terms of its discretionary judgment.[81] Nonetheless, Torquemada argues, in order to avoid a schism the two parties should issue a decision in harmony. And even if it is generally dangerous "to leave our faith to the discretion (*arbitrium*) of one single person" (the pope), one should not forget that occasionally one man, and in particular the pope, is able to judge a subject better than all the bishops. One must in this case follow the individual, whether it be simply one person (*unus homo*) or the pope—and according to a long tradition, there was a good example of just such a possibility: between Christ's death and the resurrection it was the Virgin Mary alone who preserved the faith, since the apostles and even St. Peter himself had lost theirs.[82]

According to Torquemada, it is clear that in principle both councils and popes, as individuals, are open to the possibility of error, and that they have in fact erred. The criterion of truth cannot therefore rest with them. The decision of a council has authority only when it has been approved through the Apostolic See, which as the *Tribunal Christi* has the privilege of not erring in matters of faith. The Apostolic See (as opposed to a few of its individual popes) has never strayed from right belief and has always stayed on the path of truth.[83] The promise made in Christ's prayer to the followers of Peter (Luke 22:32), Torquemada stresses anew, is not valid for every pope as an individual person, but rather is addressed to the See and its office.[84] "See" and *cathedra* alone are the constant forces that guarantee that the church will remain in truth.[85]

Finally, Torquemada also addresses the question of who constitutes the "seat," that is, the Roman church. His answer, more familiar to him than to us, is that it is, the faithful of Rome together with their shepherds.[86] The judgment of the Roman church expresses itself in a decree of the pope, which he advances in his capacity as pontiff. What is the criterion for such an official act in the name of the See? A series of conditions must be met so that the pope can make a true judgment that binds the entire church. The judgment must not be made by the pope alone, without consultation. And it is not enough for the pope simply to consult theologians who are favorites at the papal court. Put positively, the pope must seek the counsel of wise men, among whom the cardinals have an important place. In fact, it should be noted that Torquemada is one of the few theologians to view the College of Cardinals as a divine institution.[87] As the highest representative of the Roman church, the pope is free from error in his judgments only when he meets these criteria.[88] Agreement with theologians and cardinals as it emerges from the necessary consultations is the sole guarantee of dogmatic certainty. Precisely how and whence the church knows that the pope has prepared a judgment according to this definition, however, is not discussed—and as we will see, this would be a problem for later generations. Torquemada clearly did not pose such a question for himself. For him, the public character of the discussions and consultations leading up to the definition was sufficient.

Also worthy of mention is Torquemada's view that if the pope is guilty of heresy, he is automatically deposed. His "decision" would then be his private opinion, not a decree of the Apostolic See.[89] A council or the College of Cardinals would merely have the job of declaring (without causing) the deposition. Because of the difficulties inherent in such a solution, however, his contemporaries did not follow Torquemada on this point.[90]

As we have seen, Torquemada did not succeed in developing a coherent, unambiguous doctrine of papal teaching authority. But in my view he never had any intention of even attempting such a synthesis, because from his studies and from his participation at councils Torquemada knew, like no other, the many historical and substantive difficulties of the issues before him. Historians have often minimized the inconsistencies in Torquemada's *Summa de Ecclesia* in an attempt to make him a classical representative, if not a pivotal figure, of papal infallibility. Yet it is without question that for Torquemada, the Roman See had never deviated from the path of truth. Later, in the discussions in the sixteenth and seventeenth centuries, the close relationship between pope and Roman church was to lose its importance. As we will see, this also had consequences for the obligation of the pope to seek consultation and advice from theologians and synods. The conditions of papal dogmatic decisions and the problem related to it dominated the discussions of the modern era.

The ecclesiology of the Dominican theologians in the late Middle Ages is, of course, more complex than I have presented it here. To be exhaustive, one would have to include John Quidort of Paris and his famous treatise *De potestate regia et papali*, a key document of early conciliarism, as well as the works of the conciliarist John of Ragusa or the papalist Henry Kalteisen in the era of the Council of Basel.[91] Nonetheless, the choice I have made is legitimate because in a sense it represents the official, or at least the predominant, school of thought in the Dominican order. All the Dominicans presented here, like the vast majority of the theologians of their order, supported the papal primacy of jurisdiction without hesitation or restriction, even though they did not favor hierocratic ideas.

THOMAS DE VIO CAJETAN

To provide a contrast to the medieval Dominicans and at the same time to prepare for the transition to the Dominican School of Salamanca, a brief presentation of a few aspects of the ecclesiology of Cajetan is in order. Cajetan wrote his tract *De comparatione papae et concilii* in the autumn of 1511 against the schismatic Council of Pisa, which had gathered at the instigation of a few cardinals and the French king against Pope Julius II.[92] The synod was inspired by conciliar ideas that had been circulating with a negative sense, in the eyes of Cajetan, since the time of the Council of Basel, especially in France. Cajetan, who was at that time Master General of the Dominican order, answered with intense argumentation in support of papal teaching authority and the primacy of papal jurisdiction.

The central thought that emerges from Cajetan's conclusions relevant to our subject is that the pope retains jurisdiction over the whole church, in which the bishops merely participate.[93] From this principle there follow several consequences, which Cajetan formulates in light of Aquinas (*STh* II-II, q. 11, art. 2 ad 3): teaching authority "mainly" and "definitively" resides with the pope, such that he has the last word in matters of faith.[94] Were he to err in the faith, the church would then be poisoned by his error, since all activity central to life flows from the head to the body of the church.[95] In contrast to the medieval Dominicans, Cajetan does not mention the duty of consultation, indeed not even that it would be appropriate (though this does not mean that he disregards it). In his view the College of Cardinals plays no role. The guidance of the Holy Spirit is sufficient.[96] Infallibility has become a personal privilege of the pope.

Cajetan's stance marks a turning point in the discussions over papal authority among the theologians of his order. His conceptions are grounded in a single principle: the highest authority, possessed by the pope alone. The conciliar ideas that would make that authority contingent on certain conditions no longer had a place.

Despite the immense influence that Cajetan had both within and beyond his own order, Dominican theologians of the next generation, as we will see, went in new directions. But they took with them important elements of the medieval discussion, even as they recast them in light of new questions.

THREE

Papal Teaching Authority in the Dominican School of Salamanca

Sixteenth-century Spain witnessed a golden age of theology, and in that golden age the Dominicans were important participants.[1] In the wake of the reform of the church and the religious orders inspired by the *Reyes Católicos*, King Ferdinand and Queen Isabella,[2] a Thomistic renaissance began with Diego de Deza, while Matías de Paz wrote the first Spanish treatise on the juristic and moral problems associated with a newly discovered world across the Atlantic.[3] The order had a strong presence at both the University of Salamanca and at the University of Alcalá, founded in 1499 by Cardinal Cisneros. The latter developed into a center of humanist and biblical studies and won renown for its *Sacra Biblia Polyglotta*.[4] Worthy of mention as well is the Colegio de San Gregorio in Valladolid, a foundation for highly gifted Dominicans where many famous Spanish scholars and missionaries to both America and Asia would spend time.[5]

FRANCISCO DE VITORIA

In 1507 the superiors of the Dominican province of Castile sent the young Dominican Francisco de Vitoria to Paris to pursue his studies.[6] The decision would have important consequences. In Paris the young Vitoria came in touch with the spiritual and intellectual movements of the day, including several different theological schools, humanism, and the renaissance of Thomism represented by Peter Crockaert (Petrus Bruxellensis).[7] This Flemish scholar, who had joined the Dominican order in 1503 and become professor in the convent of St. Jacques, where Vitoria lived,[8] introduced a new method of teaching that focused on commenting on the *Summa Theologiae* of Thomas Aquinas.[9] Vitoria took this pedagogy back to Salamanca and practiced it, as he began his teaching career there in 1526.[10] The Dominicans had thus quietly replaced Peter Lombard's *Liber Sententiarum*—and they had triggered a revolution in academic teaching.

At the Sorbonne, Vitoria became familiar with the conciliar ideas of the theologian Jacques Almain,[11] ideas that strongly influenced French ecclesiastical policy as articulated at the Council of Pisa (1512).[12] The Dominicans of the convent of St. Jacques were also influenced by this brand of conciliarism. In 1506 they had printed the famous book *De potestate regia et papali (On Kingly and Papal Power)*. Composed by the Dominican Jean Quidort of Paris in 1302, this work had considerable influence on the history of political ideas and opened the way to a conciliarism that fostered an early form of Gallican ecclesiology.[13] In Paris, Vitoria also learned of the harsh reactions of Cajetan, the order's Master General, who in 1511 had published his classic *De comparatione auctoritatis papae et concilii (On the Comparison of the Authority of Pope and Council)*, a work directed against the conciliar theories of Jacques Almain and the professors of the Sorbonne.[14] It is notable that Vitoria stood at great distance from Cajetan in every phase of his theological development, but he always rejected—in accordance with Cajetan— the subjection of the pope to a council. Lastly, it should also be mentioned that Vitoria attended the courses of the Scottish theologian John Major, who, in his *Sentence Commentary* of 1510, pointed for the first time to the moral and political problems that had emerged in the wake of the discoveries of the new continent.[15]

In 1526 Vitoria was appointed professor at Salamanca. Between 1526 and 1527 he lectured on article 10 of the first question of the *Secunda Secundae*: "Who has the right to promulgate a new creed of faith?" This article became, and would for a long time remain, the *locus classicus* of ecclesiology in academic teaching. An independent dogmatic treatise, *De ecclesia,* developed from commentaries by other Dominicans on this article.[16] Theologians of various schools (the Augustinians, for example) would adopt this method—first in Spain, then also in Louvain and Rome.

What are the essentials of Victoria's doctrine? A pope faced with a dogmatic problem, he argues, does not have the ability to discern immediately whether a disputed matter of faith is right or wrong. He must approach the problem in a "human way" (*via humana*), which means he has to consider it carefully and study it seriously before making any decision. Only if he strives for intellectual insight in this way will God's help follow and save the pope from error.[17] This means, on the other hand, that if he wants to make a decision in matters of faith by himself, without asking the council beforehand or without having verified the matter in the light of Holy Scripture and tradition, the pope could indeed err. Hence, he must seek assistance. If a given controversy should prove to be less complicated or of minimal theological import, it is sufficient for the pope to consult distinguished theologians. If, however, the question is highly controversial and cannot be decided by clear scriptural proofs, a council must be summoned, and the issue must be thoroughly examined and discussed.[18] Only if this has been done, and only if the pope and his counselors have begged for God's assistance, can there be certainty of a truthful definition. To put the matter in more general terms, the pope, counselors, and synods must do their utmost; otherwise, they cannot expect God's assistance.[19] This well-known principle, "to do one's utmost" (*facere quod est in se*), required from the pope and his advisers every measure of preparation and diligence. Vitoria was of course well aware how difficult it could be to determine precisely when "the utmost" had actually been done. The certainty the church desired, he responds, does not lie in our hands, but is granted only by God, who would never allow pope and council to render judgment before having in fact done "the utmost."[20]

Within this context, Victoria's opinion concerning the superiority of the council over the pope is of great importance. The *Galli* and the *Germani* are in his eyes the representatives of conciliarism, and their theory is grounded in a twofold teaching: the pope is subject to the councils, and he can err in matters of faith. Are the *Galli* and the *Germani* therefore heretics? Vitoria formulates his answer with care: they are not heretics so long as they render obedience to the head of the church and recognize his jurisdiction.[21] The Fifth Lateran Council, Vitoria continues, taught the superiority of the papacy, so it would be dangerous to deny this, although the council rendered no definitive judgment and did not declare that superiority a matter of faith.[22] In this case, the doctrine that the pope is superior to the councils is "more secure."[23]

As we will see, Vitora's urgent desire for church reform deserves special attention, because from the late Middle Ages church reform had been closely bound up with the role of general councils. From whom did the authority of the councils derive? Vitoria answers: "I think it is better to say that [the authority] emanates directly from God, even if the pope forever remains pastor of the church and stands above all."[24] This answer must be considered from two angles. On the one hand, the recognition of papal jurisdiction is necessary and indisputable; on the other hand, the pope's teaching authority can be questioned. This leads to a further problem: what if a majority of bishops at a council unanimously advocates a certain doctrine and only the pope disagrees? Who is right? With whom should one side? If such dissent really occurred, Vitoria argues, the majority of the council should be supported, because unlike theologians, bishops are not mere counselors but genuine judges.[25] Not surprisingly, this is a problem that would remain a longstanding occasion of controversy.

The *Relectio De potestate papae et concilii* of 1534 is the most important and interesting text for studying Vitoria's ecclesiology. In this *relectio*, a special form of scholastic lectures at Salamanca, he laid the theological foundations for a reform of the church.[26] As is clear from my presentation thus far, Vitoria took a moderate stance on papal teaching authority, one obviously marked by conciliarism. His moderate ideas were even more evident in his thought on ecclesiology and church reform, which he developed with an eye to uniting conciliarists and papalists. His core argument in the *Relectio* was that only by a common effort could the two parties set about the greatest task of his day, the reform of the church. Leaving aside the question whether such a reconciliation would have had any real chance of success, even the attempt to bring together such bitterly divided parties deserves mention, because it was a step that many considered indispensable, and it was a crucial one on the difficult road to the Council of Trent.[27]

Vitoria understood that the reform of the church was closely connected with papal teaching authority. For him reform meant not only changes in organization and administration. More deeply, it touched issues that were part of the *ius divinum*, essential matters that concerned the constitution of the church. One example was the famous question of whether a bishop's duty of permanent residence in his diocese belongs to the *ius divinum* or merely to the *ius positivum*, from which a bishop could easily be dispensed by the pope. For Vitoria, as for Cajetan, Dominicus Soto, Bartolomé Carranza, and other Spanish theologians, there was no doubt that the residence belonged to the *ius divinum*.[28] Vitoria firmly believed that if a council obliged the bishops to observe their residency, this would be a dogmatic decision, not merely an administrative act of church legislation. Looking at the problem from this angle, the debate on church reform was also a discussion about the supreme teaching authority. The issue thus raised another question: Can the council define a doctrine as *ius divinum* against the pope? Vitoria answered without hesitation: "If the council declares something as matter of faith or divine right, the pope cannot decide differently or change the decision. This is especially true if such a law touches the faith or the morals of the whole church."[29] To support his argument he cited Luke 22:32 and Matthew 18:20. From both texts it was clear, in his view, that councils could not err. The Holy Spirit was working in his day no less than it had in the days of the apostolic councils.[30]

Vitoria tried to confirm his argument by working from an absurd supposition. If a council could err in matters of faith, so too could the pope. But if both could err, it would be better to adhere to the decision of a council. After the council of the apostles had decided that the commandments of the Old Testament had lost their validity, Saint Peter could no longer decide differently, and this applied equally to every subsequent council.[31] If such a guarantee of truth did not exist, the church would have remained in unbearable uncertainty concerning matters of faith and morals. Only councils could provide absolute certainty, and should there be any dissent between council and pope, the council was to prevail.

DOMINICUS SOTO

Between the thought of Vitoria and that of Dominicus Soto (1495–1560), professor at Salamanca and theologian of the Council of Trent, there are at once both striking similarities and notable differences.[32] Soto, too, commented on *STh* II-II, q. 1, art. 10 in 1539, and he emphasized the well-known sentiment that church, pope, and council are dependent on human means of finding truth—in other words, on theological reflection grounded in Holy Scripture. If the institutions and people in search of the truth do all that is in their power, they will reach the right decisions. When faced with difficult problems, the pope must therefore consult renowned theologians, and to that end it is at times appropriate to call a council.[33] Where Vitoria had spoken of the "necessity" of a council (*oportet*), Soto, however, spoke only of its "benefits" (*expedit*).

In reference to the relationship between pope and council, Soto preferred a middle way that ran between the conciliarists and the "two cardinals," Torquemada and Cajetan.[34] Soto argued that by virtue of their office, the bishops at a council under the presidency of the pope had the authority of the church. Whenever they gather officially and publicly, they can be assured of the infallibility of their teaching.[35] At such a council the pope is only a part of the whole, and is therefore obliged to follow its judgment.[36] Soto does not mention the name of the Flemish theologian Albert Pigge (†1542), although he notes that "a few contemporary theologians" have represented the opinion that in principle the pope could not fall into heresy. He himself held to the traditional teaching, however, which accounted for the possibility of an erroneous, private judgment in matters of faith.[37]

With Dominicus Soto an epoch in the School of Salamanca came to an end, and with Soto, Vitoria's influence on important aspects of our problem ended as well. Vitoria, too, was honored in the coming years, but his students passed over in silence the heart of his ecclesiological thought and the arguments about church reform that were inseparable from it. Moreover, conciliar ideas in general had become suspect. Vitoria's importance for the Spanish church and the Council of Trent soon fell into oblivion.[38]

MELCHIOR CANO

The silence of Vitoria's followers about his ecclesiology was no negligent omission; it was a program. This can best be observed in Vitoria's most prominent student, Melchior Cano.[39] After holding a professorship in Alcalá (1543–46), Cano became Vitoria's successor in Salamanca in 1546. The humanist climate in Alcalá had awakened in him a sense of history, even as it encouraged his suspicions about new ideas, especially in the field of exegesis.[40] Vitoria had recognized the great intellectual ability of his student early on, but he also saw a dangerous intellectual pride and overconfident carelessness. Indeed Cano himself, not without some self-satisfaction, tells of Vitoria's fear (notable in our context) that Cano would "boldly and freely trample over the footsteps of his teacher."[41] Cano's intolerance also became evident when he accused Archbishop Carranza of Toledo, himself a Dominican, of teaching errors in his *Catecismo Christiano,* which was eventually placed on the Spanish Index (1559).[42]

Vitoria's judgment reflected more than the usual emancipation of a student from his teacher. It reflected a deeper change taking place in Spain in those years. Protestantism, spreading secretly and rapidly across the Spanish landscape, now posed a serious threat to the Spanish Crown, which since the reign of the *Reyes Católicos* had been intensely focused on preserving the political and religious unity of the monarchy.[43] In Seville, Valladolid, and Burgos, in the heart of Castile, there were Protestant groups entertaining real or presumed contacts with members of the church hierarchy (Archbishop Carranza, for example).[44] As a consequence, the importing of books and their production were sharply controlled, and studying abroad was strictly prohibited.[45]

It was in this climate that Melchior Cano wrote parts of his *Loci Theologici,* through which he intended to provide ecclesiastical tribunals with guidelines for competent judgment. In this context, he developed several criteria for appropriate theological censorship. Precise theological censures, Cano realized, required an exact description of doctrine, which in turn had to be derived from proper definitions of the church's teaching authority. But a council or even a larger assembly was far too slow-moving an instrument for quick doctrinal decisions. Inquisitors and theologians confronted with the subtleties of Protestant or humanist ideas therefore had to be armed with both unambiguous doctrine and clear instructions.[46] Cano thus cautioned early on against the dangers of humanist Bible study and textual criticism, and, for example, pleaded for the Vulgate as the proven old translation, to be used as the only basis of scriptural exegesis.[47]

When Cano had been nominated a conciliar theologian by Emperor Charles V and arrived in Trent in 1551, he wrote the books of the *Loci Theologici* most relevant for our current purposes—Books III and IV.[48]

The shifting of ecclesiological ground that had begun in Vitoria's day is notably visible in Cano's treatise on the councils and their relationship to the pope. The binding character of synods and councils is completely dependent on the involvement of the pope. Their decrees are secure as rules of faith only when they have received the highest approval.[49] The fact that the pope's approval remains the sole criterion of legitimacy places the highest teaching authority in the head of the church. The number of fathers who agree to a determination is irrelevant.[50] Pope and bishops are not inspired in dogmatic decisions; they must therefore use the normal means of finding the truth. Interestingly, the College of Cardinals and the Roman curia are not mentioned as participants in the decision process—most likely in order to exclude historical reminders of their participation. Divine assistance, human effort, and foundational study of subject matter had to work together. But there was no question of dogmatic uncertainty. God Himself ensured that all participants would meet the conditions necessary for a proper decision.[51]

Cano decidedly rejected the distinction, taught by many authors, between the Roman church and the Roman pontiff, a distinction that had long held a firm place even in the ecclesiological teaching of the Dominican theologians. When we turn to the Apostolic See for clarity in matters of faith, he argued, we do not turn to the Roman faithful or the Roman church in the form of a council. Rather, we seek the judgment of the pope.[52] The legal and teaching authority has been given over to one person, not to a church. Thus, councils are not approved by the faithful of the city of Rome, but by the Roman bishop.[53]

Even Cano concedes that the pope can fall into heresy. The historical arguments that Albert Pigge offers for his thesis—that by divine assistance no pope could ever become a heretic, even as a private person—are for Cano without merit. The objections that arise from the possibility of a papal heresy can be refuted through a simple distinction. Peter had been given two privileges: one that concerned him as an individual, and one that had been given to him for the benefit of the church. With reference to our problem, this means that Peter had the personal privilege of protecting inner belief for his whole life, while also having the privilege of remaining free from error in his official teaching. His successors, however, enjoyed only the privilege granted to Peter as head of the church.[54] Since the church depends not on the private, inner beliefs of the pope, but on his official knowledge alone, heresy thus offers no principal difficulties.[55]

Soon after its publication in 1563, Cano's *Loci Theologici* became a much-quoted work that had considerable influence for centuries to come. His dissociation from Vitoria and from the late medieval heritage is therefore as important as it is clear. Cano sought to build an unassailable bastion from which Catholic theologians could defend the church against both conciliar theory and the Reformation, with their rejection of papal teaching authority, and also against the dangers of humanism, with its new methods of biblical criticism.

JUAN DE LA PEÑA

In 1559—the same year that the rigorous Spanish Index of prohibited books was published—the Dominican Juan de la Peña gave a noteworthy lecture in Salamanca.[56] It was the first great commentary on *STh* II-II, q. 1, art. 10, and it addressed all of the themes that from then on would be part of the standard academic repertoire. In it Juan also answered arguments that were closely related to Luther and the Reformation. Even more interesting in our context is that in this lecture, for the first time, tendencies appear that were both new among the Dominicans and also soon to be of great influence because they so clearly spoke to contemporary intellectual circumstances. But the fact that we have two different versions of the lecture, one "modern," which distances itself from the common doctrine of the Dominicans, and one "traditional," which comes back to the common doctrine of the Dominican school, makes clear that this is a transitional text, one whose author was not sure which way he should go.

Vitoria's, Soto's, and Cano's opinions about papal definitions stressed the necessity of diligent and appropriate preparation. Juan de la Peña deviated from their common doctrine in his earlier, "modern" version and opened the door for major changes. Although he considered the traditional view as "probable" (*probabilis*), he developed a new approach, one he liked to call "more probable" (*probabilius*). He eliminated any limitations or conditions impinging on a pope who rendered judgment in matters of faith. Regardless of how well or how poorly they had prepared to make their decision, a pope and a council could never err. Of course, a pope who failed to consult with others or to inform himself would commit a grave sin, but his determination nevertheless remained correct and valid because Christ had both given the assistance of the Holy Spirit and prayed for Peter unconditionally (Luke 22:32).[57] Juan also saw an analogy between his model and sacramental theology: as long as a priest celebrating the Eucharist is properly attentive to both form and *materia* and acts according to the intention of the church, he will always consecrate infallibly, even if he sins by disregarding liturgical rubrics.[58]

Juan de la Peña was apparently the first to articulate such a strong theory of infallibility. Why he should have done so is easy to guess: wanting to eliminate any risk resulting from procedural conditions somehow unfulfilled by the pope or the council, he excluded appeals to a higher court. There was no longer any need to rely on God to guarantee procedures that themselves were no longer necessary.

This position provoked opposition very early. A marginal note in one of the manuscripts containing Juan's lecture voiced serious concerns about its arguments. If the pope receives no divine illumination, the unknown reader argued, the assistance of the Holy Spirit is bound to previous efforts of human circumspection, diligence, and prudence. The assumption that the pope would sin if he failed to prepare dogmatic definitions is justified only if his preparation serves as a means to the end. If there is no obligation for due preparation, then neither is there any culpability in not having properly prepared.[59] The *Lectura* and this marginal note present clearly the two competing positions which would dominate the discussion for centuries to come.

A further example clearly illustrates the transitional nature of Juan de la Peña's position. In the later version of his *Lectura* he addressed the problem anew, yet he reversed himself and embraced the traditional Dominican teaching on the necessity of preparation. He grounded his position in the practice of the church, which had always held that fitting preparation was a necessary precondition of rendering judgment—for example, the cooperation of the College of Cardinals, the theologians, and the councils.[60]

A second point, no less interesting, is the problem of a heretical pope. Albert Pigge's view had so far met with no positive response from Dominican theologians. Juan de la Peña addressed the problem by arguing that whoever counts on the possibility of a papal heresy must consider the consequent risks. Who can pretend with certainty, he asked, that the pope who passed the verdict on Luther was not himself a heretic? Can dogmatic certainty ever be achieved if a pope is prone to heresy? This danger can be excluded only if one assumes that a pope would always define the truth, even if he did so against his personal conviction.[61] This is confirmed by the following argument: the words of Christ to Peter (Luke 22:32) make reference not only to the person of Peter in his relation to the church, but also to Peter as an individual, so that he never lost the faith, even during the time of Jesus' passion.[62] Lastly, the privilege was given to him not as an apostle but as future pope. And this was a privilege for all of his successors as well, since these, like Peter, have the duty of strengthening their brothers in the faith.[63] The conclusion from this exegesis is clear: anyone who has such a function in the eyes of the church must also enjoy this certainty as a person. There is no difference in this case between "private" and "public." Juan de la Peña knew that theologians who rejected Pigge's innovations relied on historical examples. In his opinion, only the case of Pope Honorius poses any difficulty, since we have no *authentica historia* for any of the other examples.[64] He conceded that the Council of Constantinople (680–81) had actually judged the pope a heretic, but the council had not discussed the question of whether or not a pope can become a heretic. A decision in the matter was therefore not handed down at the time. The theological problem emerged only when one began to discuss arguments for and against it.[65]

The conclusion from such considerations is revealing of the new tendencies in ecclesiology. Despite the prevailing opinion of his day that Honorius was heretical, Juan de la Peña deemed it "much more probable" (*forte probabilius*) that the pope had been innocent. A defense of the impossibility of a papal heresy was also fitting for Juan de la Peña because the current holder of the Apostolic See (Pius IV) was beset on all sides with great difficulties. The Holy Spirit had therefore given "some theologians" the inspiration to reject the possibility of a heretical pope. The apologetic tendency of this line of argumentation is all too obvious.

Juan de la Peña's *Lectura* holds an important place in the School of Salamanca because it so clearly indicates a change of course. And even though it was a course that other Dominicans would not necessarily follow, as we will show, the *Lectura* represented a general trend that powerfully influenced theologians from the Jesuit order.[66]

Dominicus Báñez

Along with Cano's *Loci Theologici*, the *Commentarii Theologici* (1585) of Dominicus Báñez also played an important role in the history of ecclesiology.[67] For Báñez, the teaching that the pope could not err in his public judgments had already taken the shape of an apostolic tradition that had found general acceptance until the Council of Constance.[68] Only since that time had conciliar ideas begun to spread. Should one put the question before a council nowadays, argued Báñez, it would be resolved without question in favor of the pope's authority. The situation had thus changed in recent years. It was now necessary for the welfare of the church that the pope enjoyed the privilege of the highest teaching authority, since it could not wait for a council to resolve explosive controversies in need of quick resolution. As such remarks reveal, the impact of the Counter-Reformation is quite unmistakable. The passionate discussions at Trent concerning the relationship between pope and episcopate are mentioned, notably, only in passing. Faced with the errors of the day, the pope has proven himself as the sole guarantor of proper belief, and for Báñez his authority in matters of faith is no longer a matter of controversy, at least in Spain. The following argument confirms this: all heresies condemned in the church had been condemned by the Roman bishop, so that the faith would fall into the gravest danger should one deny or even weaken the teaching authority of the Apostolic See. Accordingly, it is no surprise that

Báñez, while avoiding exaggerations and one-sided arguments and while seeking to respect the historical facts, nevertheless favored theses that offered the greatest possible dogmatic certainty.

In the matter of papal heresy Báñez thus adopted the conservative stance of his school. Of particular relevance in this connection is a story often told in the late Middle Ages that raises questions in connection with the issue of reception, an issue to which theology in our own day has devoted great attention. This is the story of Joan, the alleged female pope, which circulated among theologians and is found in the chronicles of two Dominicans, Johannes de Malliaco and Martinus Polonus. As the story goes, a female scholar disguised as a man was elected pope in 855.[69] The legend's strange history subsequently induced even serious theologians to reflect upon the many ecclesiological implications of such a *papissa*. In a certain way, the inventors of the legend deserve our gratitude, since fiction sometimes helps the historian to develop an idea by clarifying underlying or hidden problems.

For John Torquemada, the existence of a *papissa* was just as imaginable as the election of a heathen or a Jew as pope. But such unfitting candidates, he argued, could not destroy the church. Even facing an illegitimate pope, the church would enjoy God's protection.[70] The solution suggested by Báñez is more interesting. He, too, seemed to allow the possibility of a *papissa*, but he turned this special problem into a general one. Should an illegitimate or dubious pope reign over the church (perhaps one who had not been baptized or whose election was somehow deficient), and should this false pope proclaim an error, it would be rendered invalid. Either the church would never accept the error, Báñez argues, or it would be revealed at once as an error, or the pope would die before having the opportunity to render a definitive judgment.[71] In any case there would be no negative consequences for the faith. Báñez then provided a further, and simpler, solution. If the pope were to define something *de fide*, it would be absolutely certain that he is the legitimate pope. Any doubt about the validity of his election would be impossible.[72]

Notable in these considerations is that the reception of a judgment or of a pope represents an important and even decisive criterion for the truth. This means that there are situations and times in which it is not yet certain whether a decision of the teaching office has become obligatory. The church's acceptance or rejection of a judgment, which naturally can be established only after a certain time, is therefore the last criterion of truth. This means that the universal church, and not the determination of a pope, represents the most certain bulwark against error and fault in the highest office.[73] We must add, however, that such thoughts soon would disappear from the discussions of the highest teaching authority.

Báñez is the last figure of the Dominican School of Salamanca who earned a great reputation in the church. The theologians after him are of interest only to historians of ecclesiology. None of them exerted any influence outside Spain. Nevertheless, two further Dominicans deserve mention, because they brought a new argument into the discussion.

PEDRO DE LEDESMA

Pedro de Ledesma often replaced Báñez at the University of Salamanca during Báñez's absences, and from 1606 to 1616 he held the second chair of theology given to the Dominicans at the university, the *cátedra* founded by the Duque de Lerma.[74] In a *lectura* on *STh* II-II, q. 1, art. 10, he represented the conventional theses of his school.[75] In his *Tractatus de divinae gratiae auxiliis*, published in 1611, a new argument appears, however, which had its genesis in contemporary controversies over the essence and the effect of grace.[76] For Pedro, the faith of the pope enjoys an inner perfection that participates in the divine vision (*visio Dei*) and renders the pope's judgments infallible. This was not a matter of God's mere assistance, but a matter of a divine inspiration that "compelled" the pope (*necessitat*) to render the proper judgment.[77] In this view, the pope's judgment participates in the divine light, and error is therefore absolutely out of the question. There could be no greater guarantee for the truth of his judgments.

FRANCISCO DE ARAÚJO

The last Spanish Dominican worthy of mention in the history of ecclesiology is Francisco de Araújo (1580–1646). From 1617 to 1644 he held the first chair of theology given to the Dominicans at the University of Salamanca.[78] He, too, argued for the highest degree of certainty in the issue of infallibility. According to Araújo, through the special assistance of the Holy Spirit and through divine help, the will of the pope is so fixed while in the act of rendering judgment that he cannot choose to judge falsely. His faith is so firmly established that it is made infallible; his intellect so enlightened that nothing false could be proposed to him in the guise of truth.[79] Divine intervention so guards him from every kind of uncertainty or deception that his judgment enjoys absolute certainty. This divineassistance and enlightenment are strictly personal privileges of the pope, in which other people and institutions do not participate. For Araújo, conceptions such as those that had earlier been bound up with the idea of the *sedes apostolica* no longer play any role.

Araújo knew, in any case, that the historical reality of the papal teaching office is more complicated than its theory. Thus, according to Araújo, the church has "often" not followed the decrees of the popes because it held the judgments they rendered as private. The church, for example, had not generally accepted the decretal *Aeternus ille*, in which Sixtus V declared as canonical the edition of the Vulgate that had been corrected at his command. The theologians and cardinals were convinced the pope had issued the decree as a private person.[80]

JOHANNES AB ANNUNTIATIONE

At the end of our overview we turn briefly to the work of a Carmelite who was representative of a stark Thomism. He was personally acquainted with the Dominicans of San Esteban and can be numbered among the followers of that school. Johannes ab Annuntiatione (1633–1701) is the author of the *Disputationes de fide* in the *Cursus Theologicus Salmanticensis*.[81] Because of the theological depth of the work of the Spanish Carmelites, the *Cursus* has enjoyed great renown down to the modern era. Johannes, too, tries to explain infallibility with arguments drawn from contemporary discussions concerning the effectiveness of grace. Two of his ideas are important in this context. Because of the aid afforded the pope by the Holy Spirit, the infallible judgment that falls to the pope in his official capacity (*in cathedra*) is of a binding nature. Its effectiveness is incompatible with error. This does not mean, however, that the nature of the pope is somehow "changed"—the possibility of error and even heresy remains with him. It means only that he cannot err at the moment of rendering official judgment.[82] The impossibility of an erroneous judgment is guaranteed not through participation in a special grace that grounds the pope's intellect, but through divine assistance alone.[83] The fact that the pope can become heretical prohibits all exaggeration, such as a theory that the pope's mind is changed or that he enjoys divine illumination.[84] It is sufficient that the pope has the ability to guarantee the faith of the church, and to that end only the outward act of faith is necessary. To accomplish this, God can prevent the pope from rendering a false judgment in many ways (an idea Guido Terreni had first brought into the discussion).[85] Johannes ab Annuntiatione stresses that the faith of the church is assured, so long as the pope is free from error in rendering official judgment.[86]

—Seen from a later standpoint, Cano and Báñez especially developed a consistent doctrine of papal infallibility whose greatest merit was to dispel the widespread conciliar ideas of the late Middle Ages, at least outside France. Their efforts gave the papacy of the sixteenth century and the Counter-Reformation an ecclesiological foundation that helped stabilize the post-Tridentine church and set up a doctrinal bulwark against a variety of heresies. Nevertheless, by the end of the century the Dominicans had lost their former influence to their opponents and rivals, namely, the theologians from the Jesuit order, who in many ways took up the legacy of the School of Salamanca and then modified it in many essential ways.

The distinctions and subtleties we have taken great pain to treat in detail here had a long doctrinal epilogue. Whereas the Dominicans insisted that appropriate preparation—including consultations, discussions, and even councils—is essential to a proper papal definition, Robert Bellarmine and Gregory of Valencia modified this stance in a very important way. In their view, the pope merely had a moral obligation to prepare properly. If he were to neglect doing so, he would commit a sin. But proper preparation was not an indispensable condition for the validity of his decisions.[87]

There is a second difference between the two schools. Francisco Suárez, Bellarmine, and Gregory of Valencia dissociated themselves from the common doctrine that the pope could become a heretic. In their eyes, this was impossible even for the pope as a private person—although they cautiously qualified their opinion as "pious" and "probable."[88] This slight restriction notwithstanding, the fact remains that a longstanding orthodox tradition with many remarkable ecclesiological implications had come to an end. The possibility of a heretical pope had disappeared from canon law and from manuals of ecclesiology.

In view of the influence of the Jesuit order on the First Vatican Council, it is not surprising that an effort to exclude the greatest number of risks dominated the discussions. This was clear during the debates over the heresy of Pope Hono-rius. Representatives of a rigorous concept of infallibility sought to solve the problem with the same arguments that Albert Pigge had used.[89] The controversies surrounding the conditions the pope had to observe before rendering a definition were of great theological weight. Here, we encounter almost all of the objections and distinctions that we have come to know since Vitoria's first *lectura*. The in-tervention of the Dominican cardinal Filippo Maria Guidi, who looked to the theologians of his order on this point, was met with the vehement opposition of a majority who wanted no part of binding the pope with any conditions.[90] Their arguments, too, are known to us from our history. The view that Vitoria and his school so powerfully taught—that there was not merely a moral obligation, but a necessary relationship between preparation and determination—had become suspect and was brought within the orbit of Gallican ideas. Many now saw in the *via humana* an intolerable limitation of papal sovereignty, one that raised the dan-ger of seeking ultimate certainty in a council. Only through vigorous counter-arguments, many had come to believe, could such conciliar ideas be eradicated forever.

Abbreviations

AAug	*Analecta Augustiniana*
AD	*Archivo Dominicano*
AFH	*Archivum Franciscanum Historicum*
AFP	*Archivum Fratrum Praedicatorum*
AHC	*Annuarium Historiae Conciliorum*
AHDL	*Archives d'histoire doctrinale et littéraire du moyen âge*
AHP	*Archivum Historiae Pontificiae*
AHR	*American Historical Review*
AKG	*Archiv für Kulturgeschichte*
ALKGMA	*Archiv für Literatur- und Kirchengeschichte des Mittelalters*
AMRhKG	*Archiv für mittelrheinische Kirchengeschichte*
AnAn	*Anthologica Annua*
Ang	*Angelicum*
AnGr	Analecta Gregoriana
ATA	Alttestamentliche Abhandlungen
ATG	*Archivo Teológico Granadino*
BEFAR	Bibliothèques des Ecoles Françaises d'Athènes et de Rome
BGPhMA	Beiträge zur Geschichte der Philosophie und Theologie des Mittelalters
BiblThom	Bibliothèque Thomiste

BRHE	Bibliothèque de la Revue d'Histoire Ecclésiastique
BSC	Biblioteca Seraphico-Capuccina
BTE	Biblioteca de Teólogos Españoles
CEFR	Collection de l'Ecole Française de Rome
CFan	Cahiers de Fanjeaux
CFr	*Collectanea Franciscana*
Comp	*Compostellanum*
CrStor	*Cristianesimo nella storia*
CTom	*Ciencia Tomista*
DH	Dissertationes Historicae
DHEE	*Diccionario de Historia Eclesiástica de España*
DHGE	*Dictionnaire d'histoire et de géographie ecclésiastiques*
DIP	*Dizionario degli Istituti di Perfezione*
Div	*Divinitas*
DS	*Dictionnaire de Spiritualité*
DT(Fr)	*Divus Thomas (Freiburg/S.)*
DT(P)	*Divus Thomas (Piacenza)*
EE	*Estudios Eclesiásticos*
FChLDG	Forschungen zur christlichen Literatur- und Dogmengeschichte
FKRG	Forschungen zur kirchlichen Rechtsgeschichte und zum Kirchenrecht
FranzFor	*Franziskanische Forschungen*
FrS	*Franciscan Studies*
FS	*Franziskanische Studien*
FS.B	Franziskanische Studien. Beiheft
FZPhTh	*Freiburger Zeitschrift für Theologie und Philosophie*
Gr	*Gregorianum*
HJ	*Historisches Jahrbuch*
HS	Historische Studien
HThR	*Harvard Theological Review*
IThQ	*Irish Theological Quarterly*
IThS	Innsbrucker Theologische Studien
KHAbh	Kölner Historische Abhandlungen
KKTS	Konfessionskundliche und Kontroverstheologische Studien
Laur	*Laurentianum*

LF	*Liceo Franciscano*
LThK	*Lexikon für Theologie und Kirche.* 3d ed.
MDom	*Memorie Domenicane*
MGH	Monumenta Germaniae Historica
MIC.C	Monumenta Iuris Canonici, Series B: Corpus Collectionum
MiscFranc	*Miscellanea Franciscana*
MKHS	Münchener kirchenhistorische Studien
MM	*Miscellanea Mediaevalia*
MOPH	Monumenta Ordinis Fratrum Praedicatorum Historica
MS	*Mediaeval Studies*
MSHTh	Münchener Studien zur historischen Theologie
MSR	*Mélanges de science religieuse*
MThZ	*Münchener Theologische Zeitschrift*
OTHE.S	Opucula et Textus. Series scholastica
PG	Patrologiae cursus completus, series Graeca
PL	Patrologiae cursus completus, series Latina
PS	*Picenum Seraphicum*
PuP	Päpste und Papsttum
QFGDO	Quellen und Forschungen zur Geschichte des Dominikanerordens
RHEF	*Revue d'Histoire de l'Eglise de France*
RMab	*Revue Mabillon*
RöHM	*Römische Historische Mitteilungen*
RoJKG	*Rottenburger Jahrbuch für Kirchengeschichte*
RQ	*Römische Quartalschrift*
RSCI	*Rivista di storia della Chiesa in Italia*
RSPhTh	*Revue des sciences philosophiques et théologiques*
RSR	*Recherches de science religieuse*
RST	Reformationsgeschichtliche Studien und Texte
RThAM	*Recherches de théologie ancienne et médiévale*
RThom	*Revue Thomiste*
Sa	*Salesianum*
Scr	*Scriptorium*
ScrinTheol	Scrinium Theologicum
ScrTh	*Scripta Theologica*

SHCT	Studies in the History of Christian Thought
SMGH	Schriften der Monumenta Germaniae Historica
SMRT	Studies in Medieval and Reformation Thought
Spec	*Speculum*
SpicBon	Spicilegium Bonaventurianum
SSFr	Subsidia Scientifica Franciscalia
STGMA	Studien und Texte zur Geistesgeschichte des Mittelalters
StGra	*Studia Gratiana*
STh	Thomas Aquinas, *Summa Theologiae*
STPIMS	Studies and Texts. Pontifical Institute of Mediaeval Studies
StT	Studies and Texts
StudMed	*Studi Medievali*
Thom	*The Thomist*
ThomStud	Thomistische Studien
ThPh	*Theologie und Philosophie*
ThQ	*Theologische Quartalschrift*
Tr	*Traditio*
TRE	*Theologische Realenzyklopädie*
UnSa	Unam Sanctam
VGI	Veröffentlichungen des Grabmann-Institutes
VIEG	Veröffentlichungen des Instituts für Europäische Geschichte, Mainz
VRF	Vorreformationsgeschichtliche Forschungen
WBTh	Wiener Beiträge zur Theologie
WiWei	*Wissenschaft und Weisheit*
WSAMA	Walberberger Studien der Albertus-Magnus-Akademie
WSAMA.P	Walberberger Studien, Philosophische Reihe
WSAMA.T	Walberberger Studien, Theologische Reihe
ZRGKA	*Zeitschrift für Rechtsgeschichte. Kanon. Abteilung*

Notes

Foreword

1. Paul Strohm's Conway lectures have appeared in print as *Politique: Languages of Statecraft between Chaucer and Shakespeare* (Notre Dame: University of Notre Dame Press, 2005). Other Conway volumes are forthcoming with the tentative titles *Perceptions of the Past in the Early Middle Ages* (Rosamond McKitterick) and *Grasping the Wind: Words for Melodies in South-German Liturgical Music, 800–1200* (Calvin Bower), both to be published by the University of Notre Dame Press.

2. *Die Trinitäts- und Gotteslehre des Robert von Melun* (Mainz, 1974) and *Gesetz und Evangelium. Das Alte Testament in der Theologie des Robert von Melun* (Paderborn, 1971).

3. *Papst, Konzil, Unfehlbarkeit. Die Ekklesiologie der Summenkommentare von Cajetan bis Billuart* (Mainz, 1978).

4. *Unfehlbarkeit und Geschichte. Studien zur Unfehlbarkeitsdiskussion von Melchior Cano bis zum I. Vatikanischen Konzil* (Mainz, 1982).

5. *Zwischen Konziliarismus und Reformation. Studien zur Ekklesiologie im Dominikanerorden* (Rome, 1985) and *Autorität und Immunität des Papstes. Raphael de Pornassio OP und Julianus Tallada OP in der Auseinandersetzung mit dem Basler Konziliarismus* (Paderborn, 1991).

6. *Die Diskussion um die Immaculata Conceptio im Dominikanerorden. Ein Beitrag zur Geschichte der theologischen Methode* (Paderborn, 1987). See also "*Nova Opinio* und *Novelli Doctores.* Johannes de Montenigro, Johannes Torquemada und Raphael de Pornassio als Gegner der Immaculata Conceptio," in *Studien zum 15. Jahrhundert. Festschrift für Erich Meuthen,* ed. Helmrath and H. Müller (Munich, 1994), vol. 1, 169–91.

7. *Evangelische Armut und Kirche. Thomas von Aquin und die Armutskontroversen des 13. und beginnenden 14. Jahrhunderts,* Quellen und Forschungen zur Geschichte des Dominikanerordens 1 (Berlin, 1992). See also *Bischöfe und Ordensleute. 'Cura principalis animarum' und 'via perfectionis' in der Ekklesiologie des hl. Thomas von Aquin* (Berlin, 1999).

8. *Evangelische Armut und päpstliches Lehramt. Minoritentheologen im Konflikt mit Papst Johannes XXII. (1316–34)* (Stuttgart, 1996).

9. Francisco de Vitoria, *Vorlesungen (Relectiones). Völkerrecht, Politik, Kirche,* ed. Ulrich Horst, H.-J. Justenhoven, and J. Stüben, 2 vols. (Stuttgart, 1995). Horst's biographical essay is in vol. 1, 14–99.

10. *Die Lehrautorität des Papstes und die Dominikanertheologen der Schule von Salamanca,* Quellen und Forschungen zur Geschichte des Dominikanerordens 11 (Berlin, 2003).

11. *Die Gaben des heiligen Geistes nach Thomas von Aquin* (Berlin, 2001).

Introduction

1. H. J. Sieben, *Die Konzilsidee des lateinischen Mittelalters (847–1378)* (Paderborn, 1984), 255.

Chapter One.   Thomas Aquinas on Papal Teaching Authority

1. See T. Kaeppeli, "Vie du frère Martin Donadieu de Carcassonne OP (1299). Écrite par Bernard et Pierre Gui," *AFP* 26 (1956): 288.

2. On the situation in southern France see A. Friedlander, *The Hammer of the Inquisitors: Brother Bernard Délicieux and the Struggle against the Inquisition in Fourteenth-Century France,* Cultures, Beliefs and Traditions 9 (Leiden, 2000), and D. Burr, *The Spiritual Franciscans: From Protest to Persecution in the Century after Saint Francis* (Philadelphia, 2001), 191–96.

3. See A. Dondaine, "La collection des oeuvres de saint Thomas dite de Jean XXII et Jacquet Maci," *Scr* 29 (1975): 127–52; A. Maier, "Annotazioni autografe di Giovanni XXII in codici vaticani," *RSCI* 6 (1952): 317–32.

4. William of Tocco, *Ystoria sancti Thome de Aquino de Guillaume de Tocco (1323). Edition critique et notes,* ed. C. le Brun-Gouanvic, STPIMS 127 (Toronto 1996), c. XXI, 140 ff.: "Cuius sectatores simul et inventores se nominant fraterculos de vita paupere . . . Quorum mentes, dum non probant utrum ex Deo sit spiritus, sic mendax spiritus dementavit ut sub uno capite Christo duas fingant ecclesias: unam carnalem, super quam summus Romanus pontifex presidet." The allusion to contemporary circumstances is clear. The expression *fraticelli seu fratres de paupere vita* is first used in the bull *Sancta romana* of 30 December 1317. See D. Burr, *Spiritual Franciscans,* 281. See also the articles by C. Schmitt: "Fraticelli," *DIP* 4:807–21, and *"Fraticelles," DHGE* 18:1063–1108.

5. On the *ecclesia carnalis* see D. Burr, *Olivi's Peaceable Kingdom: A Reading of the Apocalypse Commentary* (Philadelphia, 1993), 214–16.

6. On the canonization see P. Mandonnet, "La canonisation de Saint Thomas d'Aquin 1317–1323," in *Mélanges Thomistes,* BiblThom 3 (Le Saulchoir, 1923), 1–48; A. Walz, "Papst Johannes XXII. und Thomas von Aquin. Zur Geschichte der Heiligsprechung des Aquinaten," in *St. Thomas Aquinas, 1274–1974: Commemorative Studies,* vol. 1 (Toronto, 1974), 29–47; L. V. Gerulaitis, "The Canonization of Saint Thomas

Aquinas," *Vivarium* 5 (1967): 25–46; A. Vauchez, *La sainteté en Occident aux derniers siècles du moyen âge d'après les procès de canonisation et les documents hagiographiques*, BEFAR 241 (Rome, 1988), index.

7. See M.-H. Laurent, *Fontes Vitae S. Thomae Aquinatis*, Processus canonizationis S. Thomae, Neapoli, Fossae-Novae. De canonizatione S. Thomae Aquinatis (Saint-Maximin, 1937), 513 ff.: ". . . et (papa) sermonem fecit; dicens eum (Thomam) in sancto ordine Praedicatorum apostolicam vitam duxisse; qui ordo, sive fratres, nichil habens proprium, *licet aliquid habeant in communi sicut apostoli habuerunt, et apostolicam vitam ducunt.* . . ." Throughout, emphases within quotations are mine unless otherwise noted.

8. I have treated this problem thoroughly in my *Evangelische Armut und Kirche. Thomas von Aquin und die Armutskontroversen des 13. und beginnenden 14. Jahrhunderts*, QFGDO n.s. 1 (Berlin, 1992), 35–54; "Mendikant und Theologe. Thomas v. Aquin in den Armutsbewegungen seiner Zeit (zu Contra retrahentes c. 15)," *MThZ* 47 (1996): 13–31; "Christ, *Exemplar Ordinis Fratrum Praedicantium*, according to Saint Thomas Aquinas," in *Christ Among the Medieval Dominicans: Representations of Christ in the Texts and Images of the Order of Preachers*, ed. K. Emery, Jr., and J. Wawrykow (Notre Dame, 1998), 256–70, esp. 264–66; "Evangelische Armut und Kirche. Ein Konfliktfeld in der scholastischen Theologie des 13. Jahrhunderts," *MM* 27 (2000): 308–20.

9. *STh* II-II, q. 188, art. 7: "perfectio non consistit essentialiter in paupertate, sed in Christi sequela . . . paupertas autem est sicut instrumentum vel exercitium perveniendi ad perfectionem." On the vows see U. Horst, *Bischöfe und Ordensleute. Cura principalis animarum und via perfectionis in der Ekklesiologie des hl. Thomas v. Aquin* (Berlin, 1999), 113–28.

10. *STh* II-II, q. 188, art. 7: "Si autem consideretur per comparationem ad speciales fines religionum, sic praesupposito tali fine, paupertas maior vel minor est religioni accommoda; et tanto erit unaqaeque religio secundum paupertatem perfectior, quanto habet paupertatem magis proportionatam suo fini. Manifestum est enim quod ad exteriora et corporalia opera vitae activae indiget homo copia exteriorum rerum; ad contemplationem autem pauca requiruntur . . . Sic ergo patet quod religio quae ordinatur ad actiones corporales activae vitae . . . imperfecta esset si communibus careret divitiis. Religiones autem quae ad contemplativam vitam ordinantur, tanto perfectiores sunt, quanto eorum paupertas minorem eis sollicitudinem ingerit. Tanto autem sollicitudo temporalium rerum magis impedit religionem, quanto sollicitudo spiritualium maior ad religionem requiritur. Manifestum est autem quod maiorem sollicitudinem spiritualium requirit religio quae est instituta ad contemplandum et contemplata aliis tradendum per doctrinam et praedicationem, quam illa quae est instituta ad contemplandum tantum. Unde talem religionem decet paupertas talis quae minimam sollicitudinem ingerit."

11. Ibid.: "Illis autem quae ordinantur ad contemplata aliis tradendum competit vitam habere maxime ab exterioribus sollicitudinibus expeditam. Quod quidem fit dum modica quae sunt necessaria vitae, congruo tempore procurata conservantur."

12. Ibid.: "Utrum habere alquid in communi diminuat perfectionem religionis." On the interpretation, see U. Horst, *Evangelische Armut und Kirche*, 123–32.

13. Ibid. That a convent could have *modica* is clear from the model of Christ himself: "Et hoc Dominus, paupertatis institutor, docuit suo exemplo; habebat enim loculos Iudae commissos, in quibus recondebantur ei oblata."

14. See Y. Congar, "Aspects ecclésiologiques de la querelle entre mendiants et séculiers dans la seconde moitié du XIIIᵉ siècle et le début du XIVᵉ," *AHDL* 28 (1961): 35–151.

15. See K. Schleyer, *Anfänge des Gallikanismus im 13. Jahrhundert. Der Widerstand des französischen Klerus gegen die Privilegierung der Bettelorden*, HS 314 (Berlin, 1937); P. Glorieux, "Prélats français contre religieux mendiants," *RHEF* 11 (1925): 309–31, 471–95.

16. *Contra impugnantes Dei cultum et religionem, Opera Omnia*, ed. Leon., vol. 41 (Rome, 1970), A5–A181. See J.-P. Torrell, *Initiation à saint Thomas d'Aquin* (Fribourg-Paris, 1993), 109–22; M.-M. Dufeil, *Guillaume de Saint-Amour et la polémique universitaire parisienne 1250–1259* (Paris, 1972); idem, *Saint Thomas et l'histoire* (Aix-en-Provence, 1991), 445–550; J. D. Dawson, "William of Saint Amour and the Apostolic Tradition," *MS* 40 (1978): 223–38; E. Faral, "Les 'Responsiones' de Guillaume de Saint-Amour," *AHDL* 25–26 (1950/51): 337–94; A. G. Traver, *The Opuscula of William of Saint-Amour: The Minor Works of 1255–1256*, BGPhMA 63 (Münster, 2003); idem, "Rewriting History? The Parisian Secular Masters' Apologia of 1254," *History of Universities* 15 (1997/99): 9–45.

17. For *De periculis* of William of Saint-Amour see the edition of M. Bierbaum, *Bettelorden und Weltgeistlichkeit an der Universität Paris*, FS.B 2 (Münster, 1920), 1–36. On the chronology see M.-M. Dufeil, *Guillaume de Saint-Amour*, 212–27. For Thomas's response see *Contra impugnantes*, ed. Leon., Introduction A7–A13.

18. See H. E. Feine, *Kirchliche Rechtsgeschichte*, vol. 1, *Die katholische Kirche*, 3rd ed. (Weimar, 1955), 323–29, 355–64; J. Gaudemet, *Eglise et cité. Histoire du droit canonique* (Paris, 1994), 412–51; *Histoire du droit et des institutions de l'Eglise en Occident*, ed. G. Le Bras and J. Gaudemet. Vol. VIII, 2, *Le gouvernement de l'Eglise à l'époque classique. II. part. Le gouvernement local*, by J. Gaudemet (Paris, 1979), 105–202; 223–30; 312–18.

19. Yvo de Chartres, *Ep.* 36, PL 116:49. The expression comes from Jerome, *Contra Vigilantium*, no. 15, PL 23:351B: "Monachus autem non doctoris habet, sed plangentis officium." Thomas cites this in *Contra impugnantes*, c. 2, arg. 2, ed. cit., A55, and ad 2, ed. cit., A60. See P. Delhaye, "L'organisation scolaire au XIIᵉ siècle," *Tr* 5 (1947): 211–68, here 213–17; M. Peuchmaurd, "Le prêtre ministre de la parole dans la théologie du XIIᵉ siècle (Canonistes, moines et chanoines)," *RThAM* 29 (1962): 52–76; idem, "Mission canonique et prédication. Le prêtre ministre de la parole dans la querelle entre mendiants et séculiers au XIIIᵉ siècle," *RThAM* 30 (1963): 122–44, 251–76.

20. On the conflict at other universities see M. W. Sheehan, "The Religious Orders, 1220–1370," in *The History of the University of Oxford*, vol. 1, *The Early Oxford Schools*, ed. J. I. Catto (Oxford, 1984), 192–221; W. A. Hinnebusch, *The Early English Friars Preachers*, DH 14 (Rome, 1951), 3–11; A. G. Little, *The Grey Friars in Oxford*, Oxford Historical Society 20 (Oxford, 1892); J. R. Moorman, *The Grey Friars in Cambridge* (Cambridge, 1938); A. D'Amato, *I Domenicani e l'università di Bologna* (Bologna, 1988), 79–89.

21. Reference should be made here to a few simple but very important innovations. Preachers and Minorites did not bind themselves through profession to any one place (*stabilitas loci*). The outward sign for this is that they professed their vows not in the

hands of a local superior, but in those of the *magister ordinis*, who had the power to send them anywhere. The Dominican formula of profession reads: "Ego N. facio professionem et promitto obedientiam Deo et beate Marie et tibi N., magistro ordinis Predicatorum, et successoribus tuis . . ." or "priori talis loci N., *vice magistri ordinis Predicatorum.*" See A. H. Thomas, *De oudste constituties van den Dominicanen. Vorgeschiedenis. Text, bronnen, ontstaan en ontwikkeling (1215–1237) met uitgave van de text*, BRHE 42 (Leuven, 1965), D. I, c. 16, ed. cit., 326f. For another characterization see the classic description of H. Denifle, "Die Constitutionen des Prediger-Ordens vom Jahre 1228," *ALKGMA* 1 (1885): 165–93. See also R. Creytens, "Les constitutions des frères prêcheurs dans la rédaction de s. Raymond de Peñafort," *AFP* 18 (1948): 5–68. On the history of associations see I. W. Frank's detailed overview, *Franz von Assisi. Frage auf eine Antwort* (Düsseldorf, 1982), 199–214. On the constitution of the order see S. Tugwell, "The Evolution of Dominican Structures of Government. I. The First and Last Abbot," *AFP* 69 (1999): 5–60; idem, "The Evolution of Dominican Structures of Government. II. The First Dominican Provinces," *AFP* 70 (2000): 5–109; idem, "The Evolution of Dominican Structures of Government. III. The Early Development of the Second Distinction of the Constitutions," *AFP* 71 (2001): 5–182; idem, "The Evolution of Dominican Structures of Government. IV. Election, Confirmation and 'Absolution' of Superiors," *AFP* 72 (2002): 27–159.

22. See the articles "Travail," *DS* 15:1208–37 (P. Vallin), and "Arbeit (Mittelalter)," *TRE* 3:626–35 (J. Le Goff). See also J. Dubois, "Le travail des moines au moyen âge," in *Le travail au moyen âge. Une approche inter-disciplinaire*, ed. J. Hamesse and C. Muraille-Samaran (Louvain-la Neuve, 1990), 61–100, and K. Esser, "Die Handarbeit in der Frühgeschichte des Minderbrüderordens," *FS* 40 (1958): 145–66.

23. William of Saint-Amour, *De periculis*, c. 2, ed. cit. (Bierbaum), 7–9: "In hanc domum intrat per ostium rector animarum, qui curam habet ab ecclesia sibi commissam . . . Alienus autem, qui curam non habet, in hac domo recipi non debet . . . et ideo dicitur penetrare domum tanquam fur et latro . . . Ab ecclesia recte eliguntur episcopi, qui apostolis successerunt; et parochiales presbyteri, qui discipulis 72 successerunt, et eorum loca tenent . . . Nec plures sunt in ecclesia gradus ad regendam ecclesiam constituti."

24. On the interest of Aquinas in pastoral duties see L. E. Boyle, "The Quodlibets of St. Thomas and Pastoral Care," *Thom* 38 (1974): 232–56.

25. See *Contra impugnantes*, c. 4, §§ 9–12, ed. cit., A76–A81.

26. *Contra impugnantes*, c. 2, § 3, ed. cit., A57: "illi maxime sunt idonei ad docendum qui maxime divina per contemplationem capere possunt."

27. Ibid., A58: "Eis autem competit docere qui notitiam habent Scripturarum; ergo religiosi qui paupertatem profitentur maxime competit docere."

28. See J. A. Watt, "The Theory of Papal Monarchy in the Thirteenth Century," *Tr* 20 (1964): 179–317; K. Pennington, *Pope and Bishops: The Papal Monarchy in the Twelfth and Thirteenth Centuries* (Philadelphia, 1984), esp. 43–74; K. Schatz, "Papsttum und partikularkirchliche Gewalt bei Innozenz III. (1198–1216)," *AHP* 8 (1970): 61–111.

29. U. Horst, *Evangelische Armut und Kirche*, 58–61. On Thomas of York see A. G. Traver, "Thomas of York's Role in the Conflict between Mendicants and Seculars at Paris," *FrS* 57 (1999): 179–202.

30. This is precisely the point at which William of Saint-Amour raises his objections. The pope has no right to violate the jurisdiction of the bishops. *De periculis*, c. 2, ed. cit., 10: "Respondemus, quod de potestate domini papae aut episcoporum nolumus disputare; verumtamen, cum secundum iura, tam divina quam humana, in una ecclesia non possit esse nisi unus, alioquin non esset sponsa, sed scortum [cf. C. 21, q. 2, c. 4, *Sicut in unaquaque*, in *Corpus Iuris Canonici*, ed. Friedberg, 1:855]. Et in una ecclesia non debeant esse plura capita, ne fit monstrum [cf. C. 14.X. I 31, *Quoniam in plerisque*, ed. Friedberg, 2:191 ff.] . . . Si forte dominus papa aliquibus personis concedat potestatem predicandi ubique, intelligendum est, ubi ad hoc fuerit invitati, quia etiam episcopi, nisi invitati fuerint ad hoc, ultra diocesim accedere non debent super aliquibus ecclesiasticis disponendis [C. 9, q. 2, c. 11, *Non invitati*, ed. Friedberg, 1:605]. Non enim princeps per mandata sua vult preiudicem iurisdictionis alterius generari."

31. *De periculis*, c. 2, ed. cit., 11: "Non est veresimile, quod dominus papa, contra doctrinam apostoli Pauli, infinitis vel pluribus licentiam concedat praedicandi plebibus alienis, nisi a plebanis fuerint invitati . . . Quod si Romanus pontifex, 'quod docuerunt Apostoli et prophetae, destruere, quod absit, niteretur, non sententiam dare, sed magis errare convinceretur'. . . Item, si una persona vel infinitae persone habeant potestatem praedicandi ubique, non invitati, cum hoc sit potissimum officium episcoporum, iam erunt infiniti episcopi universales, quod est contra iura."

32. *Contra impugnantes*, c. 4, § 15, ed. cit., A84.

33. Ibid., § 8, ed. cit., A76: "Item, legati papae et eorum paenitentiarii confessiones audiunt non petita licentia a presbyteris parochialibus, et etiam auctoritate papae ubique praedicant; et ita patet, quod praedicare et audire confessiones potest aliis committi sine licentia sacerdotum parochialium." On legates, see W. Plöchl, *Geschichte des Kirchenrechts*, vol. 2 (Vienna-Munich, 1955), 95–99; R. C. Figueira, "'Legatus apostolicae sedis': The Pope's 'alter ego' According to Thirteenth Century Canonists," *StudMed* 27 (1986): 527–74. Because his opponents deployed arguments mainly drawn from canon law, Thomas had to respond similarly with juristic authorities. See J. McIntyre, "Aquinas, Gratian and the Mendicant Controversy," in *Proceedings of the Ninth International Congress of Medieval Canon Law, Munich, 13–18 July 1992*, ed. P. Landau and J. Müller (Vatican City, 1997), 1101–35.

34. *Committere* is the key word for Thomas. *Contra impugnantes*, c. 4, § 15 ad 5, ed. cit., A85: "ex hoc ipso quod papa committit alicui officium praedicandi ille habet exe-cutionem officii, quicumque sit." C. 4, § 13 ad 8, ed. cit., A82: "dicendum quod nusquam possunt [fratres] audire [confessiones] propria auctoritate, possunt tamen audire ubicumque eis commissum fuerit; et si committeretur eis quod ubique audirent ab eo qui toti Ecclesiae praeest, possent ubique audire."

35. A. H. Thomas, *De oudste constituties van den Dominicanen*, D. II, c. 23, 358: "Conventus citra numerum duodenarium et sine licentia capituli et sine priore et doctore non mittatur. See I. W. Frank, "Die Grundlegung des intellektuellen Profils des Predigerordens in seinen Anfängen," *RoJKG* 17 (1998): 13–34; M. M. Mulchahey, "*First the Bow is Bent in Study . . .*": *Dominican Education before 1350*, STPIMS 132 (Toronto,

1998). On the development of the Franciscan order see D. Berg, *Armut und Wissenschaft. Beiträge zur Geschichte des Studienwesens der Bettelorden* (Düsseldorf, 1977), 43–56, 76–85; idem, "Studien und Bildungsfragen im Franziskanerorden," in *Armut und Geschichte. Studien zur Geschichte der Bettelorden im Hohen und Späten Mittelalter*, Saxonia Franciscana 11 (Kevelaer, 2001), 51–123.

36. It was of some historical consequence that already in the early days of his community, St. Dominic sent the first brothers to Paris with this commission: "misit [Dominicus] hunc testem [Ioannem Hispanum] Parisius cum quinque fratribus clericis et uno converso, *ut studerent et predicarent et conventum ibi facerent . . .*" *Acta canonizationis S. Dominici*, ed. A. Walz, MOPH 16 (Rome, 1935), 143 ff. Also in MOPH 16, cf. Jordanus de Saxonia, *Libellus de principiis Ordinis Praedicatorum*, ed. H. C. Scheeben, nos. 51 and 55, 50 ff.

37. *Chartularium Universitatis Parisiensis*, ed. H. Denifle and E. Chatelain, vol. 1 (Paris, 1889), nos. 247, 279–85. See Dufeil, *Guillaume de Saint-Amour*, 152–56.

38. See C. Ferruolo, *The Origins of the University: The Schools of Paris and Their Critics, 1100–1215* (Stanford, 1985), 288–95; O. Lewry, "Papal Ideas and the University of Paris, 1170–1303," in *The Religious Role of the Papacy: Ideals and Realities, 1150–1300*, ed. C. Ryan (Toronto, 1989), 363–88; W. Maleczek, "Das Papsttum und die Anfänge der Universität im Mittelalter," *RöHM* 27 (1985): 85–143.

39. See O. Weijers, *Terminologie des universités au XIIIᵉ siècle* (Rome, 1987), 46–51; M. Teeuwen, *The Vocabulary of Intellectual Life in the Middle Ages* (Turnhout, 2003), 88–91; A. Bernstein, "Magisterium and License: Corporate Autonomy against Papal Authority in the Medieval University of Paris," *Viator* 9 (1978): 291–307; P. R. McKeon, "The Status of the University of Paris as *Parens Scientiarum*: An Episode in the Development of Its Autonomy," *Spec* 39 (1964): 651–75; A. Michaud-Quantin, *Universitas. Expressions du mouvement communautaire dans le moyen âge latin*, L'église et l'état au moyen âge 13 (Paris, 1970), 11–57; G. Post, "Alexander III, the *Licentia docendi* and the Rise of the Universities," in *C. H. Haskins Anniversary Essays in Medieval History*, ed. C. H. Taylor and J. L. La Monte (Boston, 1929), 255–77; P. Delhaye, "L'organisation," 258–60.

40. *Contra impugnantes*, c. 3, § 3, ed. cit., A64: "mali homines et seductores (i.e. magistri) . . . non contenti religiosorum infamia etiam apostolicam auctoritatem evacuare conantur, dicentes quod nec etiam apostolica auctoritate cogi possunt ut ad suam societatem religiosos admittant, quia secundum iuris civilis ordinationem nullus ad societatem compelli debet, cum societas voluntate firmetur, unde nec ipsi compelli possunt aliqua auctoritate ut religiosos ad suam societatem admittant." On the point of view of the *magistri* see P. Michaud-Quantin, "Le droit universitaire dans le conflit parisien de 1252–1257," *StGra* 8 (1962): 577–99; G. Post, "Parisian Masters as a Corporation, 1200–1246," *Spec* 9 (1934): 421–45; O. Gierke, *Das deutsche Genossenschaftsrecht*, vol. 3, *Die Staats- und Korporationslehre des Alterthums und des Mittelalters und ihre Aufnahme in Deutschland* (Berlin, 1881), especially § 416–644.

41. *Contra impugnantes*, c. 3, § 7, ed. cit., A68: "In his autem quae sequuntur in quibus apostolicae potestati derogant, non solum falsitatis sed etiam haeresis crimen

incurrunt, quia, ut dicitur in Decretis dist. XXII cap. 'Omnes', 'qui romanae ecclesiae privilegium ab ipso summo omnium ecclesiarum capite traditum auferre conantur, hic procul dubio in haeresim labitur,' et infra 'Fidem quippe violat qui adversus illam agit quae est fidei mater.'"

42.   Ibid.: "Hoc autem privilegium Christus romanae ecclesiae contulit ut omnes ei sicut Christo obediant."

43.   Ibid.: "'. . .ut membra maneamus in capite nostro apostolico throno romanorum pontificum, a quo nostrum est quaerere quid credere et quid tenere debeamus, ipsum venerantes, ipsum rogantes pro omnibus quoniam ipsius solum est reprehendere, corrigere, statuere, disponere, solvere et loco illius ligare qui ipsum aedificavit et nulli alii quod suum est plenum sed ipsi soli dedit, cui omnes iure divino caput inclinant et primates mundi tamquam ipsi Domino Iesu obediunt.' Unde patet quod quicumque dicit non esse obediendum his quae per papam statuuntur in haeresim labitur."

44.   Ibid.: "Et sic patet quod ordinare de studio pertinet ad eum qui praeest rei publicae, et praecipue ad auctoritatem apostolicae sedis qua universalis Ecclesia gubernatur, cui per generale studium providetur."

45.   St. Dominic is only once mentioned in a sermon together with St. Francis. "Sermo 'Homo erat dives qui habebat vilicum,'" ed. J.-B. Raulx, in *Divi Thomae Aquinatis doctoris angelici sermones et opuscula concinatoria*, vol. 2 (Luxemburg, 1881), 354–64: "Item suscitavit gloriosos ministros, scilicet beatum Dominicum et Franciscum, qui administraverunt salutem hominum, et ad hoc fuit ipsorum spirituale studium, ut homines ducerent ad salutem (364). St. Francis's stigmata are similarly mentioned in an unedited sermon. See L.-J. Bataillon, "Les stigmates de saint François vus par Thomas d'Aquin et quelques autres prédicateurs dominicains," *AFH* 90 (1997): 341–47, here 342. Thomas offers no discussion of any theological consequences. On the veneration of St. Dominic in the early days of the order see L. Canetti, *L'invenzione della memoria. Il culto e l'immagine di Domenico nella storia dei primi frati Predicatori*, Biblioteca di Medioevo latino 19 (Spoleto, 1996). Cf. S. Tugwell in the introduction to *Miracula Sancti Dominici mandato magistri Berengarii collecta. Petri Calo legendae Sancti Dominici*, MOPH 26 (Rome, 1997), 21–189.

46.   See U. Horst, *Bischöfe und Ordensleute*, 146–54; idem, "Thomas von Aquin und der Predigerorden," *RoJKG* 17 (1998): 35–52. An interesting detail is worthy of mention here. The *exemplum* for poverty in the *Contra impugnantes* is not St. Dominic, but Benedict and Alexius. Cf. c. 7, § 6, ed. cit., A110 ff., and c. 7, § 8, ed. cit., A114. Bonaventure mentions Dominic in the argument over mendicancy: *Quaestio reportata de mendicitate cum annotationisbus Gulielmi de S. Amore*, ed. F. Delorme, in *S. Bonaventurae Collationes in Hexaëmeron* (Quaracchi, 1934), nos. 16 and 17, 338 ff.

47.   See W. Dettloff, "Die franziskanische Vorentscheidung im theologischen Denken des hl. Bonaventura," *MThZ* 13 (1962): 107–15; idem, "Die Rückkehr zum Evangelium in der Theologie. Franziskanische Grundanliegen bei Bonaventura," *WiWei* 38 (1975): 26–40.

48.   On the writings about the order see B. Distelbrink, *Bonaventurae scripta. Authentica, dubia vel spuria critice recensita*, SSFr 5 (Rome, 1975), 31–53; I. Brady, "The Writ-

ings of Saint Bonaventure Regarding the Franciscan Order," *in San Bonaventura Maestro di vita francescana e di sapienza cristiana a cura di A. Pompei. Atti Congresso Internazionale per il VII centenario di San Bonaventura di Bagnoregio*, vol. 1 (Rome, 1976), 89–112; S. Clasen, *Der Hl. Bonaventura und das Mendikantentum. Ein Beitrag zur Ideengeschichte des Pariser Mendikantenstreites (1252–72)* (Werl, 1940).

49. Bonaventura, *Legenda maior S. Francisci, Opera Omnia*, vol. 8 (Quaracchi, 1898), 504–64; see also *Fontes Franciscani*, ed. E. Menestò and S. Brufani (Porziuncula, 1995), 777–967. On tendencies and intentions see S. Clasen, "S. Bonaventura S. Francisci Legendae maioris compilator,"*AFH* 54 (1961): 241–72; 55 (1962): 3–58, 289–319; idem, *Franziskus Engel des sechsten Siegels. Sein Leben nach den Schriften des heiligen Bonaventura*, Franziskanische Quellenschriften 7 (Werl, 1962); idem, "Einteilung und Anliegen der Legenda maior S. Fancisci Bonaventuras," *FrS* 27 (1967): 115–62.

50. Text in A. G. Little, "Definitiones capitulorum generalium Ordinis Fratrum Minorum, 1262–1282," *AFH* 7 (1914): 676–82: "Item precipit generale capitulum per obedientiam, quod omnes legende de beato Francisco olim facte deleantur et, ubi extra Ordinem inveniri poterunt, ipsas fratres studeant amovere, cum illa legenda que facta est per generalem ministrum, fuerit compilata prout ipse habuit ab ore eorum, qui cum b. Francisco quasi semper fuerunt et cuncta certitudinaliter sciverunt et probata ibi sunt posita diligenter (678)." See G. Abate, "Le 'diffinitiones' del capitulo generale di Parigi del 1266," *MiscFranc* 32 (1932): 3–5. On the intentions of Bonaventure and the order concerning the approval of the Legenda maior and the destruction of other legends see C. Frugoni, *Francesco e l'invenzione delle stimmate. Una storia per parole e immagini fino a Bonaventura e Giotto* (Torino, 1993), 24–34; E. Pástor, "S. Bonaventura: biografo di S. Francesco? Contributo alla 'questione francescana,'" *Doctor Seraphicus* 27 (1980): 83–107; G. Miccoli, *Francesco d'Assisi. Realtà e memoria di un'esperienza cristiana* (Torino, 1991), 264–302, esp. 286 ff.; J. Dalarun, *La malaventure de François d'Assise. Pour un usage historique des légendes hagiographiques* (Paris, 2002), esp. 211–46; F. Uribe, *Introduzione alla fonti agiografiche di san Francesco e santa Chiara d'Assisi (secc. XIII–XIV)* (Assisi, 2002), 234–69. The Dominican order had a similar problem, but found a far less radical solution. At the general chapter in Strassburg in 1260, Master General Humbert commanded that in the future only the legend of Dominic that he himself had authored was to be used officially. The older legends were not to be copied any more. See *Acta capituli generalis*, ed. B. M. Reichert, MOPH 3 (Rome, 1898), 105: "Item. Mandat magister, quod fratres utantur legenda beati Dominici que inserta est in lectionario, et alie deinceps non scribantur." There is therefore no question of a "decisione identica," as C. Frugoni claims in *Francesco*, 45, n. 103.

51. Bonaventura, *Quaestiones disputatae De perfectione evangelica*, q. 2, *De paupertate*, a. 2 ad 2, *Opera Omnia*, vol. 5 (Quaracchi, 1891), no. 4, 153: "Quod autem pro *regula* approbet, patet per illud scriptum superius allegatum, de Excessibus praelatorum, *Nimis prava*, ubi dicitur, quod 'ordinem et regulam fratrum Praedicatorum et Minorum Sedes apostolica noscitur approbasse.'" Emphasis in edition.

52. Ibid.: "Patet etiam per regulam beati Francisci a domino Honorio approbatam et confirmatam, ubi dicitur, quod fratres 'vadant pro eleemosyna confidenter.'"

Cf. K. Esser and E. Grau, *Die Opuscula des hl. Franziskus von Assisi. Neue textkritische Edition*, 2d ed., SpicBon 13 (Grottaferrata, 1989), c. 6, 369.

53. *Quaestiones disputatae De perfectione evangelica*, q. 2, a. 2 ad 2, no. 4, ed. cit., 153: "Sed si erravit [Honorius] hoc approbando—et constat, eum hoc approbasse et confirmasse; constat etiam, quod universalis Ecclesia per totum mundum huiusmodi ordines et status acceptat—concludendum est ergo secundum dictum huius hominis unius, quod universalis Ecclesia tota erravit et decepta fuit; et qui huiusmodi statum erroneum invenerunt et approbaverunt, omnes damnati sunt; quod est horribilissimum et incredibilissimum, quod Deus permitteret sic errare universaliter populum sanctum suum et tantam multitudinem sapientium, qui haec tempora praecesserunt." See J. Ratzinger, "Zum Einfluß des Bettelordensstreites auf die Entwicklung der Primatslehre," in his *Das neue Volk Gottes. Entwürfe zur Ekklesiologie* (Düsseldorf, 1969), 49–71.

54. *Quaestiones disputatae De perfectione evangelica*, q. 2, a. 2 ad 2, no. 4, ed. cit., 153: "Mira est haec *sapientia*, quae omnium ostendit insipientiam; et mira *iustitia*, quae ceteros condemnat. Quodsi hoc non est sapientia, sed potius temeritas Sedem apostolicam velle iudicare, quae a solo Deo iudicatur, et eius iudicium et sententiam reprobare et tot viros sanctos in infernum retrudere et in barathrum damnationis." Emphasis in edition.

55. But what would happen, one may ask, if some day the pope should have the intention to modify the approbation of the Franciscan order and to repeal parts of the rule or to dispense from its observation?

56. Bonaventura, *Apologia pauperum*, c. 11, no. 15, *Opera Omnia*, vol. 8 (Quaracchi, 1898), 315a: "Sed constans est, quod beatus Franciscus non ob aliud possessionem seu contrectationem pecuniae imitatoribus suis inhibuit, nisi quia in hoc aliquam esse sanctitatem et pia fide credidit et certa veritate cognovit; non quia mala sit pecunia . . . sed quia inter cetera, quae possidentur, pecunia maxime est illecebrosa et de facili est illectiva et distractiva non solum imperfectorum, sed etiam perfectorum, et quia Spiritu sancto dictante percepit, quod sanctitatis est non tantum peccata cavere, verum etiam ocasiones peccatorum refugere: ideo veraciter in hoc sanctitatem esse credidit et non erravit." L. Hardick, "Pecunia et denarii. Untersuchungen zum Geldverbot in den Regeln der Minderbrüder," *FS* 40 (1958): 193–217, 313–28; 41 (1959): 268–90; 43 (1961): 216–44. On the discussions see *Expositio quatuor magistrorum super regulam Fratrum Minorum (1241–1242). Accedit eiusdem regulae textus cum fontibus et locis parallelis*, ed. L. Oliger (Rome, 1950), c. 4, 141–48; O. Langholm, *Economics in the Medieval Schools: Wealth, Exchange, Value, Money and Usury according to the Paris Theological Tradition, 1200–1350*, STGMA 29 (Leiden, 1992), 142–67. On the problem of money in Thomas Aquinas see F. Wittreck, *Geld als Instrument der Gerechtigkeit. Die Geldrechtslehre des Hl. Thomas von Aquin in ihrem interkulturellen Kontext* (Paderborn, 2002).

57. *Apologia pauperum*, c. 11, no. 15, ed. cit., 315a: "Qui igitur hunc Christi imitatorem praecipuum, ipsius insignitum stigmatibus, ascriptum catalogo Sanctorum et ab universa Ecclesia in veneratione susceptum asserit errore deceptum fuisse, maxime in professione et observantia evangelicae vitae, non solum ipsum impugnat, verum etiam

universalem Ecclesiam, et quod plus est, Magistri veritatis et Apostolorum eius doctrinam blasphemat et vitam."

58.   It is not necessary to address here the problem of the historicity of the stigmata. It is sufficient to make reference to the discussion. Older literature: O. von Rieden, "De S. Francisci Assisiensis stigmatum susceptione. Disquisitio historico-critica luce testimoniorum saec. XIII," *CFr* 33 (1963): 210–66, 392–422; 34 (1964): 5–62, 241–338; A. Vauchez, *La sainteté en Occident*, 514–18. The discussion has entered a new phase with C. Frugoni, *Francesco e l'invenzione*. A good summary is C. Frugoni, *Francis of Assisi: A Life* (London, 1998), 119–47. On the controversy over the thesis see A. Vauchez, "Autour de la stigmatisation de saint François," *RMab* 5 (1994): 270–74; P. Zerbi, "L' 'ultimo sigillo' (Par. XI, 107). Tendenze della recente storiografia italiana sul tema delle stigmate di S. Francesco. A proposito di un libro recente," *RSCI* 48 (1994): 7–42; G. Miccoli, "Considerazione sulle stimmate," in *Franciscana I (Bolletino della Società internazionale di studi francescani)* (Spoleto, 1999), 101–21. It is interesting that Thomas Aquinas speaks of the *indicia passionis Christi* that St. Francis had on his body. See L.-J. Bataillon, "Les stigmates," 342.

59.   *Apologia pauperum*, c. 11, no. 16, ed. cit., 315b: "*Exsurge igitur, sancta mater* [Ecclesia Romana], et *iudica causam tuam* [Ps 73, 22] [emphasis in edition], quia, si pauperum hic Ordo Minorum recte profitetur veritatem Evangelii, tuum est; si a veritate in professione a te sancita deviat, tuum est; ac per hoc, si professioni huiusmodi sanctae error impingitur, *tu, quae illam sanxisti, errasse assereris, et quae magistra veritatis hactenus exstitisti, nunc de approbatione erroris argueris et quibusdam modernis praesumtoribus velut iuris divini et humani nescia derideris*" (emphasis mine).

60.   *Quaestiones de quolibet*, ed. R.-A. Gauthier, ed. Leon., vol. 25 (Rome-Paris, 1996), 118 ff.

61.   See S. Kuttner, "La réserve papale du droit de canonisation," *Revue historique du droit français et étranger* 17 (1938): 172–228; R. Klauser, "Zur Entwicklung des Heiligsprechungsverfahrens bis zum 13. Jahrhundert," *ZRGKA* 60 (1954): 85–101; E. W. Kemp, *Canonization and Authority in the West* (Oxford, 1948); M. Ries, "Heiligenverehrung und Heiligsprechung in der Alten Kirche und im Mittelalter. Zur Entwicklung des Kanonisationsverfahrens," in *Bischof Ulrich von Augsburg, 890–973. Seine Zeit—sein Leben—seine Verehrung. Festschrift aus Anlaß des tausendjährigen Jubiläums seiner Kanonisation im Jahre 993*, ed. M. Weitlauff (Weissenhorn, 1993), 143–67, esp. 148–63; A. Vauchez, *La sainteté en Occident*, 25–67; R. Paciocco, *"Sublimia negotia." Le canonizzationi dei santi nella curia papale e il nuovo Ordine dei Frati Minori* (Padova, 1996); M. Bihl, "De canonizatione S. Francisci (occasione VII centenarii: 1228–1928)," *AFH* 21 (1928): 468–514.

62.   *Quodlibet* IX.16, ed. cit., 119: "Dico ergo quod iudicium eorum qui presunt ecclesie errare in quibuslibet, si persone eorum tantum respiciantur, possibile est. Si vero consideretur divina providentia que ecclesiam Spiritu sancto dirigit ut non erret, sicut ipse promisit [Jo 16:13] quod *Spiritus* adveniens doceret *omnem veritatem*, de necessariis scilicet ad salutem, certum est quod iudicium ecclesie universalis errare in hiis que ad fidem pertinent, impossibile est." Emphasis in edition. For more details see U. Horst, "Die

Lehrautorität des Papstes nach Augustinus von Ancona," *AAug* 53 (1991): 271–303, esp. 285–89.

63. *Quodlibet* IX.16, ed. cit., 119: "Unde magis est standum sentencie Pape, ad quem pertinet determinare de fide, quam in iudicio proferret, quam quorumlibet sapientum hominum in sacris scripturis opinioni." See M. Schenk, *Die Unfehlbarkeit des Papstes in der Heiligsprechung*, ThomStud 9 (Freiburg/Schw., 1965).

64. *Quodlibet* IX.16, ed. cit., 119: "cum Cayphas, quamvis nequam, tamen quia pontifex legatur etiam inscius prophetasse." The example of the prophesying Caiaphas had a broad resonance in scholastic literature. See M. Schlosser, *Lucerna in caligonoso loco. Aspekte des Prophetie-Begriffes in der scholastischen Theologie*, VGI 43 (Paderborn, 2000), 154–61 (Index: Kajaphas); Thomas Aquinas, *Super Ioannem*, c. 11, lectio 7, ed. R. Cai (Torino, 1952), nos. 1578–79, 294 ff.; *STh* II-II, q. 173, art. 4; *Ad Titum*, c. 1, lectio 3, ed. R. Cai (Torino, 1953), no. 30, 308.

65. *Quodlibet* IX.16, ed. cit., 119: "Canonizatio vero sanctorum medium est inter haec duo; quia tamen honor quem sanctis exhibemus quedam professio fidei est, qua sanctorum gloriam credimus, *pie credendum est quod nec etiam in hiis iudicium ecclesie errare possit.*"

66. Ibid.: "Ad primum ergo dicendum quod pontifex, cuius est canonizare sanctos, potest certificari de statu alicuius per inquisitionem vite et attestationem miraculorum, et *precipue per instinctum Spiritus sancti, qui omnia scrutatur, etiam profunda Dei.* Ad secundum dicendum quod divina providentia preservat ecclesiam ne in talibus per fallibile testimonium hominum fallatur." (Emphasis mine and in edition.) See M. Seckler, *Instinkt und Glaubenswille nach Thomas von Aquin* (Mainz, 1961); J. Alfaro, "Supernaturalitas fidei iuxta S. Thomam, II: Functio 'interioris instinctus,'" *Gr* 44 (1963): 731–87; U. Horst, *Die Gaben des Heiligen Geistes nach Thomas von Aquin*, VGI 46 (Berlin, 2001), esp. 71–79.

67. See C. Conticello, "San Tommaso ed i Padri: La Catena aurea super Ioannem," *AHDL* 65 (1990): 31–92; U. Horst, "Thomas von Aquin: Professor und Consultor," *MThZ* 48 (1997): 205–18, here 207–10; L.-J. Bataillon, "Saint Thomas et les Pères: de la Catena aurea à la Tertia Pars," in *Ordo sapientiae et amoris (Festschrift J.-P. Torrell)* (Fribourg, 1993), 15–36; T. Prügl, "Patristische Fundamente der Ekklesiologie des Thomas von Aquin," in *Väter der Kirche. Ekklesiales Denken von den Anfängen bis in die Neuzeit (Festgabe H. J. Sieben)*, ed. J. Arnold, R. Berndt, and M. W. Stammberger (Paderborn, 2004), 745–69.

68. See U. Horst, "Albertus Magnus und Thomas von Aquin zu Matthäus 16, 18f. Ein Beitrag zur Lehre vom päpstlichen Primat," in *Albertus Magnus. Zum Gedenken nach 800 Jahren. Neue Zugänge, Aspekte und Perspektiven*, ed. W. Senner, QFGDO n.s. 10 (Berlin, 2001), 553–71, esp. 562–67.

69. *Catena aurea in quatuor evangelia*, ed. A. Guarienti (Torino, 1953), vol. 1, *In Mt. XVI*, 252a. Cf. *Liber de fide trinitatis*, ed. Leon., vol. 40, A145s: "Secundum autem hanc Domini promissionem, Ecclesia Apostolica Petri ab omni seductione haereticaque circumventione manet immaculata, super omnes praepositos et episcopos, et super omnes primates ecclesiarum et populorum in suis pontificibus, in fide plenissima et auctoritate

Petri. Et cum aliae ecclesiae, quorumdam errore sint verecundatae, stabilita inquass-
abiliter ipsa sola regnat, silentium imponens, et omnium obturans ora haereticorum: et
nos necessario salutis, non decepti superbia, neque vino superbiae inebriati, typum veritatis et sanctae apostolicae traditionis una cum ipsa confitemur et praedicamus."

    70. Albertus Magnus, *Super Lucam*, ed. Borgnet, vol. 23 (Paris, 1895), c. 22, 32, 685:
"*Ait autem Dominus:* Qui ipse principalis fuit: et ideo sibi dicitur, ut per ipsum haec con-
fortatio ad alios ordinate derivetur. *Rogavi autem ut non finaliter deficiat fides tua.* Hoc argumentum efficax est pro sede Petri et successore ipsius, quod fides eius non *finaliter*
deficiat." Hugo of St. Cher, *Postilla in totam Bibliam. Sexta pars huius operis continens postillam domini Hugonis super quatuor evangelia* (Basil, 1506–1508), c. 22: "*Ego autem rogavi*
quasi sathanas temptabit me permittente sed non prevalebit et hoc non erit ex vobis sed
ex me qui hoc rogavi. Sed *ut non deficiat fide* . . . Qualiter ergo rogavit? Solutio. Non dixit
dominus ut non neges sed ut non deficiat fides tua ut non *finaliter periret*. Beda: Non ait
non tempteris sed ne deficiat fides tua ut post lapsum negationis ad pristinum statum
penitendo resurgas."

    71. *Catena aurea, In Lucam*, ed. cit., vol. 2, c. 22, 289b: "Non autem dixit: Rogavi, ut
non neges, sed ne deseras fidem. Theophylactus. Nam et si *paululum* agitandus sis, habes
tamen reconditum semem fidei: quamvis deicerit folia spiritus tentatoris, viget tamen
radix. Petit ergo Satanas te laedere tamquam invidens tibi de mea dilectione; sed quamvis
egomet pro te sim deprecatus, tu tamen delinques; unde sequitur: *Et tu aliquando conversus confirma fratres tuos*; quasi dicat: Postquam me negato ploraveris ac poenitentueris,
corrobora ceteros, cum te principem apostolorum deputaverim: hoc enim decet te qui
mecum robur es et petra Ecclesiae . . . ne scilicet aliquis credentium diffidat, videns eum
qui, cum esset apostolus, denegavit, ac iterum per poenitentiam obtinuit praerogativam,
ut esset antistes mundi." Cf. Theophylactus, *Enarrationes in evangelium Lucae*, c. 22, PG
123, no. 471, 1074.

    72. For more details see H.-F. Dondaine in the introduction to the critical edition,
Contra errores Graecorum, ed. Leon., vol. 40 (Rome, 1969), A5–A65.

    73. *Contra errores Graecorum*, ed. cit., P. II, c. 36, A103: "Et Maximus in Epistola Ori-
entalibus directa [PG 91: 137D] dicit: 'Omnes fines orbis qui Dominum sincere receperunt
et ubique terrarum catholici veram fidem confitentes in ecclesiam Romanorum tamquam
in solem respiciunt, et ex ipsa lumen catholicae et apostolicae fidei recipiunt.'"

    74. Döllinger was first to be convinced that the infallibility of the pope was an in-
vention of the fourteenth and fifteenth centuries. Under the impression of the Pseudo-
Cyrillic texts and the convocation of the First Vatican Council, he wrote in August 1869 in
Der Papst und das Konzil (Leipzig, 1869), 286 ff.: "he [Thomas v. Aquin] introduced the
teaching of the pope and his infallibility . . . into the doctrinal tradition . . . a step whose
importance and complete success can hardly be overestimated." Cf. F. X. Bischof, *Theologie und Geschichte. Ignaz von Döllinger (1799–1890) in der zweiten Hälfte seines Lebens.
Ein Beitrag zu seiner Biographie*, MKHS 9 (Stuttgart, 1997), 146–69; C. Oeyen, "Döllinger
und die pseudo-kyrillischen Fälschungen," in *Geschichtlichkeit und Glaube. Zum 100.
Todestag Johann Joseph Ignaz von Döllingers (1799–1890)*, ed. G. Denzler and E. L. Grasmück

(Munich, 1990), 341–90. F. H. Reusch offered the definitive proof of forgery, in Reusch, *Die Fälschungen in dem Traktat des Thomas von Aquin gegen die Griechen Opusculum contra errores Graecorum ad Urbanum IV.*, Bayerische Akademie der Wissenschaften/Historische Klasse: Abhandlungen, vol. 18, 8 (Munich, 1889), 676–742. M. B. Crowe has said all that is necessary concerning the uncritical and superficial arguments of Hans Küng (*Unfehlbar? Eine Anfrage* [Zürich-Cologne, 1970], 94–98) in his "St. Thomas and the Greeks: Reflections on an Argument in Hans Küng's *Infallible?*," *IThQ* 39 (1972): 253–75.

75.   H. Fuhrmann, *Einfluß und Verbreitung der pseudoisidorischen Fälschungen. Von ihrem Auftauchen bis in die neuere Zeit*, SMGH 24, I (Stuttgart, 1972), 64–136.

76.   See U. Horst, "Albertus Magnus," 568–70.

77.   *Super evangelium S. Matthaei lectura*, ed. R. Cai (Torino, 1951), c. 16, no. 1385, 212. "Ecclesia tamen Romana non fuit ab haereticis depravata quia supra petram erat fundata. Unde in Constantinopoli fuerunt haeretici et labor apostolorum amissus erat: sola Petri ecclesia inviolata permansit (Lc 22:32). Et hoc non solum refertur ad Ecclesiam Petri, sed ad fidem Petri, et ad totam occidentalem Ecclesiam. Unde credo quod occidentales maiorem reverentiam debent Petro quam aliis Apostolis."

78.   See U. Horst, *Papst, Konzil, Unfehlbarkeit. Die Ekklesiologie der Summenkommentare von Cajetan bis Billuart*, WSAMA 10 (Mainz, 1978).

79.   *STh* II-II, q. 1, art. 10: "nova editio symboli necessaria est ad vitandum insurgentes errores. Sed contra . . . editio symboli facta est in synodo generali."

80.   See H. J. Sieben, "Lateran IV," *TRE* 20:485–89.

81.   See J.-P. Torrell, *Initiation*, 183 ff. Thomas's text: ed. Leon., vol. 40 (Rome, 1969), E30–44.

82.   See I. Backes, *Die Christologie des hl. Thomas v. Aquin und die griechischen Kirchenväter*, FChLDG 17 (Paderborn, 1931); G. Geenen, "En marge du Concile de Chalcédoine. Les textes du quatrième concile dans les oeuvres de Saint Thomas," *Ang* 29 (1952): 43–59; idem, "Doctrinae Concilii Chalcedonensis usus et influxus in theologia S. Thomae Aquinatis," *DT(P)* 56 (1953): 319–42; Editores operum Alexandri de Hales, *Summa Theologica*, vol. 4, 1.3 (Quaracchi, 1948), XC: "Profecto nonnisi opera ac merito S. Thomae et post an. 1260 Acta primorum Conciliorum generalium scriptaque S. Cyrilli Alexandrini prima vice scholasticis innotuerunt, scilicet in Catena aurea (1262–1267) Aquinatis et in eius Summa Theologica (1267–1273)." Aquinas made use of the *Collectio Cassinensis* containing the Latin translation of Rusticus. See R.-A. Gauthier, *Somme contre les Gentils* (Paris, 1993), 101 ff.; M. Morard, "Une source de Saint Thomas d'Aquin: Le deuxième Concile de Constantinople (553)," *RSPTh* 81 (1997): 21–56; G. Emery, "Le photinisme et ses précurseurs chez saint Thomas," *RThom* 95 (1995): 371–89.

83.   *De potentia*, q. 10, a. 4 ad 13: "doctrina catholicae fidei sufficienter tradita fuit in symbolo Nicaeno; unde sancti patres in sequentibus synodis non intenderunt aliquid addere, sed propter insurgentes haereses id quod implicite continebatur explicare studuerunt."

84.   Ibid.: "dicendum est, quod processio Spiritus sancti a Filio implicite in symbolo Constantinopolitano continetur . . . Sed propter insurgentes errores . . . conveniens fuit ut in symbolo poneretur, non quasi aliquid additum, sed explicite interpretatum quod im-

plicite continebatur . . . *Sicut autem posterior synodus potestatem habet interpretandi symbolum a priore synodo conditum ac ponendi aliqua ad eius explanationem, ut ex praedictis patet; ita etiam Romanus pontifex hoc sua auctoritate potest, cuius auctoritate sola synodus congregari potest et a quo sententia synodi confirmatur et ad ipsum a synodo appellatur. Quae omnia patent ex gestis Chalcedonensis Synodi.*" See G. Geenen, "Doctrinae Concilii Chalcedonensis," 322–24; G. Emery, "La procession du Saint-Esprit a Filio chez saint Thomas d'Aquin," *RThom* 96 (1996): 531–74, esp. 555–58. On the role of councils see M. Morard, "Thomas d'Aquin lecteur des conciles," *AFH* 98 (2005): 211–365.

85. *De potentia*, q. 10, a. 4 ad 13: "Nec est necessarium quod ad eius expositionem faciendam universale concilium congregetur, cum quandoque id fieri prohibeant bellorum dissidia, sicut in septima synodo [Constantinopolitanum III] legitur, quod Constantinus Augustinus dixit, quod propter imminentia bella universaliter episcopos congregare non potuit; sed tamen illi qui convenerunt, quaedam dubia in fide exorta, sequentes sententiam Agathonis papae determinaverunt."

86. On the interpretation of the article see Y. Congar, "Saint Thomas Aquinas and the Infallibility of the Papal Magisterium (Summa Theol., II-II, q. 1, a. 10)," *Thom* 38 (1974): 81–105. On the conciliar teaching of the canonists see H. J. Sieben, *Die Konzilsidee des lateinischen Mittelalters (847–1378)* (Paderborn, 1984), 252–68. He summarizes it as follows (255): "There is virtually no general council without the pope. But there certainly is a pope without a general council! If papal permission is constitutive of the determinations of a general council, then a general council is in its essence subordinate to the papacy. If the general council is without papal license *nullius momenti* (Huguccio), then the pope is essentially superior to the council."

87. In the contemporary canonistic literature such tensions are, however, discussed. A few examples from that literature illustrate Thomas's position. One is Alanus Anglicus on C. IX, q. 3, c. 17: "Set queritur cum ipse concilio vel cardinalibus questionem fidei ventilat et contingit papam aliam habere sententiam, aliam cardinales, cuius sententia prevalebit? R. concilii vel cardinalium si omnes in concilium opinione concordent. Immo etiamsi maior pars set si cum papa tanta pars concordaverit quanta est que consensit, pape adhereo, et hoc in questione fidei tantum. In aliis autem controversiis iudicialibus pape sententiam omnem aliorum sententiis prefero." Cited by J. A. Moynihan, *Papal Immunity and Liability in the Writings of the Medieval Canonists*, AnGr 120 (Rome, 1961), 82, n. 106. Alanus Anglicus was a defender of papal monarchy. See A. M. Stickler, "Alanus Anglicus als Verteidiger des monarchischen Papsttums," *Sa* 21 (1959): 346–406. Another example is Huguccio, *Summa decretorum*, C. IX, q. III, c. 17, cited by M. Ríos Fernández, "El primado del romano pontífice en el pensamiento de Huguccio de Pisa decretista," *Comp* 11 (1966): 49: "Sed ecce congregatum est concilium de toto orbe; oritur dubitatio, fertur una sententia a solo papa, alia ab omnibus aliis . . . Si tamen papa precipiat ut sua sententia teneatur et non teneatur sententia concilii, obediendum est ei et sua sententia est tenenda et non illa . . . Hoc intelligo verum esse de articulis fidei vel de aliis que non pendunt de arbitrio aliorum. . . . Johannes Teutonicus: Arg. Quod sententia totius ecclesie preferenda est Romae si in aliquo sibi contradicant . . . sed contrarium credo . . . nisi erraret Romana ecclesia quod non credo posse fieri, quia Deus non permitteret." Cited by B. Tierney,

Foundations of the Conciliar Theory: The Contribution of the Medieval Canonists from Gratian to the Great Schism (Cambridge, 1968), 253. Another voice is cited by J. Watt, "The Early Medieval Canonists and the Formation of Conciliar Theory," *IThQ* 24 (1957): 28: "Argumentum, auctoritas pape maiorem esse cum sinodo quam eiusdem solius . . . Solutio, maior est cum sinodo quam sine . . . Ergo ad novam heresim dampnare, opus est congregatione concilii."

88. *STh* II-II, q. 1, art. 10: "Ad illius ergo auctoritatem pertinet editio symboli ad cuius auctoritatem pertinet finaliter determinare ea quae sunt fidei." See Y. Congar, "Saint Thomas Aquinas," 84: *determinare* is the term habitually employed by St. Thomas to signify "define."

89. See B. C. Bazàn, "Les questions disputées, principalement dans les facultés de théologie, de droit et de médecine," in *Les questions disputées et les questions quodlibétiques dans les facultés de théologie, de droit et de médecine,* ed. J. W. Wippel, G. Fransen, and D. Jacquart,Typologie des sources du moyen âge occidental, fasc. 44–45 (Turnhout, 1985), 58–70; O. Weijers, *Le maniement du savoir. Pratiques intellectuelles à l'époque des premières universités (XIIIᵉ–XIVᵉ siècles)* (Turnhout, 1996).

90. Note this interesting text from St. Albert the Great: "Si urgeret necessitas adhuc posset papa *convocato concilio peritorum* et invocato Spiritu sancto aliquid quod implicite continetur in symbolo Apostolorum explanare et ponere inter articulos fidei explicitos: quia hoc non esset novum articulum invenire, sed eum qui semper erat explicare." *Super III Sent.,* ed. Borgnet, vol. 28 (Paris, 1894), d. 24, a. 7 ad 7, 464.

91. *STh* II-II, q. 1, art. 10: "ut ab omnibus inconcussa fide teneatur." Cf. *De potentia,* q. 10, a. 4 ad 13: "unde in determinatione Chalcedonensis Synodi dicitur: Praesens nunc sancta et magna atque universalis Synodus praedicationem hanc ab initio *inconcussam* docens." Cf. *Gestorum Chalcedonensium versio a Rustico edita,* in *Concilium Universale Chalcedonense,* vol. 3, pars altera, Actiones II–VI, ed. E. Schwarz (Berlin-Leipzig, 1936), 136. Thomas used the *Codex Cassinensis.*

92. D. 18, c. 5, *Corpus Iuris Canonici,* ed. Friedberg, 1:52: "Multis denuo apostolicis et canonicis atque ecclesiasticis instruimur regulis, non debere absque sententia Romani Pontificis concilia celebrari . . . Maiores vero et difficiliores questiones . . . ad sedem apostolicam semper deferantur."

93. *STh* II-II, q. 1, art. 10: "Unde et Dominus, Luc. 22, 32, Petro dixit, quem summum pontificem constituit *Ego pro te rogavi, Petre, ut non deficiat fides tua; et tu aliquando conversus confirma fratres tuos.* Et huius ratio est quia una fides debet esse totius ecclesiae . . . Quod servari non posset nisi quaestio fidei exorta determinetur per eum qui toti ecclesiae praeest, ut sic eius sententia a tota ecclesia firmiter teneatur."

94. See B. Tierney, *Foundations of the Conciliar Theory,* 35, n. 1: "in figura ecclesie dixit Christus Petro Ego rogavi . . . ; in eius persona enim universalis ecclesia significatur . . . in persona Petri intelligebatur ecclesia, in fide Petri fides universalis ecclesie que nunquam in totum deficit vel deficiet usque in diem iuditii." Cf. Thomas Aquinas, *Scriptum super sententiis IV,* ed. M. F. Moos (Paris, 1947), D. 20, a. 3, 1024: "Ecclesia generalis non potest errare; quia ille qui 'in omnibus exauditus est pro sua reverentia' (Hebr 5, 7)

dicit Petro, super cuius confessione ecclesia fundata est: 'Ego pro te rogavi, Petre, ut non deficiat fides tua'. . . . Sed ecclesia generalis indulgentias approbat et facit. Ergo indulgentiae aliquid valent."

95. B. Tierney, "A Scriptural Text in the Decretales and in St. Thomas: Canonistic Exegesis of Luke 22:32," *StGra* 20 (1976): 361–78, here 363. Huguccio: "(Ut non deficiat fides tua) intelligitur finaliter et irrecuperabiliter, licet enim ad tempora defecerit, tamen factus est postea fidelior, vel tunc in persona Petri intelligebatur ecclesia, in fide Petri fides universalis ecclesie que numquam in totum deficit vel deficiet usque in diem iuditii." Quoted by B. Tierney, *Origins of Papal Infallibility, 1150–1350: A Study on the Concepts of Infallibility, Sovereignty and Tradition in the Middle Ages*, SHCT 6 (Leiden, 1972), 34, n. 4. See also p. 36, n. 1, a quotation from the *Summa Cantabrigiensis*: "'Ut non deficiat fides tua,' i.e. ecclesie que est tua fides, enim ecclesia nunquam deficit quia etiam in morte domini fuit, saltem in beata virgine."

96. Unlike its place among the canonists, the famous c. *Si papa* (D. 40, c. 6, *Corpus Iuris Canonici*, ed. Friedberg, 1:146) plays no role. See T. Prügl, "Der häretische Papst und seine Immunität im Mittelalter," *MThZ* 47 (1996): 197–215.

97. See P. Rodríguez, "'Infallibilis?' La respuesta de Santo Tomás de Aquino. (Estudio de la terminología 'infallibilis-infallibiliter-infallibilitas' en sus tratados 'de fide,'" *ScrTh* 7 (1975): 51–123.

98. See U. Betti, "Assenza dell'autorità di S. Tommaso nel Decreto Vaticano sull' infallibilità pontificia," *Div* 6 (1962): 407–22.

Chapter Two.   The Medieval Thomist Discussion

1. I list the most important commentaries from the period relevant to our theme: *Expositio quatuor magistrorum super regulam Fratrum Minorum (1241–1242). Accedit eiusdem regulae textus cum fontibus et locis parallelis*, ed. L. Oliger (Rome, 1950), c. 4: 141–48, c. 6: 152–58; *Hugh of Digne's Rule Commentary*, ed. D. Flood, SpicBon 14 (Grottaferrata, 1979), c. 4: 122–38, c. 6: 145–68; Bonaventura, *Expositio super Regulam Fratrum Minorum*, *Opera Omnia*, vol. 8 (Quaracchi, 1898), c. 4: 411–19, c. 6: 420–25. The authorship is contested. Cf. C. Harkins, "The Authorship of a Commentary on the Franciscan Rule Published among the Works of St. Bonaventure," *FrS* 29 (1969): 157–248; S. Clasen, "Bonaventuras Expositio super Regulam Fratrum Minorum," in *S. Bonaventura 1274–1974*, vol. 2 (Grottaferrata, 1973), 531–70; B. Distelbrink, *Bonaventurae scripta. Authentica, dubia vel spuria critice recensita*, SSFr 5 (Rome, 1975), 47 f. See also Bonaventura, *Epistola de tribus quaestionibus*, *Opera Omnia*, vol. 8 (Quaracchi, 1898), 331–36, and D. Flood, *Peter Olivi's Rule Commentary. Edition and Presentation*, VIEG 67 (Wiesbaden, 1972), c. 4: 141–45, c. 6: 158–75. On pages 92–103, Flood gives an overview of other commentaries on the *Rule*.

2. *Testamentum S. Francisci*, in *Die Opuscula des Hl. Franziscus von Assisi*, ed. K. Esser and E. Grau, 2d ed., 2:441: "Praecipio firmiter per obedientiam fratribus universis, quod ubicumque sunt, non audeant petere aliquam litteram in curia Romana, per se

neque per interpositam personam. . . ." 4:443 f.: "Et generalis minister et omnes alii ministri et custodes per obedientiam teneantur, in istis verbis non addere vel minuere. Et semper hoc scriptum habeant secum iuxta regulam. Et in omnibus capitulis quae faciunt, quando legunt regulam, legant et ista verba."

3. Thomas Eccleston reports this. *Fratris Thomae vulgo dicti de Eccleston Tractatus de adventu fratrum minorum in Anglia*, ed. A. G. Little, 2d ed. (Manchester, 1951), collatio XVIII:66.

4. H. Grundmann, "Die Bulle 'Quo elongati' Papst Gregors IX.," *AFH* 54 (1961): 3–25, here 21: "dubietatem de vestris cordibus amovendo ad mandatum illud vos dicimus non teneri, quod sine consensu fratrum et maxime ministrorum, quos universos tangebat, obligare nequivit nec successorem suum quomodolibet obligavit, cum non habeat imperium par in parem." On the problem of papal interpretation of the *Rule*, cf. F. Elizondo, "Pontificiae interpretationes regulae franciscanae usque ad annum 1517," *Laur* 1 (1960): 324–58; idem, "Doctrinales regulae franciscanae expositiones usque ad annum 1517," *Laur* 2 (1961): 449–92; idem, "Bullae 'Quo elongati' Gregorii IX et 'Ordinem vestrum' Innocentii IV. De duabus primis regulae franciscanae authenticis declarationibus," *Laur* 3 (1962): 349–94.

5. On the problems associated with *Quo elongati*, cf. M. D. Lambert, *Franciscan Poverty: The Doctrine of the Absolute Poverty of Christ and the Apostles in the Franciscan Order 1210–1323*, rev. ed. (New York, 1998), 86–88 and 134–36.

6. *Bullarium Franciscanum*, vol. 1, ed. J. H. Sbaralea (Rome, 1759), 401b: "cum tam immobilium quam mobilium hujusmodi jus, proprietas et dominium (illis solis exceptis in quibus expresse donatores seu translatores sibi proprietatem et dominium reservasse constiterit) nullo medio ad Eccesiam ipsam spectent; cui domus et loca praedicta cum ecclesiis ceterisque suis pertinentiis (*quae omnia in jus et proprietatem Beati Petri suscipimus*) omnino tam in spiritualibus quam temporalibus immediate subesse noscuntur." Cf. Lambert, *Franciscan Poverty*, 103–7; K. Balthasar, *Geschichte des Armutsstreites im Franziskanerorden bis zum Konzil von Vienne*, VRF 6 (Münster, 1911), 40–49.

7. We do not yet have a history of ideas of poverty among the Dominicans. See, however, the overview in W. A. Hinnebusch, *The History of the Dominican Order: Origins and Growth to 1500*, vol. 1 (New York, 1966), 157–68. See also F. A. Mathes, "The Poverty Movement and the Augustinian Hermits," *AAug* 31 (1968): 5–154; 32 (1969): 5–116. Nor do we have a history of poverty among the Carmelites. See, however, the isolated remarks in A. Jotischky, *The Carmelites and Antiquity: Mendicants and Their Pasts in the Middle Ages* (Oxford, 2002).

8. *Bullarium Franciscanum*, ed. cit., vol. 1, 487 ff.

9. Cf. F. M. Delorme, "Diffinitiones capituli generalis O.F.M. Narbonensis (1260)," *AFH* 3 (1910): 491–504, here no. 13, 503: "Declaratio domini Innocentii maneat suspensa, sicut fuit in capitulo Methensi; et inhibemus districte ne aliquis utatur in hiis, in quibus declaratio domini Gregorii contradicit." Cf. B. Distelbrink, *Bonaventurae scripta*, 33 f.

10. Here see the important passage of the *Apologia pauperum*, c.11, no. 8, ed. cit., 313a: "Sane, quemadmodum essentiale cuilibet Religionis statui esse dignoscitur, quod nulla persona privata possideat aliquid proprium; sic nec huiusmodi pauperum religio

tota, quae quidem quantum ad abdicationem proprietatis censetur sicut una persona. Quemadmodum igitur monachus vel quivis religiosus utitur vestibus, calceamentis et cibis et ceteris, quae usu consumuntur, ita tamen quod nihil sibi appropriat quoad privatum dominium, nec propter talem usum efficitur proprietarius, quia proprietas semper collegio reservatur; sic et de collegio istiusmodi pauperum summoque Pontifice intelligere debet quicumque de professione ipsorum sentire vult tam vere quam pie. Et propterea, sicut illud quod datur monacho, qualiscumque sit intentio dantis, non in ipsius transit dominium, sed totius collegii et subiacet dispositioni abbatis, etiam si dans nihil de collegio cogitet; *sic quidquid datur congregationi Minorum Fratrum in ius, dominium et proprietatem summi Pontificis et Romanae Ecclesiae transit*; praecipue cum ipsi Fratres ius seu proprietatem rei alicuius sibi acquirere nulla ratione intendant." Cf. V. Mäkinen, *Property Rights in the Late Medieval Discussion on Franciscan Poverty*, RThAM, Bibliotheca 3 (Leuven, 2001), 57–94. On the later discussion cf. M. Kriechbaum, *Actio, ius und dominium in den Rechtslehren des 13. und 14. Jahrhunderts*, Münchener Universitätsschriften. Abhandlungen zur Rechtswissensschaftlichen Grundlagenforschung 77 (Ebelsbach, 1996), esp. 40–89.

11. Bonaventura, *Apologia pauperum*, c. 7, no. 4, ed. cit., 273a: "Cum enim duplex sit rerum dominium, privatum scilicet et commune, unum quidem spectans ad determinatam personam, alterum vero ad determinatum collegium; et primum abdicari possit, retento secundo, possit etiam abdicari secundum cum primo: duplex erit secundum hunc duplicem modum paupertatis perfecta professio, una videlicet, qua quis, temporalium omnium privato seu personali abdicato dominio, sustentatur de non suo; id est, non sibi proprio, communi tamen iure cum aliis participato et simul possesso; *alia vero, qua quis, omni rerum abdicato dominio, tam in proprio quam in communi, sustentatur de non suo, id est non sibi proprio, sed alieno, pie tamen et iuste ab alio sibi pro sustentatione collato*." No. 5: "Secundae autem paupertatis exemplar et forma in vita praeecessit Apostolorum, quam perfectionis magister Christus eisdem instituit, quando ipsos ad praedicandum misit . . . (Mt 10:9s)." See G. Tarello, "Profili giuridici della questione della povertà nel francescanesimo prima di Ockham," in *Università degli studi di Genova*. Annali della facoltà di giurisprudenza, vol. 3 (Milan, 1964), 338–448, esp. 387–94.

12. *Apologia pauperum*, c. 8, nos. 35–40, ed. cit., 284–86.

13. Cf. L. Oliger, "Die theologische Quaestion des Johannes Pecham über die vollkommene Armut," *FS* 4 (1917): 127–76, here 145ff.: "Paupertas eorum (scl. Praedicatorum et Minorum) est altissima." Those who deny this attack the Apostolic See: "Tu dicis, quod est (paupertas) infima, ergo . . . directe impugnas sententiam apostolicam. Sed quicumque est illi pertinaciter contrarius, est hereticus." Later (ca. 1270) Pecham saw that Thomas Aquinas had abandoned the same position. Cf. F. M. Delorme, "Quatre chapitres inédits de Jean de Pecham, O.F.M., sur la perfection religieuse et autres états de perfection," *CFr* 14 (1944): 84–120, here 117. Cf. U. Horst, *Evangelische Armut und Kirche*, 168–71.

14. *Fratris Johannis Pecham quondam archiepiscopi Cantuariensis Tractatus tres*, ed. C. L. Kingsford, A. G. Little, and F. Tocco (Aberdeen, 1910), 131–46. Cf. A. G. Little, *The Grey Friars in Oxford*, 320–35; E. M. F. Sommer-Seckendorff, *Studies in the Life of Robert Kilwardby O.P.*, DH 8 (Rome, 1937), 50–52.

15. See M.-T. D'Alverny, "Un adversaire de Saint Thomas: Petrus Ioannis Olivi," in *St. Thomas Aquinas 1274–1974: Commemorative Studies*, vol. 2 (Toronto, 1974), 179–218 (commentary on Matthew 10:9, 207–18); U. Horst, *Evangelische Armut und Kirche*, 171–76; D. Burr, *Olivi and Franciscan Poverty: The Origins of the Usus Pauper Controversy* (Philadelphia, 1989), 55, n. 36.

16. Cf. G. Fussenegger, "Definitiones Capituli Generalis Argentinae celebrati 1282," *AFH* 26 (1933): 127–40, here 139. On the controversy over the "Correctoria" see U. Horst, *Evangelische Armut und Kirche*, 177–89, and D. Burr, "The Correctorium Controversy and the Origins of the Usus Pauper Controversy," *Spec* 60 (1985): 331–42.

17. Cf. MOPH, vol. 5, 100–104.

18. See J. Moorman, *A History of the Franciscan Order from Its Origins to the Year 1517* (1968; repr. Oxford, 1998), 179–81, and Lambert, *Franciscan Poverty*, 149–56.

19. See V. Maggiani, "De relatione scriptorum quorumdam S. Bonaventurae ad Bullam 'Exiit' Nicolai III (1279)," *AFH* 5 (1912): 3–21, and F. Elizondo, "Bulla 'Exiit qui seminat' Nicolai III (14 augusti 1279)," *Laur* 4 (1963): 59–117.

20. *Corpus Iuris Canonici*, ed. Friedberg, 2:1109–21: "dicimus, quod abdicatio proprietatis huiusmodi omnium rerum non tam in speciali, quam etiam in communi propter Deum meritoria est et sancta, quam et Christus, viam perfectionis ostendens, verbo docuit et exemplo firmavit . . . Nec his quisquam putet obsistere, quod interdum dicitur, Christum loculos habuisse (1112)."

21. Ibid., 2:1120: "Super ista constitutione glossae non fiant, nisi forsan, per quas verbum et verbi sensus, seu constructio, vel ipsa constructio quasi grammaticaliter ad literam vel intelligibilius exponatur."

22. Ibid., 2:1121: "Sed si quid penes aliquem in his ambiguitatis emerserit, ad culmen praedictae sedis apostolicae deducatur, ut ex auctoritate apostolica sua in hoc manifestetur intentio, cui soli concessum est in his statuta concedere et edita declarare."

23. D. Burr, *The Spiritual Franciscans*.

24. Bernardus Guidonis, *Practica inquisitionis heretice pravitatis*, ed. C. Douais (Paris, 1886), 126. Cf. R. Manselli, "Bernard Gui face aux Spirituels et aux Apostoliques," in *Bernard Gui et son monde*, CFan 16 (Toulouse, 1981), 265–78.

25. Bernardus Guidonis, *Practica inquisitionis heretice pravitatis*, no. 5, 268. On the quasi-identification of the gospel with the *Rule* of St. Francis, See R. B. Brooke, ed. and trans., *Scripta Leonis, Rufini et Angeli, Sociorum S. Francisci: The Writings of Leo, Rufino et Angelo, Companions of St. Francis* (Oxford 1990), no. 113, 286: "Tunc audita est vox in aëre Christi respondentis: 'Francisce, nichil est in Regula de tuo; sed totum est meum quicquid est ibi.'" See also J. M. Pou y Marti, *Visionarios, Beguinos y Fraticelos catalanes siglos XIII–XV* (Vich, 1930): "certum est quod regula facta per beatum Franciscum est veraciter et proprie vita evangelica, quam Christus servavit . . . et hoc certum est per scripturas sacras et per testimonium beati Francisci." And, "quod clerici et religiosi habentes aliqua in communi sunt in errore et male sentiunt de veritate evangelii." Cf. D. Nimmo, *Reform and Division in the Medieval Franciscan Order: From Saint Francis to the Foundation of the Capuchins*, BSC 33 (Rome, 1987), 152–58; R. Manselli, *Spirituali e Beghini in Provenza*, Studi

storici 31–34 (Rome, 1959), 152–58; G. Leff, *Heresy in the Later Middle Ages: The Relation of Heterodoxy to Dissent c. 1250–1450*, 2 vols. (Manchester, 1967), 1:195–230; J. Schlageter, "Die Kirchenkritik des Petrus Johannis Olivi und ihre ekklesiologische und soziale Relevanz," *FS* 65 (1983): 19–34; idem, "Die Entwicklung der Kirchenkritik des Petrus Johannis Olivi von der 'Quaestio de altissima paupertate' bis zur 'Lectura super Apocalypsim,'" *WiWei* 47 (1984): 99–131.

26. Cf. J. M. Pou y Marti, *Visionarios*, 509: "contra Fatrem Thomam et alios dicit: quod tenentes quod alta paupertas, id est, non habere in proprio et in communi, non sit perfectio necessario evangelica et quod non cadat sub voto regule evangelice Christi, est reprobandum et sunt magistri carnales pleni errore."

27. W. H. May, "The Confession of Prous Boneta: Heretic and Heresiarch," in *Essays in Medieval Life and Thought Presented in Honor of Austin Patterson Evans*, ed. J. H. Mundy, R. W. Emery, and B. N. Nelson (New York, 1955), 3–30, here 24: "et alius qui est Caym fuit iste frater Thomas de Aquino de ordine Praedicatorum, qui fuit nuper canonizatus; et sicut Caym interfecit Abel fratrem suum corporaliter, ita iste frater Thomas interfecit fratrem suum, scilicet dictum fratrem Petrum Joannis, spiritualiter, id est eius scripturam." Cf. L. A. Burnham, "The Visionary Authority of Na Prous Boneta," in *Pierre Jean Olivi (1248–1298). Pensée scolastique, dissidence spirituelle et société*, ed. A. Boureau and J. Piron (Paris, 1999), 319–39; D. Burr, "Na Prous Boneta and Olivi," *CFr* 67 (1997): 277–300.

28. On the biography of the pope see N. Valois, "Jacques Duèse, pape sous le nom de Jean XXII," in *Histoire littéraire de la France*, vol. 34 (Paris, 1914), 391–630; C. A. Lückerath, "Johannes XXII," *TRE* 17:109–12; P. Levillain, "Jean XXII," in *Dictionnaire de la papauté* (Paris, 1994), 943–47; J. E. Weakland, "John XXII before His Pontificate, 1244–1316: Jacques Duèse and His Family," *AHP* 10 (1972): 161–85; M. D. Lambert, "The Franciscan Crisis under John XXII," *FrS* 32 (1972): 123–43. On Avignon and the papal court see B. Guillemain, *La cour pontificale d'Avignon 1309–1379. Etude d'une société* (Paris, 1966).

29. For the text of the bull see J. Tarrant, ed., *Extravagantes Iohannis XXII*, MIC.C 6 (Vatican City, 1983), 217–21; also G. Gál and D. Flood, eds., *Nicolaus Minorita: Chronica. Documentation on Pope John XXII, Michael of Cesena and the Poverty of Christ with Summaries in English. A Source Book* (New York, 1996), 64 ff.

30. G. Gál and D. Flood, *Nicolaus Minorita*, 64 ff.: "non debet reprehensibile iudicari si canonum conditor canones a se vel a suis praedecessoribus editos, revocare, modificare vel suspendere studeat, si ea obesse potius viderit quam prodesse . . . Nos autem, attendentes quod argumentis et collationibus latens veritas aperitur, quodque sub eadem littera saepe latet multiplex intellectus."

31. *Littera capituli generalis*, in G. Gál and D. Flood, *Nicolaus Minorita*, 67 f.: "Visis et examinatis dicta quaestione cum allegationibus, quae pro et contra fiunt, diligentique et matura deliberatione digestis, *determinationi sanctae Romanae Ecclesiae firmiter et totaliter inhaerentes*, concorditer et unanimiter dicimus et fatemur, quod dicere et adserere quod Christus, viam perfectionis ostendens, et apostoli eiusdem perfectionis viam sequentes . . . nihil iure proprietatis, dominii seu iuris proprii, in speciali vel in communi

habuerint, non est haereticum; sed sanum, catholicum et fidele, maxime cum sancta Romana Ecclesia catholica, quae a tramite apostolicae traditionis numquam deviasse aut errasse probatur . . . hoc expresse dicat, affirmet et determinet manifeste." On this chapter and its consequences see A. Bartoli Langeli, "Il manifesto francescano di Perugia del 1322 alle origini dei Fraticelli 'De opinione,'" *PS* 11 (1974): 204–61; U. Horst, *Evangelische Armut und päpstliches Lehramt*, 28–30; P. Nold, *Pope John XII and His Franciscan Cardinal: Bertrand de la Tour and the Apostolic Poverty Controversy* (Oxford, 2003), 91–118.

    32. J. Tarrant, *Extravagantes*, 228–57.

    33. Hervaeus Natalis, "*De paupertate Christi et apostolorum*," ed. J. G. Sikes, *AHDL* 12/13 (1937/38): 209–97; J. Miethke, "Das Votum *De paupertate Christi et apostolorum* des Durandus von Sancto Porciano im theoretischen Armutsstreit. Eine dominikanische Position in der Diskussion um die franziskanische Armut (1322/3)," in *Vera Lex Historiae. Studien zu mittelalterlichen Quellen (Festschrift D. Kurze)* (Cologne-Vienna, 1993), 149–96; U. Horst, "Raimundus Bequin und seine Disputation *De paupertate Christi et apostolorum* aus dem Jahr 1322," *AFP* 64 (1994): 101–18. On the vows found in MS Vat. lat. 3740 see L. Duval-Arnould, "Les conseils remis à Jean XXII sur le problème de la pauvreté du Christ et des apôtres (Ms. Vat. lat. 3740)," in *Miscellanea Bibliothecae Apostolicae Vaticanae III*, StT 333 (Vatican City, 1989), 121–201.

    34. L. Oliger, "Fr. Bonagratia de Bergamo et eius Tractatus de Christi et apostolorum paupertate," *AFH* 22 (1929): 292–335, 487–511; U. Horst, *Evangelische Armut und päpstliches Lehramt*, 36–42. See also the recent monograph of L. E. Wittneben, *Bonagratia von Bergamo. Franziskanerjurist und Wortführer seines Ordens im Streit mit Papst Johannes XXII*, SMRT 90 (Leiden, 2003).

    35. *Bullarium Franciscanum*, vol. 5, ed. C. Eubel (Rome, 1898), 237–46; cf. U. Horst, *Evangelische Armut und päpstliches Lehramt*, 44–48; L .E. Wittneben, *Bonagratia von Bergamo*, 164–85.

    36. J. Tarrant, *Extravagantes*, 255–57. Cf. L. Duval-Arnould, "La Constitution 'Cum inter nonnulos' de Jean XXII sur la pauvreté du Christ et des apôtres: Rédaction préparatoire et rédaction definitive," *AFH* 77 (1984): 406–20; idem, "Elaboration d'un document pontifical: Les travaux préparatoires à la constitution apostolique *Cum inter nonnullos* (12 novembre 1323)," in *Aux origines de l'état moderne: Le fonctionnement administratif de la papauté d'Avignon. Actes de la table ronde. Avignon (23–24 janvier 1988)*, CEFR 138 (Rome, 1990), 385–409.

    37. J. Tarrant, *Extravagantes*, 255 ff.: "assertionem huiusmodi pertinacem . . . deinceps erroneum fore censendum et hereticum de fratrum nostrorum consilio hoc perpetuo declaramus edicto."

    38. J. Schwalm, ed., *Ludovici appellatio tertia contra processum pontificis*, MGH, Legum sectio IV, *Constitutiones et acta publica imperatorum et regum*, vol. 5 (Hannover and Leipzig, 1909–13), 722–44, here 737: "Quod enim per clavem sciencie per Romanos pontifices semel determinatum est in fide et moribus recte vite, est inmutabile, eo quod ecclesia Romana est inerrabilis in fide et veritate nec potest dare regulam falsam vel malam in recte vivendo nec in veritatis iudicio ecclesia Romana potest sibi esse contraria. Si enim in uno

esset falsa vel sibi contraria, in omnibus vacillaret. Et super hoc fundamento generale capitulum se in predicta littera stabilivit. Nam quod semel per summos pontifices Dei vicarios per clavem sciencie est diffinitum esse de fidei veritate, non potest per successorem aliquem in dubium revocari vel eius quod diffinitum est contrarium affirmari, quin hoc agens manifeste hereticus sit censendus. Cuius veritatis racio et fundamentum est, quia fides katholica est de vero perpetuo et inmutabili prorsus. Et ideo quod semel est diffinitum verum esse in ipsa fide vel moribus, in eternum verum est et inmutabile per quemcunque. Secus autem in hiis, que statuuntur per clavem potencie." English translation by B. Tierney, *Origins of Papal Infallibility*, 182.

39. Cf. B. Tierney, *Origins of Papal Infallibility*, 183. See also H. J. Becker, *Die Appellation vom Papst an ein allgemeines Konzil. Historische Entwicklung und kanonistische Diskussion im späten Mittelalter und in der frühen Neuzeit*, FKRG 17 (Cologne-Vienna, 1988), 83–92; more recently, E. L. Wittneben, *Bonagratia von Bergamo*, 229–53.

40. Cf. F. Ehrle, "Petrus Johannis Olivi, sein Leben und seine Schriften," *ALKGMA* 3 (1887): 409–552, here 540–52; Petrus Ioannis Olivi, *Das Heil der Armen und das Verderben der Reichen. Petrus Johannis Olivi OFM. Die Frage nach der höchsten Armut*, ed. J. Schlageter, FranzFor 34 (Werl, 1989), 47–50. It is noteworthy that the *Quaestio De inerrabilitate Romani pontificis* is not cited. The Dominicans, too, about whom we will speak in the next sections, seem not to have known it: see M. Maccarone, "Una questione inedita dell'Olivi sull'infalibilità del papa," *RSCI* 3 (1949): 309–43. On this discussion cf. M. Bartoli, "Pietro di Giovanni Olivi nella recente storiografia sul tema dell'infallibilità pontificia," *Bulletino dell'Istituto Storico Italiano per il Medio Evo—Archivio muratoriano* 92/2 (1994): 149–200; Petrus Ioannis Olivi, *Petri Iohannis Olivi Quaestiones de Romano pontifice*, ed. M. Bartoli, Collectio Oliviana 4 (Grottaferrata, 2002), 67–77.

41. See U. Horst, *Evangelische Armut und päpstliches Lehramt*, 51–57.

42. See Gál and Flood, *Nicolaus Minorita*, 68.

43. See U. Horst, *Evangelische Armut und Kirche*, 215.

44. See the editions of J. G. Sikes and J. Miethke, respectively, cited above.

45. See A. de Guimarâes, "Hervé Noël (†1323). Étude biographique," *AFP* 8 (1938): 5–81; T. Kaeppeli, *Scriptores Ordinis Praedicatorum Medii Aevi*, 4 vols. (Rome, 1970–93), 2:231–44; E. Lowe, *The Contested Theological Authority of Thomas Aquinas: The Controversies between Hervaeus Natalis and Durandus of St. Pourçain*, Medieval History and Culture 17 (New York, 2003), 68–71.

46. *De potestate papae*, in Hervaeus Natalis, *Commentaria quibus adiectus est eiusdem auctoris Tractatus de potestate papae* (Paris, 1647), 365: "declarare dubia in aliquibus potest dupliciter contingere: uno modo inquisitive sicut potest quilibet ex ingenio vel habitu inquirere de dubiis alicuius scientiae, et isto modo declarare potest pertinere ad quemcumque doctum vel scientem in aliqua scientia. Alio modo potest accipi in declarare cum auctoritate aliqua, scilicet quod declaratio sua debeat haberi pro vera, ita quod non liceat oppositum tenere vel opinari."

47. Ibid.: "Et isto modo potestas vel auctoritas declarandi praedicta dubia est solum apud summum pontificem simpliciter. Et quod talis auctoritas sit simpliciter

apud papam patet sic, quia oportet ponere in ecclesia unum caput ad quod pertinet declarare ista quae sunt dubia circa quaeque ad fidem pertinentia, sive sint speculativa sive agibilia . . . oportet poni ecclesiam sic dispositam quod tota communitas universalis ecclesiae maneat in veritate fidei et in una sententia de fide, scilicet hoc non posset esse nisi tota communitas ecclesiae haberet recursum ad unum caput, scilicet ad praesidentem, apud quem esset auctoritas declarandi dubia circa ea quae sunt fidei."

48.   Ibid.: "Et si obiciatur contra hoc quod papa (cum sit singularis persona) sit potens peccare et potens errare. Apud autem potentem errare non debet esse auctoritas contra quam non liceat opinari dicendum quod licet papa sit singularis persona et proprio motu agens possit errare sicut dicitur de illo Leone contra quem ivit Hilarius Pictaviensis ad concilium generale, *tamen papa utens consilio, requirens adiutorium universalis ecclesiae Deo ordinante qui dicit Petro Ego rogavi pro te <ut> non deficiat fides tua, non potest errare nec potest esse quod universalis ecclesia tanquam verum accipiat aliquod erroneum*, nec tamen si papa ut singularis persona sententiat errorem teneat vel sequitur quod auctoritas eius obliget ad illam sententiam tenendam, nec etiam quod auctoritas illa sibi erranti subtrahatur, scilicet quod auctoritas sua non habet locum obligandi in tali casu, sed quod deest obiectum aptum natum autenticari: sicut non sequitur quod careat visu ille qui non videt saporem qui non est obiectum visus." On Hilarius and Leo cf. H. Fuhrmann, "Die Fabel von Papst Leo und Bischof Hilarius. Vom Ursprung und der Erscheinungsform einer historischen Legende," *AKG* 43 (1961): 125–62. Notable in this connection is that along with other Dominicans—Johannes Quidort among them—Hervaeus Natalis signed Philip the Fair's famous appeal to a council against Boniface VIII. See A. Dondaine, "Documents pour servir à l'histoire de la province de France. L'appel au Concile (1303)," *AFP* 22 (1952): 381–439, here no. 103, 409; W. J. Courtenay, "Between Pope and King: The Parisian Letters of Adhesion of 1303," *Spec* 71 (1996): 577–605.

49.   St. Antoninus did not, however, note its author. See U. Horst, "Papst, Bischöfe und Konzil nach Antonin von Florenz," *RThAM* 32 (1965): 76–116.

50.   See U. Betti, "L'autorità di S. Antonino e la questione dell'infallibilità pontificia al Concilio Vaticano," *MDom* 76 (1959): 173–92.

51.   See A. Maier, "Zur Textüberlieferung einiger Gutachten des Johannes de Neapoli," *AFP* 40 (1970): 5–27, here 10–15; E. Hillenbrand, "Kurie und Generalkapitel des Predigerordens unter Johannes XXII. (1316–1334)," in *Adel und Kirche. Gerd Tellenbach zum 65. Geburtstag*, ed. J. Fleckenstein and K. Schmidt (Freiburg, 1968), 499–515. *Quaestio de paupertate* is cited here from Johannes de Napoli, *Quaestiones variae Parisiis*, ed. A. Gravina (Naples, 1618), q. 42, 357–406. For references, T. Kaeppeli, *Scriptores* 2:495–98.

52.   *Quaestio de paupertate*, Punctum V, sol., ed. cit., 376: "Et per hoc patet ad confirmationem rationis, quia determinatio facta per papam Ioannem in decretalibus cap. *Inter nonnullos* et cap. *Ad conditorem* non est contraria determinationi decretalis *Exiit*, sed est ei concors seu consona. Et convenientius et rationabilius est sic tales decretales concordare quam dicere unam determinationem vel aliam esse haereticam, cum tam magna irreverentia et blasphemia Sanctae Romanae Ecclesiae et Summi Pontificis . . . Et similiter dicere

aliquam determinationem Ecclesiae in pertinentibus ad veritatem fidei esse falsam vel haereticam est enervare totam Ecclesiae auctoritatem."

53. John of Naples, *Quodlibet* II: "Ea quae facit Papa cum Cardinalibus sunt duplicis generis. Quaedam enim sunt et pertinent ad particularia facta particularium hominum . . . et in talibus potest Papa errare . . . Quaedam alia sunt, quae facit Papa, pertinentia ad statum universalem totius Ecclesiae, vel quantum ad fidem—ut sunt determinationes et declarationes, quae spectant ad fidem et articulos fidei et Ecclesiae sacramenta et omnia alia contenta in sacra Scriptura, sive quantum ad bonos mores—ut sunt statuta, decreta et decretales, et in talibus dicendum est, quod licet absolute, *pensatis solis personis Papae et Cardinalium, Papa cum ipsis errare possit,* supposita tamen divina providentia, credendum est, Papam errare non posse, quia Christus oravit pro Ecclesia, Luc. 22: Ego rogavi, Petre, ut non deficiat fides tua, et dicere quod in huiusmodi Papa errare possit, esset haereticum." Cited from M. Schenk, *Die Unfehlbarkeit des Papstes in der Heiligsprechung,* 15. John mentions neither the inspiration of the Holy Spirit nor the high priest Caiaphas as a symbol for the highest office in the church.

54. On Petrus de Palude see T. Kaeppeli, *Scriptores* 2:243–49; J. Dunbabin, *A Hound of God: Pierre de la Palud and the Fourteenth-Century Church* (Oxford, 1991).

55. *Inter cunctas: Extr. Com.* 5.7.1, *Corpus Iuris Canonici,* ed. Friedberg, 2:1296–1300.

56. In the bull *Dudum* is inserted *Super cathedram: Clem.* 3.7.2, *Corpus Iuris Canonici,* ed. Friedberg, 2:1161–64.

57. On the controversy see J. Dunbabin, *A Hound of God,* 57–68; B. Tierney, *Origins of Papal Infallibility,* 149–53; T. P. Turley, "Infallibilists in the Curia of Pope John XXII," *Journal of Medieval History* 1 (1975): 71–101, esp. 75–78; J. G. Sikes, "John de Pouilli and Peter de la Palu," *EHR* 49 (1934): 219–40; J. Koch, "Der Prozess gegen den Magister Johannes de Polliaco und seine Vorgeschichte (1312–1321)," *RThAM* 5 (1933): 391–422, esp. 349–97; L. Hödl, "Dignität und Qualität der päpstlichen Lehrentscheidung in der Auseinandersetzung zwischen Petrus de Palude (†1342) und Johannes de Polliaco (†1321) über das Pastoralstatut der Mendikantenorden," in *Bonaventura. Studien zu seiner Wirkungsgeschichte,* ed. by I. Vanderheyden (Werl, 1976), 136–45.

58. Quodlibet, Toulouse, Bibliothèque municipale, cod. 744, fol. 92ra (cited from B. Tierney, *Origins of Papal Infallibility,* 151, n. 2): "et quamvis statuta romane ecclesie sepe mutentur quia quod iustum est aliquando mutatione aliqua temporum vel personarum sit iniustum, tamen quia veritas fidei est immutabilis nunquam auditum est nec per dei gratiam audietur quod ecclesia romana retractaret declarationem a se alias factam in talibus quia tunc confiteretur se aliquando errasse vel tunc errare." Fol. 94vb (Tierney, 151, n. 3): "si tota ecclesia residua teneret unum et romana ecclesia oppositum ipsi est adherendum." Fol. 98rb (Tierney, 150, n. 2): "Et tunc illud quod romana ecclesia iudicat et determinat et declarat ab omnibus est tenendum, nec ex tunc licet aliter opinari nec in dubium revocare nec aliter iudicare."

59. Ibid., fol. 89vb (Tierney, 152, n. 2): "Notandum quod papa possit errare et in fide et in moribus sicut quidam Leo papa tempore beati Hylarii narratum fuisse hereticus

et sicut Anastasius favens hereticum divino fulmine percussus est . . . et Marcellinus . . . Sed propter hoc ecclesia romana non errat que favente deo omnium ecclesiarum capud est et magistra. Si autem capud haberet oculos erutos reliqua membra corporis nihil viderunt. *Illam autem constitutionem non solus papa fecit de capite suo imo de consilio fratrum sicut in ea dicitur.*"

60. Ibid.: "Item, etsi papa errare possit nec in suo errore sequendus sit sed corrigendus . . . tamen in dubio non praesumitur nec est cuiuslibet iudicare papam errantem sed concilii quod propter heresim ipsum deponere potest . . . Unde non sunt sequendi clave errante, sed non praesumuntur errare in dubia nec pertinet ad aliquem citra concilium ipsorum iudicium erroneum appellare."

61. See J. Dunbabin, *A Hound of God*, 164–68. I cite Peter's *De paupertate Christi et apostolorum* from MS 2206, Salamanca, Biblioteca de la Universidad: *Tractatus fratris Petri de Palude de paupertate Christi et apostolorum contra Michaelis de Cesena consticionem contra Conditorem canonum.* Cf. U. Horst, *Evangelische Armut und päpstliches Lehramt*, 131–51.

62. *De paupertate Christi et apostolorum*, fol. 70vb: "Nec ecclesia catholica erravit, quia illa decretalis *Exiit* nullum errorem continet sane intellecta et ad huius concordiam reducta modo superius declarata. Item dato quod contineret errorem, non propter hoc ecclesia catholica erravit, que illam non approbavit, sed per pacienciam tolleravit, quousque ventum est ad plenam discussionen veritatis. Item, si erravit, non tamen erravit ita evidenter, quin posset de veritate probabiliter dubitari. Et ideo sicut ecclesia non statim condempnavit errorem Grecorum, sed cum magna maturitate discussit, sic nec veritas, de qua agitur plus quam per annum in omnibus studiis generalibus et in curia Romana, per omnes cardinales et prelatos discussa est, et omnes per universalem ecclesiam veritati declarate per dominum nostrum in constitutionibus istam [fol. 71ra] materiam tangentibus concordant. . . ."

63. Ibid., fol. 71ra: ". . . [universalis ecclesia] que errare non potest, sicut dictum est Petro 'ego rogavi pro te . . .', quod non dicitur de eo pro persona sua, que erravit . . . sed hoc dictum est pro universali ecclesia generaliter, in qua similiter est Spiritus Sanctus, qui docet omnem veritatem . . . Item hoc etiam verificatur de ecclesia Romana, que disponente deo omnium ecclesiarum caput est, regula et magistra, non quando successor Petri in sede Romana possit ad horam errare sicut Petrus, sed Romana ecclesia cum capite et membris cardinalibus et prelatis creditur non errare."

64. Ibid., fol. 70ra: "Nihilominus tamen, si pontifex errat, non est cuiuslibet [fol. 71rb] eum corrigere nec ei errorem imponere, sed tantum concilii generalis, aut si quis esset Paulus ad tercium celum et in paradisum raptus a Christo doctus ille posset dicere Petro et Christi vicario, quod non recte iret ad veritatem evangelii, vel forte collaterales cardinales, sicut Christus volebat, quod apostoli eius dicerent, quid ipsi vel alii de eo dicerent vel sentirent. Similiter quia Paulus frater et coepiscopus erat Petri, episcopi catholici obsecrando ut patrem possent sibi errorem suum ostendere, quod si nollet corrigere, possent adversus eum pro fide concilium postulare. Sed alii privati et subditi, etiam catholici, non habent ad hoc vocem, quanto minus scismatici et heretici condempnati."

65. Ibid., fol. 71va: "Ita etiam nunquam visum est, quod in hiis, que sunt fidei, papa cum cardinalibus determinavit contraria, ad quod sequeretur Romanam ecclesiam aliquando errare."

66. Ibid., fol. 71va: "Sed bene visus est unus papa in fide errasse . . . Sed non propter hoc ecclesia Romana erravit nec ydolotravit."

67. Ibid., fol. 71va: "Illa igitur constitutio *Exiit* non legitur facta, ut iam dictum est, de consilio fratrum et prelatorum in Romana curia existencium sicut ista [*Ad conditorem*]. Unde si papa in illa erravit, non propter hoc Romana ecclesia vel universalis in illa, specialiter in suis erroribus, si sunt, approbavit, sed iste constituciones nove sequentes de dominio Christi et apostolorum in communi et in speciali, et quod non est usus facti licitus sine iure utendi et similia, in quibus sibi errores imponuntur, sunt facte de consilio fratrum et prelatorum in Romana curia existencium et eis in istis concordat et consentit universitas magistrorum in theologia et in decretis in generalibus studiis, ut patet per determinaciones eorum in studiis generalibus, quilibet quamplures doctores determinaverunt pro hac parte, nullus contra. Unde si in ista constitucione sunt errores, quos impugnantes sibi imponunt, quod ecclesia Romana et universalis errat, quod est hereticum et insanum."

68. Petrus de Palude, *Tractatus de potestate papae (Toulouse Bibl. de la Ville, 747)*, ed. P. T. Stella (Zürich, 1966), 191: "Hoc, autem, privilegium (Lc 22:32) dedit Deus sedi Petri, id est romane, quod scilicet non exorbitet a fide . . . Propter hoc in ipsis que sunt fidei debet semper ad ecclesiam romanam recursus haberi. . . ."

69. See B. M. Xiberta, *Guiu Terrena, Carmelita de Perpinya* (Barcelona, 1932), 71–74; idem, *De scriptoribus scholasticis saeculi XIV ex ordine Carmelitarum* (Louvain, 1931), 137–41; U. Horst, *Evangelische Armut und päpstliches Lehramt*, 109–16; T. P. Turley, "The Ecclesiology of Guido Terreni" (diss., Cornell University, 1978), 62–111.

70. Guido Terreni, *Quaestio de magisterio infallibili Romani pontificis*, ed. B. M. Xiberta, OTHE.S fasc. 2 (Münster, 1926), 25: "Propter obiecta est advertendum quod posito quod papa esset hereticus et sedes apostolica ac ecclesia romana labe heresis macularetur . . . non videtur mihi quod papa hereticus permittererur a Deo determinare aliquid contra fidem."

71. Ibid., 25 ff.: "Sed Deus sic providit illi populo, ut patet Num XXII° quod malus propheta veniens ad maledicendum populo Iudeorum prohibitus fuit a Deo, sic quod non potuit maledicere populo quem Deus benedixerat, immo vellet nollet habuit Balaam populo benediccionem dare, ne Deus mutabilis videretur. Ergo multo forcius, si esset papa hereticus, propter immutabilem veritatem Dei et fidei datam a Deo benediccionem toti ecclesie et populo Christiano non permitteret Deus eum determinare heresim aut aliquit contra fidem; sed prohiberet eum Deus aut per mortem aut per aliorum fidelium resis-tenciam aut per aliorum instruccionem aut per internam inspirationem aut aliis modis,secundum quos Deus ecclesie sancte et fidei veritati multipliciter providere potest."On *propheta malus Bileam* cf. Thomas Aquinas, *STh* II-II, q. 172, art. 6 ad 1. See also M. Schlosser, *Lucerna in caligonoso loco*, 313 (Reg.).

72.   Guido Terreni, *Quaestio de magisterio*, 26: "ut quamvis aliquis boni meriti sit, non possit benedicere nisi fuerit ordinatus, ut officium ministerii exhibeat."

73.   Ibid., 27 ff.: "Igitur per hominem Spiritus Sanctus statuit et determinat fidei infallibilitatem et indefectibilem veritatem . . . Quod vero dicitur quod summus pontifex potest errare: dicendum quod summus pontifex, etsi ut est persona singularis possit in se errare, tamen propter communitatem fidelium et universalitatem ecclesie, pro cuius fide rogavit Dominus, non permittet eum determinare aliquid contra fidem in ecclesia Spiritus Sanctus . . . immo talem papam a suo malo proposito impediret Deus sive per mortem sive per aliorum resistenciam sive per alios modos. . . ."

74.   Ibid., 30 ff.: "Non enim querimus, an papa possit esse in se hereticus, sed queritur, an papa determinando aliquid in ecclesia et obligando fideles ad fidem credendum possit errare, ut error eius non solum concernat personam pape, sed concernat omnes fideles et totam ecclesiam Christi. Quia error concernens personam potest inesse pape, non autem error concernens totam ecclesiam, que tenetur in fide determinacionem pape inconcussa fide sequi. . . ."

75.   Cf. T. Kaeppeli, *Scriptores* 3:24–42; V. Beltrán de Heredia, "Noticias y documentos para la biografía del cardenal Juan de Torquemada O.P.," *AFP* 30 (1960): 53–148; idem, "Colección de documentos inéditos para ilustrar la vida del cardenal Juan de Torquemada O.P.," *AFP* 7 (1937): 210–45; T. Izbicki, *Protector of the Faith: Cardinal Johannes de Turrecremata and the Defense of the Institutional Church* (Washington, DC, 1981); K. Binder, *Konzilsgedanken bei Kardinal Juan de Torquemada O.P.*, WBTh 49 (Vienna, 1976). From the older literature see S. Lederer, *Der spanische Kardinal Johann von Torquemada. Sein Leben und seine Schriften* (Freiburg, 1879). For more details see U. Horst, "Kardinal Juan de Torquemada und die Lehrautorität des Papstes," *AHC* 36 (2004): 395–428.

76.   *Flores Sententiarum beati Thome de auctoritate summi pontificis*, ed. T. Prügl, in his *Antonio da Canara. De potestate pape supra Concilium Generale contra errores Basiliensium*, VGI 41 (Paderborn, 1996), 141–46.

77.   The text of Torquemada's speech is in P. Massi, *Magistero infallibile del papa nella teologia di Giovanni da Torquemada*, ScrinTheol 8 (Torino, 1957), 163–76. For the details of the diet see J. Helmrath, *Das Basler Konzil 1431–1449. Forschungsstand und Probleme*, KHAbh 32 (Cologne, 1987), 297–306. See also J. W. Stieber, *Pope Eugenius IV, the Council of Basel, and the Secular and Ecclesiastical Authorities in the Empire: The Conflict over Supreme Authority and Power in the Church*, SHCT 13 (Leiden, 1978); 178 ff.; H. Hürten, "Die Mainzer Akzeptation von 1439. Ein Beitrag zur Reform- und Vermittlungspolitik der Kurfürsten zur Zeit des Basler Konzils," *AMRhKG* 11 (1959): 42–75.

78.   In P. Massi, *Magistero infallibile*, 165: "Tanta soliditate veritatis apostolicum thronum, cuius oratores nos sumus, domini et patres colendissimi, clemencia divinitatis firmavit, quod, ut sanctorum patrum attestatur doctrina, iudicium eius in hiis, que fidei sunt, errare non possit. Decebat sane, ut *sedes illa*, que superni dispositione consilii magistra fidei et cardo omnium instituebatur ecclesiarum, *in hiis, que fidei sunt hominumque necessaria saluti, ab ipso omnium auctore Deo, cuius providencia in sui dispositione non fallitur, hoc preclaro infallibilitatis munere iudicii donaretur*, in cuius rei sacramentum primo il-

lius sedis pontifici divine dispensationis nutu, nomen firmitatis imponitur, scilicet Petrus, quod syra lingua firmus interpretatur."

79. Cf. G. Hofmann, "Due discorsi di Giovanni da Torquemada O.P. a Norimberga e Magonza contro il conciliarismo," in *Miscellanea Historiae Pontificiae* II, 2 (Rome, 1940), 29: "quod apostolica sedes, fidei magistra et omnium ecclesiarum caput, in qua providente domino fidei integritas et religio christiana semper immaculata servata est, renuit et docuit et divine et institucionis et sanctorum patrum ac universalis ecclesie affirmat auctoritas." On the concept *ecclesia romana/sedes apostolica* see T. A. Weitz, *Der Traktat des Antonio Roselli "De Conciliis ac Synodis Generalibus."* *Historisch-kanonistische Darstellung und Bewertung* (Paderborn, 2002) (index); B. Tierney, *Foundations of the Conciliar Theory*, 36–46; M. Ríos Fernández, "El primado del romano pontífice en el pensamiento de Huguccio de Pisa decretista," *Comp* 6 (1961): 47–97, here 91–97; Y. Congar, "Ecclesia Romana," *CrStor* 5 (1984): 225–44; T. Prügl, *Die Ekklesiologie Heinrich Kalteisens OP in der Auseinandersetzung mit dem Basler Konziliarismus*, VGI 40 (Paderborn, 1995), 184–95.

80. P. Massi, *Magistero infallibile*, 174: "Nec obstat huius dignitatis privilegio apostolice sedis, aliquos summos pontifices quandoque male sensisse, *quoniam hoc privilegium non est personarum secundum se, sed sedis, hoc est iudicii publici.*"

81. Johannes Torquemada, *Summa de Ecclesia*, bk. III, c. 64 (Lyon, 1496), fol. 231v (Glossa): "que ita habet papa tenetur requirere concilium episcoporum, ubi de fide agitur et tunc synodus maior est papa quod intelligendum est maioritate discretivi iudicii secundum quod non dubium [est] quin regulariter concilium sit maius Romano pontifice." Bk. III, c. 46 ad 20, fol. 218v: "respondetur quod glossa intelligitur quod ubi de fide agitur conventus synodalis patrum ecclesie est maior non maioritate potestatis sed maioritate iudicii discretionis superior ac maior ipso papa sive maioritate approbationis secundum quod qui maiore ratione utitur maioris auctoritatis eius verba esse videntur . . . glossa in c. Multi d. XL maior autem discretio et iudicium verisimiliter regularius arguitur esse in omnibus patribus unius synodi generalis quam apud unum solum hominem etiam si sit papa et propter hoc cum casus est valde dubius et habet fortes pro utraque parte defensores recurrendum est ad synodum, quoniam ut ait Archidiaconus in hoc loco nimis periculosum esset fidem nostram committere arbitrio unius hominis." Cf. B. Tierney, "'Only the Truth Has Authority': The Problem of 'Reception' in the Decretists and in Johannes de Turrecremata," in *Law, Church, and Society: Essays in Honor of Stephan Kuttner*, ed. K. Pennington and R. Somerville (University Park, PA, 1977), 69–96, esp. 86–89.

82. Johannes Torquemada, *Summa de Ecclesia*, bk. III, c. 64, fol. 231v: "Diximus autem regulariter quia non esset impossibile quod quandoque unus homo et maxime papa multiplici respectu in aliqua materia melius sentiret ceteris omnibus unde secundum communem doctrinam doctorum in sola beata Virgine fides mansit inviolata catholica in triduo et sanctitas ecclesie."

83. Johannes Torquemada, *Oratio synodalis de primatu*, ed. E. Candal, Concilium Florentinum documenta et scriptores, Series B, vol. 4, fasc. 2 (Rome, 1954), no. 65, 55: "licet universalis ecclesia privilegium habeat non errandi in fide, hoc tamen privilegium universalia concilia non habent; cum multa eorum errasse legamus, cum a doctrina apostolice sedis, in qua semper immaculata christiane fidei est religio servata, declinaverint.

Ymo si alicuius auctoritatis esset racio facta clare concluderet in oppositum, cum apostolica sedes, iuxta illud Luce XXII 'Ego rogavi . . .' et iuxta sanctorum patrum doctrinam exponencium hunc locum, privilegium habeat a Christo, utpote tribunal Christi in terris, in iudicio fidei non errandi, quod concilia universalia ab apostolica sede separata non habent."

84.   Torquemada, *Summa de Ecclesia*, bk. III, c. 112 ad 1, fol. 173v.

85.   Ibid., fol. 174r: "Habuit autem amplius singulariter Petrus super omnes alios apostolos, ut privilegium non errandi in fide se extenderet ad sedem sive cathedram eius ita quod in cathedra sua semper catholica vigeret doctrina et in sede sua iudicium in his quae fidei sunt ab omni macula erroris esset alienum."

86.   Ibid., ad 5, fol. 174v: "Secundo dicitur quod ecclesia romana in qua religio christiana a tempore apostolorum Petri et Pauli semper immaculata dicitur perstitisse et usque in finem seculi debere persistere vocatur congregatio populi fidelis Romani cum suo pastore . . . Hec apostolica Christi ecclesia per dei omnipotentis gratiam a tramite apostolice traditionis numquam errasse perhibetur." Cf. E. S. Morris, "The Infallibility of the Apostolic See in Juan de Torquemada," *Thom* 46 (1982): 242–66.

87.   Ibid., ad 6, fol. 174v–175r: "Hinc etiam Agato papa in c. Sic d. XIX inquit: Sic omnes apostolice sedis sanctiones accipiende sunt tanquam ipsius divina voce Petri firmate. Super quo dicit Archidiaconus: Caute dicit apostolice sedis et non dicit apostolici. Sedis autem apostolice sanctiones sive sententia in iudicio prolata a Romano pontifice intelligitur non que occulte, maliciose aut inconsulte per solum Romanum pontificem aut etiam que per ipsum cum paucis sibi faventibus aliis in fraudem contemptis sive non vocatis ad partem proferur, *sed que a Romano pontifice qui maturo et gravi virorum sapientum et maxime dominorum cardinalium primo concilio digesta et maturata sancitur et proferur.*" For Torquemada, the cardinals are of divine institution: *Summa de Ecclesia*, bk. I, c. 80, fol. 68v: "Est enim cardinalium status a Christo solo originaliter et primordialiter institutus." Fol. 69r: "ita dominorum cardinalium consilio et assensu summus pontifex regit, disponit atque gubernat universalem ecclesiam." Fol. 68v: "status dominorum cardinalium representat apostolorum statum in hoc quod assistunt Romano pontifici . . . tanquam principales assessores, consiliarii atque cooperatores et in executione sacerdotalis officii coadiutores existunt. . . ." Bk. I, c. 81, fol. 69v: "*Hoc magisterium fit ex eo quod cardinales pars corporis pape esse dicuntur . . . Nulli autem dubium est quod hi qui una persona censentur cum summo pontifice omnibus aliis prelatis honore merito veniant preferendi.*" Cf. J. Leclerc, "'Pars corporis pape.' Le sacré collège dans l'ecclésiologie médiévale," in *L'homme devant Dieu. Mélanges offerts au Père Henri de Lubac*, vol. 2 (Paris, 1964), 183–98; A. Paravicini-Bagliani, *Il trono di Pietro. L'universalità del papato da Alessandro III a Bonifacio VIII* (Rome, 1996), 51–67; M. García Miralles, "El cardenalato, de institución divina, y el episcopado en el problema de sucesión apostólica según Juan de Torquemada," in *XVI Semana Española de Teología* (Madrid, 1957), 251–74. Useful as well is J. B. Sägmüller, *Die Thätigkeit und Stellung der Cardinäle bis Bonifaz VIII historisch-canonistisch untersucht und dargestellt* (Freiburg, 1896), 215–49.

88.   Torquemada, *Summa de Ecclesia*, bk. II, c. 122, 175r: "Quibus omnibus consideratis, videlicet infallibilitate divine promissionis, efficacia orationis Christi, meritorum af-

fluentia beatissimi apostoli Petri et maturitate consilii quam in huiusmodi arduis materiis, que fidem tangunt, cum dominis cardinalibus et aliis doctis patribus Romanus pontifex semper habet, sine dubio tenendum est hoc quod de apostolice sedis iudicio dictum est, videlicet quod in his que fidei sunt deficere non possit." On the differences between Guido Terreni and Torquemada cf. T. Izbicki, "Infallibility and the Erring Pope: Guido Terreni and Johannnes Turrecremata," in *Law, Church, and Society: Essays in Honor of Stephan Kuttner*, ed. Pennington and Somerville, 97–111.

89. Ibid., fol. 175r: "Si Romanus pontifex efficitur hereticus ipso facto quo cadit a fide Petri cadit a cathedra et sede Petri et per consequens iudicium quod faceret talis hereticus non esset iudicium apostolice sedis immo nec iudicium alicuius auctoritatis est dicendum aut momenti, quia cum per heresim cecidisset a prelatione per consequens auctoritate iudicandi privatus esset." The following text is important, both for the problem of heresy and for the question of the teaching authority of the pope: *Ioannis a Turrecremata in Gratiani decretorum primam doctissimi commentarii*, D. 19, "Secundum ecclesiae," no. 10, vol. 1 (Venice, 1578), 176b: "Ad hanc dicendum iuxta Huguccionem quod Romana ecclesia quandoque dicitur tota ecclesia, et tunc in totum non errat, quia illa in totum errare non potest. Vel potest intelligi ecclesia Romana pro papa et cardinalibus, adhuc illa non potest in totum errare, sed bene aliqui errant, sicut hic papa [Anastasius] erravit, non cardinales, imo ipsi intelligentes eum errare communicando Photino haeretico et volendo occulte revocare Achacium recesserunt ab eo." For a severe criticism of Torquemada's point of view see J. B. Sägmüller, *Ein Traktat des Bischofs von Feltre und Treviso Teodoro de'Lelli über das Verhältnis von Primat und Kardinalat* (Rome, 1893).

90. For the discussion in the context of the Council of Basel see T. Prügl, *Ekklesiologie Heinrich Kalteisens*, 184–94; U. Horst, *Autorität und Immunität des Papstes. Raphael de Pornassio OP und Julianus Tallada OP in der Auseinandersetzung mit dem Basler Konziliarismus*, VGI 34 (Paderborn, 1991), esp. 42–52.

91. Johannis (Stojković) de Ragusio, *Tractatus de Ecclesia*, ed. Fr. Šanjek (Zagreb, 1983). Cf. Z. Strika, *Johannes von Ragusa (†1443). Kirchen- und Konzilsbegriff in der Auseinandersetzung mit den Hussiten und Eugen IV.* (Augsburg, 1998); J. S. Madrigal Terrazas, *La eclesiología de Juan de Ragusa O.P. (1390/1443). Estudio e interpretación de su Tractatus de Ecclesia* (Madrid, 1995).

92. For literature on conciliarism of the sixteenth century, see the following chapter.

93. Thomas de Vio Cajetan, *De comparatione auctoritatis papae et concilii cum Apologia eiusdem*, ed. V. I. Pollet (Rome, 1936), c. IX, no. 137, 69: "*sed potestas Papae est tota potestas Ecclesiae universalis* et aliae potestates sunt participationes ipsius in partem sollicitudinis datae." Cf. J. A. Domínguez Asensio, "Infalibilidad y potestad magisterial en la polémica anticonciliarista de Cayetano," *Communio* (Sevilla) 14 (1981): 205–26; idem, "Infalibilidad y 'determinatio de fide' en la polémica antiluterana del Cardenal Cayetano," *ATG* 44 (1981): 5–61; U. Horst, *Papst, Konzil, Unfehlbarkeit*, 24–26; A. Walz, "Von Cajetans Gedanken über Kirche und Papst," in *Volk Gottes (Festgabe J. Höfer)* (Freiburg, 1967), 336–60.

94. *De comparatione* c. XII, no. 197, 94 f.: "Amplius: auctoritas Ecclesiae determinativa de his quae sunt fidei, principaliter residet in Summo Pontifice, et non solum

principaliter, sed finaliter, ita quod ad ipsum spectat finalis de fide determinatio, nec exspectat Concilium, sed Concilii sententia a Papa confirmatur. . . ." C. IX, no. 134, 68: "quia auctoritas determinandi de fide competens universali Ecclesiae principaliter residet in Romano Pontifice, ut sanctus Thomas in IIa IIae, q. 11, a. 2 ad 3 dicit."

95. Ibid., c. IX, no. 132, 67: "error Papae in definitiva sententia fidei est error totius Ecclesiae."

96. Ibid., no. 133, 68: "Papa in huiusmodi iudicio est rectissimus propter assistentiam Spiritus Sancti in iudicio fidei, propter universale bonum Ecclesiae."

Chapter Three.   Papal Teaching Authority in the Dominican School of Salamanca

1. V. Beltrán de Heredia, *Historia de la reforma de la provincia de España (1450–1550)*, DH 11 (Rome, 1939); idem, *Las corrientes de espiritualidad entre los dominicos de Castilla durante la primera mitad del siglo XVI*, BTE 29 (Salamanca, 1960).

2. Cf. M. Andrés, *La teología española en el siglo XVI*, 2 vols. (Madrid, 1976); T. de Azcona, "Reforma del episcopado y del clero de España en tiempo de los Reyes Católicos y de Carlos V (1475–1558)," in *La Iglesia en la España de los siglos XV y XVI*, ed. José Luis González Novalín, Historia de la Iglesia de España 3 (Madrid, 1980), 114–210; idem, *Isabel la Católica. Estudio crítico de su vida y reinado*, 3d ed. (Madrid, 1993), 568–631, 703–74; M. A. Ladero Quesada, *La España de los Reyes Católicos* (Madrid, 1999), 254–99; J. Pérez, *Histoire de l'Espagne* (Paris, 1996), 151–83; idem, *Isabelle et Ferdinand. Rois Catholiques d'Espagne* (Paris, 1988); J. García Oro, "Conventualismo y observancia. La reforma de las órdenes religiosas en los siglos XV y XVI," in *La Iglesia en la España de los siglos XV y XVI*, 211–349; idem, *El cardenal Cisneros. Vida y empresa*, 2 vols. (Madrid, 1992–93).

3. On Diego de Deza see K. Reinhardt, *Bibelkommentare spanischer Autoren (1500–1700)*, vol. 1 (Madrid, 1990), 138–41. His important work is *Novarum defensionum doctrine angelici doctoris beati Thome de Aquino super libris sententiarum questiones profundissime ac utilissime*, 4 vols. (Seville, 1517); on Matías de Paz see V. Beltrán de Heredia, "El tratado del Padre Matías de Paz OP acerca del dominio de los Reyes de España sobre los Indios de América," *AFP* 3 (1933): 133–81.

4. See J. García Oro, *La universidad de Alcalá de Henares en la etapa fundacional (1458–1578)* (Santiago de Compostela, 1992); J. H. Bentley, *Humanists and Holy Writ: New Testament Scholarship in the Renaissance* (Princeton, 1983), 70–111; F. Domínguez Reboiras, *Gaspar de Grajal (1530–1575). Frühneuzeitliche Bibelwissenschaft im Streit mit Universität und Inquisition*, RST 140 (Münster, 1998), 21–34; M. Bataillon, *Erasmo y España*, 2d ed. (México, 1966), 19–23, 33–43.

5. See Gonzalo de Arriaga, *Historia del Colegio de S. Gregorio de Valladolid, editada, corregida y documentada por M. M. Hoyos*, 3 vols. (Valladolid, 1928–40).

6. See R. Hernández, *Un español en la ONU. Francisco de Vitoria* (Madrid, 1977); idem, *Francisco de Vitoria. Vida y pensamiento internacionalista* (Madrid, 1995); L. G. A. Getino, *El Maestro Francisco de Vitoria. Su vida, su doctrina e influencia*, 2d ed.

(Madrid, 1930); V. Beltrán de Heredia, *Francisco de Vitoria* (Barcelona, 1939); C. G. Noreña, *Studies in Spanish Renaissance Thought* (The Hague, 1975), 36–149; U. Horst, "Leben und Werke Francisco de Vitorias," in Francisco de Vitoria, *Vorlesungen I (Relectiones). Völkerrecht, Politik, Kirche*, ed. U. Horst, H.-G. Justenhoven, and J. Stüben (Stuttgart, 1995), 14–99.

7. Fundamental is G. Villoslada, *La Universidad de Paris durante los estudios de Francisco de Vitoria O.P. (1507–1522)*, AnGr 14 (Rome, 1938).

8. Ibid., 232–44, 261–64.

9. This method had its origins in Cologne. See M. Grabmann, "Der belgische Thomist Johannes Tinctoris (†1469) und die Entstehung des Kommentars zur 'Summa Theologiae' des hl. Thomas von Aquin," in *Studia mediaevalia in honorem A. R .P. Raymundi Josephi Martin O. P.* (Bruges, 1948), 409–36; E. Höhn, "Köln als Ort der ersten Kommentare zur 'Summa Theologiae' des Thomas von Aquin," in *Thomas von Aquino. Interpretation und Rezeption. Studien und Texte*, ed. W. P. Eckert, WSAMA.P 5 (Mainz, 1974), 641–55; I. W. Frank, "Der Wiener Dominikaner Johannes Werd (†1510) als Verfasser von Thomaskommentaren," in ibid., 609–40; H. Wilms, *Der Kölner Universitätsprofessor Konrad Köllin*, QFGDO o.s. 39 (Cologne, 1941), 47–64.

10. See Francisco de Vitoria, *Comentarios a la Secunda Secundae de Santo Tomás*, ed. V. Beltrán de Heredia, 6 vols. (Salamanca, 1932–52); C. Zimara, "Einblicke in die Unterrichtsweise des Franz de Vitoria O.P.," *DT(Fr)* 24 (1946): 429–46; 25 (1947): 192–224, 255–89.

11. See O. de la Brosse, *Le pape et le concile. La comparaison de leurs pouvoirs à la veille de la Réforme*, UnSa 58 (Paris, 1965); F. Oakley, "Almain and Major: Conciliar Theory on the Eve of the Reformation," *AHR* 70 (1964/65): 673–90; idem, *The Conciliarist Tradition: Constitutionalism in the Catholic Church, 1300–1870* (Oxford, 2003), 113–29; A. Ganoczy, "Jean Major, exégète gallican," *RSR* 56 (1968): 457–95.

12. The council was deliberately directed against the pope. See H. Jedin, *Geschichte des Konzils von Trient*, vol. 1, *Der Kampf um das Konzil* (Freiburg, 1949), 84–92; A. Landi, *Concilio e papato nel Rinascimento (1449–1516). Un problema irrisolto* (Torino, 1997), 241–365; N. H. Minnich, "The Healing of the Pisan Schism (1511–13)," *AHC* 16 (1984): 59–192; J. Goñi Gaztambide, "Concilio de Pisa y España," *DHEE* (Supl.), 211–19; F. Oakley, *The Conciliarist Tradition*, 111–29.

13. The modern edition is Johannes Quidort, *Über königliche und päpstliche Gewalt (De regia potestate et papali)*, ed. F. Bleienstein (Stuttgart, 1969). The first printed edition is *De utraque potestate papali scilicet et regali* (Paris, 1506). Cf. R. Scholz, *Die Publizistik zur Zeit Philipps des Schönen und Bonifaz' VIII* (Stuttgart, 1903), 253 ff. (n. 3). It seems very likely that Jean Quidort influenced Vitoria.

14. Thomas de Vio Cajetan, *De comparatione auctoritatis papae et concilii cum apologia eiusdem tractatus*, ed. cit. See J. K. Farge, *Orthodoxy and Reform in Early Reformation France: The Faculty of Theology in Paris, 1500–1543*, SMRT 32 (Leiden, 1985), 222 ff.

15. John Major, *In Secundum Sententiarum*, d. 44, q. 3 (Paris, 1510), fol. 96r–96v. See P. Leturia, "Maior y Vitoria ante la Conquista de América," *EE* 11 (1932): 44–82; M. Beuchot,

"El primer planteamiento teológico-jurídico sobre la conquista de América: John Maior," *CTom* 103 (1976): 213–30.

16.   See U. Horst, *Papst, Konzil, Unfehlbarkeit*, esp. 64–142, 143–57.

17.   The texts of Vitoria have been published by C. Pozo, "Una teoría en el siglo XVI sobre la relación entre infalibilidad pontificia y conciliar," *ATG* 25 (1962): 257–324, here 278: "Nec enim summus pontifex habet illam potestatem ut, proposita quacumque propositione de materia fidei, statim agnoscat an sit vera falsa, sed oportet prius *via humana* procedere, qua diligenter facta, sequetur auxilium divinum quod papam errare non permittet. *Sic ergo, si papa per semetipsum vellet determinare propositiones fidei non adhibito concilio nec examinata prius ex scriptura veritate, posset profecto errare.*" It is worthy of mention that John Major also teaches that a monarch *in causis arduissimis* had also to consult those *pares sui regni*: "Rex autem regulariter in positivis dispensat et ad nutum de officiis in temporalibus et bello subeundo disponit *licet cogatur in causis arduissimis* consulere pares sui regni et qui vicem gerunt totius communitatis. . . ." Cited from H. Burns, *"Politia regalis et optima*: The Political Ideas of John Maior," *History of Political Thought* 2 (1981): 31–62, here 37, n. 30.

18.   C. Pozo, "Una teoría," 279: "Si autem res sit gravis et in qua sint difficultates grandes, in quibus viri boni et docti dubitant, nec satis patet ex scripturis, *tunc opus est congregare concilium.*"

19.   Ibid.: "Sed oportet prius examinare dictas propositiones ex sacris litteris, item relationibus et disputationibus virorum doctorum, quo facto et oratione praemissa, procedere potest ad determinandum. *Oportet igitur ut faciat quod in se est,* non enim datur auxilium speciale nisi in necessitate et quando diligentia humana non sufficit nec potest sufficere.*"

20.   Ibid.: "Sed tunc insurgit dubium, quia si oportet ut praemittat talem examinationem, ergo si non faciat, poterunt aliquando errare in determinando. Respondeo: profecto verum est, si non faciat, sed oportet dicere, postquam Deus subiecit omnes fideles summo pontifici et Ecclesiae et oportet nos obedire illis, quod sint aliquo pacto infallibiles; *et sic dico quod Deus numquam permittet quod procedat ad determinationem antequam faciat quod in se est et sic numquam poterunt errare.*" On the origins of the formula *facere quod est in se* cf. A. M. Landgraf, "Das Axiom 'facienti quod est in se Deus non denegat gratiam,'" in *Dogmengeschichte der Frühscholastik*, Part 1, vol. 1 (Regensburg, 1952), 249–64; H. A. Oberman, *"Facientibus quod in se est Deus non denegat gratiam.* Robert Holcot O.P. and the Beginning of Luther's Theology," *HThR* 55 (1962): 317–42.

21.   C. Pozo, "Una teoría," 281f.: "Respondeo quod non, modo non subtrahant obedientiam papae nec negent papae suam iurisdictionem."

22.   Ibid., 282: "Sed concilium non condemnavit hoc esse de fide vel oppositum haereticum."

23.   Ibid.: "securius est quod est supra concilium."

24.   Ibid.: "Respondeo: *credo quod melius est dicere quod a Deo immediate,* licet papa semper maneat pastor et supra omnes."

25.   Ibid.: "Respondeo: papa, licet posset esse contrariae opinionis, tamen in decernendo non posset esse contrariae opinionis, *et sequenda est maior pars patrum, quia non*

solum sunt consiliarii, sed etiam iudices, quod patet, quia doctores et alii, qui vocantur ad concilium, non ferunt sententiam, sed solum praelati." Vitoria commented again on *STh* II-II, q. 1, art. 10 in 1534, but his teaching did not change. See U. Horst, *Papst, Konzil, Unfehlbarkeit,* 33–35.

26. Vitoria, *Relectio De potestate papae et concilii,* in *Vorlesungen I (Relectiones),* 352–435. *Relectiones,* originally called *Repetitiones,* were academic events in which the Magister discussed a central theme from his lectures before a larger university public. See *Bulario de la Universidad de Salamanca (1219–1549),* vol. 2, ed. V. Beltrán de Heredia (Salamanca, 1966), no. 13, 186: "unam repetitionem quolibet anno facere teneatur circa materiam quam lecturus sit vel legerit illo anno."

27. See H. Jedin, *Geschichte des Konzils von Trient,* vol. 1, 3–355.

28. As far as I am aware, Cajetan was the first theologian to teach the strict obligation of the bishops by divine law to reside in their dioceses. *Commentarii S Th* II-II 185, 5, in *S. Thomae Aquinatis opera omnia cum commentariis Thomae de Vio Cajetani,* ed. Leon., vol. 10 (Rome, 1899), 475–79. See U. Horst, *Die Lehrautorität des Papstes und die Dominikanertheologen der Schule von Salamanca,* QFGDO n.s. 11 (Berlin, 2003), 112–17. On Dominicus Soto see ibid., 85–90. On the debates at the Council of Trent see H. Jedin, *Geschichte des Konzils von Trient,* vol. 2, 269–315 and vol. 4/1, 237–47.

29. Vitoria, *Relectio De potestate papae et concilii,* no. 2, ed. cit., 372: "et ideo breviter sit secunda propositio: *Si concilium declarat aliquid esse de fide aut de iure divino, papa in hoc nihil potest aliter declarare aut immutare, maxime si tale ius spectet ad fidem vel ad mores ecclesiae universalis.*"

30. Ibid.: "Probatur: Quia in illis concilium errare non potest, iuxta promissum Lc 22: 32: *Ego rogavi pro te* etc., et Mt 18: 20: *Ubicumque fuerint duo vel tres* etc. Et non minus est Spiritus Sanctus in quocumque concilio generali quam in concilio apostolorum, ubi Spiritus Sanctus assistebat, iuxta illud Ac 15: 28: *Visum est Spiritui Sancto* etc."

31. Ibid.: "Confirmatur, quia si in illis concilium errare posset, et papa errare posset. *Et si utrumque errare posset, standum potius esset concilio.* Sicut ergo postquam determinatum fuit in concilio apostolorum, quod legalia erant extincta, non potuit Petrus aliter definire, ita in quocumque concilio generali."

32. On Soto's life and work see V. Beltrán de Heredia, *Domingo de Soto. Estudio biográfico documentado,* BTE 20 (Salamanca, 1960); J. Belda Plans, *La Escuela de Salamanca y la renovación de la teología en el siglo XVI* (Madrid, 2000), 399–500.

33. Dominicus Soto, text in C. Pozo, "Una teoría," 288: "Respondetur, quod papa potest determinare articulum fidei consulendo sacram scripturam et faciendo quod in se est more humano, aliter errasset sicut concilium ipsum et singularis persona in rebus humanis. Non facit quod in se est, nisi consulat viros probos in rebus gravissimis et ad consulendum illos expedit facere concilium."

34. Dominicus Soto, *Commentarii in Quartum Sententiarum,* vol. 1 (Salamanca, 1557/58), *In IV Sent.,* d. 20, q. 1, a. 5 ad 2, ed. cit., 944 ff.

35. Ibid.: "episcopi et qui legitimae sunt personae concilii legitime congregati praesidente Papa aut eius legatis, eo ipso quod sunt episcopi per se habent, dum publica

autoritate congregantur, autoritatem ecclesiae, sicut senatores in senatu. Quare nulla alia indigent Papae autoritate, nisi quod ipse sit praesens tanquam caput. Non quod ipsi epis-copi sint tanquam procuratores totius ecclesiae recipientes autoritatem a toto populo, sed per autoritatem episcopalem, quam a Christo susceperunt, dum publico nomine congre-gantur, habent autoritatem, quibus spiritus sanctus, ut errare nequeant, assistit."

36.   Ibid.: "Non ergo aliter concilium habet autoritatem a summo Pontifice, quam quod episcopi creantur ab ipso. Et e contrario, si aliqua ratione concilium est supra Pa-pam, non est quod ipse a concilio ullam recipiat autoritatem, *sed quia omne membrum, etiam caput, est pars totius et ideo tenetur stare decreto et sententiae totius.*"

37.   Ibid., d. 22, q. 2, a. 2, ed. cit., 1021: "Verumtamen quamvis nonnulli doctores nostri temporis contendant Papam nullatenus posse esse haereticum, nihilominus com-munis sententia a parte contraria stat. Quamvis enim in quantum Papa errare non possit, hoc est statuere errorem nequeat tanquam articulum fidei, quia spiritus sanctus id non permittet, tamen ut singularis persona errare in fide potest." Cf. Albert Pigge, *Hierarchiae ecclesiasticae assertio* (Cologne,1544), book 4, c. 16, fol. 401r–401v; R. Bäumer, "Das Kirch-enverständnis Albert Pigges. Ein Beitrag zur Ekklesiologie der vortridentinischen Kontro-verstheologie," in *Volk Gottes (Festgabe Josef Höfer)* (Freiburg, 1967), 306–22; G. Kreuzer, *Die Honoriusfrage im Mittelalter und in der Neuzeit*, PuP 8 (Stuttgart, 1975).

38.   See U. Horst, "Die Dominikanerschule von Salamanca und das Konzil von Tri-ent," *AHC* 35 (2003): 86–103.

39.   On life and works see J. Belda Plans, *La Escuela*, 503–618; J. Tapia, "La vida y la obra de Melchor Cano, marco de su reflexión eclesiológica," *AnAn* 36 (1988): 11–76.

40.   See M. Bataillon, *Erasmo y España*, 22–43; F. Domínguez Reboiras, *Gaspar de Grajal*, 21–37; J. H. Bentley, *Humanists and Holy Writ*, 70–111.

41.   Melchior Cano, *Loci Theologici, Opera Omnia*, ed. H. Serry (Bassani, 1746), book 12, prooemium, 340a: "Franciscum Victoria . . . solitum dicere audivi, postquam ab illius schola discessi, se ingenio meo quidem egregie delectari, sed id vereri, ne huius excel-lentia quadam elatus et exultans immoderate jactarer et grandior effectus, non late modo et libere ingrederer, sed temere etiam ac licenter praeceptoris vestigia conculcarem. Au-dierat enim me opinionem ipsius unam et item alteram non probasse."

42.   See U. Horst, "Die Loci Theologici Melchior Canos und sein Gutachten zum Catechismo Christiano Bartolomé Carranzas," *FZPhTh* 36 (1989): 47–92.

43.   See W. Thomas, *La represión del protestantismo en España, 1517–1648* (Leuven, 2001); idem, *Los protestantes y la Inquisición en España en tiempos de Reforma y Contrar-reforma* (Leuven, 2001); J. C. Nieto, *El renacimiento y la otra España. Visión cultural socio-espiritual*, Travaux d'Humanisme et Renaissance 315 (Geneva, 1997).

44.   See J. I. Tellechea Idígoras, *El arzobispo Carranza y su tiempo*, 2 vols. (Madrid, 1968); idem, "El proceso del arzobispo Carranza," in *Historia de la Inquisición en España y América*, ed. J. Pérez Villanueva and B. Escandell Bonet, vol. 1 (Madrid, 1984), 556–98.

45.   F. Domínguez Reboiras, *Gaspar de Grajal*, 260–65 and n. 380; A. Alcalá, *Lite-ratura y ciencia ante la Inquisición Española* (Madrid, 2001).

46.   See U. Horst, "Die Loci Theologici Melchior Canos," 53–71.

47. See F. Domínguez Reboiras, *Gaspar de Grajal*; U. Horst, "Melchior Cano und Dominicus Báñez über die Autorität der Vulgata. Zur Deutung des Trienter Vulgatadekrets," *MThZ* 51 (2000): 331–51, esp. 332–41.

48. Later they were revised. See B. Körner, *Melchior Cano De locis theologicis. Ein Beitrag zur theologischen Erkenntnislehre* (Graz, 1994), 86–89; A. Lang, *Die Loci Theologici des Melchior Cano und die Methode des dogmatischen Beweises*, MSHTh 6 (Munich, 1925), 18. On the development of Cano's teaching on papal teaching authority cf. J. Belda Plans, "La autoridad del Romano Pontífice según Melchor Cano (en los comentarios inéditos a la II-II, q. 1, a. 10)," *ScrTh* 14 (1982): 59–104; idem, "La infalibilidad 'ex cathedra' del romano pontífice según Melchor Cano. Estudio de las condiciones de la infalibilidad en cuanto al modo," *ScrTh* 10 (1978): 519–75; idem, *Los lugares teológicos de Melchor Cano en los comentarios a la Suma* (Pamplona, 1982); idem, *La Escuela*, 501–750.

49. Cano, *Loci Theologici*, bk. IV, c. 4, concl. 1–8, ed. cit., 150a–155b.

50. *Loci Theologici*, bk. IV, c. 5, ed. cit., 160b: "Non enim numero haec iudicantur, sed pondere. Pondus autem conciliis dat summi pontificis et gravitas et auctoritas: quae si adsit, centum patres satis sunt; sin desit, nulli sunt satis, sint quamlibet plurimi. Nec si major pars patrum vere sentiat, summus ecclesiae pontifex repugnabit. Id enim ad peculiarem Christi procurationem pertinet, semperque pertinuit, ne ecclesia in factiones duas dividatur. Nec Romanus unquam episcopus, si exemplum quaeritur, contra patres concilii vere sentientes dixit."

51. *Loci Theologici*, bk. V, c. 5, resp. ad 1, ed. cit., 161a–161b: "*concilium et pontifex humana via incedunt* . . . adhibere prius consilium necesse est et expendere utriusque partis argumenta: tum deinde sequetur auxilium dei, quod videlicet opus est, ut summus pontifex in recta fide contineatur. In conciliis quidem itidem non habent patres mox quasi ex auctoritate sententiam absque alia discussione dicere: sed collationibus et disputationibus re ante tractata, precibusque primum ad Deum fusis, tum vero quaestio a concilio sine errore finietur, Dei videlicet auxilio atque favore, hominumque diligentia et studio confluentibus . . . Ita numquam ego admittam, aut pontificem aut concilium diligentiam aliquam necessariam quaestionibus fidei decernendis omisisse" (163b).

52. *Loci Theologici*, bk. VI, c. 8, ed. cit., 200b: "Atque in illis argumentis, quae a principio sunt posita, theologi nonnulli, minime mali illi quidem, sed non satis acuti, quoquo modo possunt, tergiversantur. Romanam quippe Ecclesiam a Romano pontifice discernunt: ajuntque hunc in fide errare posse, illam non posse. Sic sibi videntur omnia propemodum argumenta diluere. Nam pleraque ex illis non Ecclesiae Romanae, sed summi pontificis fidem impugnant. Atqui Ecclesiam Romanam isti, non Romanum episcopum ab errore vindicant. *Verum si de errore in fidei iudicio atque decreto loquimur, ut vere loquimur, nullum ergo discrimen inter apostolicam sedem et apostolicae sedi insidentem invenio.* Primum quoniam, cum ad sedem apostolicam accedimus fidei oracula postulaturi, non singulos Romanae Ecclesiae fideles interrogamus, nec ecclesiam ipsam Romanam in concilium cogimus, sed pontificis maximi judicium quaerimus ejusque sententiam expectamus." Cano doubtless numbered Alfonso de Castro among the theologians *non satis acuti*. Castro's work *Adversus omnes haereses* is most often cited in this context. Cf. U. Horst, *Papst,*

Konzil, Unfehlbarkeit, 158–61; L. García y García, "El primado pontificio y la infalibilidad de la Iglesia en Fray Alfonso de Castro," *LF* 12 (1958): 131–65.

53.   *Loci Theologici,* bk. VI, c. 8, ed. cit., 200b–201a: "Rursum quoniam non Romanus populus est, qui ecclesiam universalem docet ea, quae ad fidem attinent, sed Romanus episcopus. Nec potestas judicandi de causis fidei, ligandi, solvendi, pascendi in populo Romano est, sed in Romano pastore, vicario Jesu Christi. Concilia quoque non exigunt confirmationem et robur ab ipsa Romana plebe, sed a plebis Romanae antistite."

54.   Ibid., 210a: "Non est igitur negandum, quin summus pontifex haereticus esse posit . . . Itaque objectioni positae hoc responsum habeto. *Aliud est in Petro, quod spectat ad hominis privatam excellentiam, aliud quod pertinet ad communem ecclesiae utilitatem.* Quod negavit Christum, hominis erat, quod confirmavit fratres, erat ecclesiae. Illud proprium, hoc commune erat. Similiter, quod fides Petri propria semper interius servaretur, hominis privilegium erat, quod vero aliis confirmandis solidam fidem proponeret, nec in fidei iudicio deficeret, ecclesiae publicum privilegium erat. Romanus igitur episcopus non fuit haeres aut privilegiorum aut culparum Petri propriarum, quae videlicet ex accidenti publicae Petri potestati conjungebantur, sed successit in his quae spectabant ad ecclesiae communes et necessarias commoditates."

55.   Ibid., 210b: "Non enim fides interior Romani pontificis ecclesiae est necessaria: nec illius occultus et privatus mentis error ecclesiae Christi nocere potest. Quapropter non est necesse, ut interioris fidei conservatione Romanis pontificibus Deus semper assistat."

56.   Juan de la Peña, *Eclesiología. Réplica a la Iglesia de Lutero,* ed. R. Hernández, BTE 30 A14 (Salamanca, 1987); V. Beltrán de Heredia, "El maestro Juan de la Peña," in *Miscelanea Beltrán de Heredia. Colección de artículos sobre la historia de la teología española,* vol. 2, BTE 26 B6 (Salamanca, 1972), 447–542; U. Horst, *Papst, Konzil, Unfehlbarkeit,* 76–99.

57.   Biblioteca de la Universidad de Sevilla, MS 333-53-1, fol. 58r: "Respondetur consequenter, quod quando papa vel concilium definit, numquam Deus permittet, quod definiat, quin prius faciat, quod in se est, ita quod Spiritus Sanctus assistit ad utrumque et ad hoc, ut faciat, quod in se est, et ad hoc, quod definiat veritatem. Itaque a posteriori scio, quod papa fecit, quod in se est, quia definivit. *Et iste modus dicendi est probabilis. Sed mihi videtur probabilius dicendum.* Dico primo, quod si papa aut concilium tentet definire aliquid ex officio, tunc de fide numquam errabit, si de facto definiat, sive fecerit, quod in se est, sive non fecerit. Secundo dico, quod istud, quod est facere vel non facere, quod in se est, refert multum, ut papa vel concilium non peccet definiendo temerarie, quia si tentet definire nulla facta diligentia, peccabit ipse mortaliter, at vero semper definiet veritatem et numquam falsitatem."

58.   Ibid.: "Ratio huius est, quia Christus absolute promisit, quod Spiritus Sanctus doceret omnem veritatem necessariam ecclesie et absolute dixit Petro 'rogavi pro te ut non deficiat fides tua.' Non dixit 'ut non deficiat gratia tua aut prudentia tua, sed fides tua.' Unde licet ille sit imprudens definiendo, tamen non definiret falsitatem. Dico ergo, quod mea sententia stat in hoc, quia sicut sacerdos rite ordinatus, si servet formam et materiam et intentionem ecclesie, infallibiliter consecrat, sive ipse peccet [fol. 58v] non servando ceremonias ecclesie aut vestes sacras aut alias."

59. Ibid. Cf. U. Horst, *Papst, Konzil, Unfehlbarkeit*, 87.

60. The text is found in MS 1852 of the Biblioteca Geral da Universidade de Coimbra, fol. 91r–v: "Sed ista sententia (si autem non premittat diligentiam, peccabit, sed tamen non errabit) est contra communem usum ecclesie, que semper premittit diligentiam et examinationem. Unde est communis sententia, quod est necessarium, ut premittat examinationem . . . Nos vero per sedem apostolicam intelligimus ipsum pontificem, sed definientem non pro suo cerebro solum, sed etiam per doctores et per concilia, et postea ille definit." Cf. U. Horst, *Papst, Konzil, Unfehlbarkeit*, 99–112.

61. MS Sevilla 333-53-1, fol. 58v: "Ad argumentum ergo dico, *quod, licet sit hereticus, si tentet definire, definiret veritatem etiam contra opinionem*. Et hoc ex promissione Christi et assistentia Spiritus Sancti, neque est miraculum hoc, sed est communis providentia Christi in lege gratie, quod sicut malus sacerdos, etiam hereticus, si attente vere consecret, ita etiam papa definiat veritatem."

62. Ibid., fol. 59r: "Alii vero tenent, quod papa non potest esse hereticus de lege, sed quod eo ipso, quod est papa, est confirmatus in fide. Hanc tenuit primo Pigius . . . Pro ista sententia est illud, quod habet Luce 22 . . . Hec verba Christi secundum communem intelligentiam doctorum non solum referuntur ad personam Petri in ordine ad ecclesiam, sed etiam in ordine ad ipsammet personam Petri; itaque fuit privilegium collatum Petro, quod non deficeret in fide etiam tempore passionis Christi, et sic est communis sententia et sanctorum doctorum, quod Petrus non amisit fidem tempore passionis, sed amisit confessionem fidei. . . ." On the problem of faith *in triduo mortis Christi* see Y. Congar, "Incidence ecclésiologique d'un thème de dévotion mariale," *MSR* 7 (1950): 277–92; K. Binder, "Thesis, in passione Domini fidem Ecclesiae in Beatissima Virgine sola remansisse, iuxta doctrinam medii aevi et recentioris aetatis," in *Acta Congressus Mariologici-Mariani in civitate Lourdes anno 1958 celebrati*, vol. 3 (Rome, 1959), 389–488.

63. MS Sevilla 333-53-1, fol. 59r–v: "Istud privilegium fuit datum Petro non inquantum erat apostolus. Ergo inquantum erat futurus pontifex . . . Si ergo Petro tamquam pape conceditur privilegium non deficiendi in fide, ut possit confirmare fratres suos, cum omnes pontifices debeant confirmare, habent etiam hoc privilegium, quod fides eorum non deficiat. Et hoc est potissimum argumentum huius sententie."

64. On the history of the problem see G. Kreuzer, *Die Honoriusfrage*; R. Bäumer, "Die Wiederentdeckung der Honoriusfrage im Abendland," *RQ* 56 (1961): 200–214; G. Kreuzer, "Honorius I," *LThK*, 3d ed., 5:265–66.

65. MS Sevilla 333-53-1, fol. 60r: "Sed tota difficultas est de Honorio pontifice, quia concilium Constantinopolitanum pro comperto habuit, quod papa potest esse hereticus, siquidem condemnavit Honorium. Respondetur tamen, quod in concilio non fuit disputatum, utrum papa possit esse hereticus necne. At vero postquam est disputatum, sunt rationes et doctores pro utraque parte et videtur esse sicut opinio de conceptione beate Virginis, quia a principio ecclesie pro comperto habebatur, quod beata Virgo habuit originale peccatum, sed postquam est disputatum, sunt rationes pro utraque parte." Cf. U. Horst, *Die Diskussion um die Immaculata Conceptio im Dominikanerorden. Ein Beitrag zur Geschichte der theologischen Methode*, VGI 34 (Paderborn, 1987), 76 ff.

66. Juan de la Peña's influence is clear in the *Lectura* of the Dominican Mancio de Corpore Christi, who considers the *opinio nova* as probable, but who ultimately gives preference to the traditional argument because it corresponds to church practice. See A. Sarmiento, ed., *La eclesiología de Mancio. Introducción y Comentario a la 2ª 2ᵃᵉ, q. 1, a. 10, del ms. 5 de la Catedral de Palencia*, 2 vols. (Pamplona, 1976), here 2:246: "Haec opinio videtur contra usum Ecclesiae, nam semper definit, praemisso diligenti examine. Unde opinio communis est quod necessario debet praemitti examen. . . ." Cf. U. Horst, *Papst, Konzil, Unfehlbarkeit*, 114–17.

67. See V. Beltrán de Heredia, "Actuación del maestro Domingo Báñez en la Universidad de Salamanca," *CTom* 25 (1922):64–78, 208–40; 26 (1922): 63–73, 199–223; 27 (1923): 40–51, 361–74; 28 (1923): 36–47; idem, "Báñez y la inquisición española," *CTom* 37 (1928): 289–309; 38 (1928): 35–58, 171–86; idem, "Vindicando la memoria del maestro fray Domingo Báñez," *CTom* 40 (1929): 312–22; 43 (1931): 193–99; idem, *Domingo Báñez y las controversias sobre la gracia. Textos y documentos*, BTE 24 (Salamanca, 1968); F. Domínguez Reboiras, *Gaspar de Grajal*, 561–97; J. Belda Plans, *La Escuela* 779–94; U. Horst, *Die Lehrautorität*, 119–61.

68. Dominicus Báñez, *Scholastica commentaria in Secundam Secundae quibus quae ad fidem, spem et caritatem spectant clarissime explicantur* (Duaci, 1615), here in q. 1, a. 1, 4. concl., 60aF: "*In publico fidei iudicio non potest summus pontifex errare.*"

69. A.-D. von den Brincken, "Johanna, angebl. Päpstin," *LThK*, 3d ed., 5:860; E. Gössmann, *Die "Päpstin Johanna." Der Skandal eines weiblichen Papstes. Eine Rezeptionsgeschichte* (Berlin, 1998); A. Boureau, *La papesse Jeanne* (Paris, 1988); K. Herbers, "Die Päpstin Johanna. Ein kritischer Forschungsbericht," *HJ* 108 (1988): 174–94.

70. Johannes Torquemada, *Summa de Ecclesia*, bk. IV, p. II, ed. cit., 257r–257v.

71. Báñez, *Scholastica commentaria*, q. I, a. 1, 5 concl., 62aCD: "etiamsi in ecclesia esset aliquis putatus pontifex qui revera non esset, nunquam tamen error ipsius definientis redundabit in ecclesiam universalem, quia vel non definiet vel definiet verum vel si falsum definiat, non recipietur ab ecclesia, sed revelabitur error definitionis vel definientis. Et hoc citra miraculum, sed secundum legem communem. . . ." 63bBC: "Caeterum quod dicitur de Ioanne illo fuisse feminam, incertum est. Et quando id semel acciderit, non tamen admittendum est, quod toti ecclesiae proponat aliquem errorem tanquam de fide credendum, et quod ab ecclesia accepetur. . . ." 63abFA: "Nunquam tamen admittendum est totam ecclesiam falli acceptando huiusmodi definitionem concilii: quin potius si tota ecclesia acceptaverit, signum certissimum erit, quod propositio definitiva vera est et ad fidem pertinet, *etiamsi ille qui habebatur summus pontifex, non esset verus papa.*"

72. Ibid., 62aEF: "Respondent aliqui . . . quod postquam papa definivit aliquid tenendum secundum fidem, tunc etiam secundum fidem est asserendum ipsum esse summum pontificem . . . Ut v.g. Gregorius XIII definiat nunc aliquam propositionem esse tenendam secundum fidem, definit etiam simul et consequenter se esse summum pontificem."

73. See A. Grillmeier, "Konzil und Rezeption. Methodische Bemerkungen zu einem Thema der ökumenischen Diskussion der Gegenwart," *ThPh* 45 (1970): 321–52; Y. Congar,

"La 'réception' comme réalité ecclésiologique," *RSPhTh* 56 (1972): 369–403; H. J. Sieben, *Die Konzilsidee der Alten Kirche* (Paderborn, 1979), 53–55, 178–81, 333–39, 340–43.

74. See J. Barrientos García, "El maestro Pedro de Ledesma y la Universidad de Salamanca," *AD* 5 (1984): 201–61; J. Belda Plans, *La Escuela*, 811 f.; I. Jericó Bermejo, "Sobre la potestad de la Iglesia postapostólica para decir infaliblemente cuál es la verdadera Sagrada Escritura, y si es la edición Vulgata. Los comentarios de Pedro de Ledesma (1581)," *ScrTh* 31 (1999): 413–35; idem, "Sobre la posible definición de una conclusión teológica. Los comentarios de Pedro de Ledesma (1581)," *Communio* (Sevilla) 32 (1999): 199–226; idem, "La definición del Romano Pontífice como regla infalible de fe, según los comentarios escolares de Pedro de Ledesma," *CTom* 125 (1998): 347–400; U. Horst, *Die Lehrautorität*, 163 f.

75. I. Jericó Bermejo, "La definición del Romano Pontífice," 356, n. 34: "Summus pontifex ut persona particularis potest errare in fide, non solum errore invincibili, verum etiam culpabili qui destruit fidem ita ut sit haereticus." But: "Summus pontifex haereticus ex coniunctione ad assistentiam Spiritus Sancti suaviter definit veritatem in ordine gratiae, quamvis oppositum sentiat."

76. Pedro de Ledesma, *Tractatus de divinae gratiae auxiliis, circa illa verba Esaiae cap. 26 Omnia opera nostra operatus es in nobis Domine: et circa Doctrinam D. Thomae multis in locis* (Salamanca, 1611). Cf. V. Beltrán de Heredia, *Domingo Báñez y las controversias*, 11–99.

77. Pedro de Ledesma, *Tractatus*, q. un., a. IX ad 4, ed. cit., 181b: "dicendum est, quod sicut gratia illorum hominum, qui in ea sunt confirmati, habet quandam perfectionem intrinsecam auferentem a confirmatis vertibilitatem ad malum, quam participat ex gratia consumata in patria, *sic etiam fidei Summi Pontificis in definiendo res fidei communicatur quaedam perfectio intrinseca ex participatione visionis Dei, cuius est velut quaedam participatio vicaria, et ratione huius perfectionis est indefectibilis in definiendo veritates fidei . . .* quod ista indefectibilitas fidei Pontificis in definiendo res fidei provenit non solum ex sola extrinseca assistentia Dei sed ex actione physica illius . . . *potest dici, quod quando Deus movet Pontificem ad determinandum res fidei necessitat illum ad sic definiendum, quia facit, quod oppositum eius, quod definiendum est, nullo modo appareat verum.*"

78. Cf. R. Hernández, "Actividad universitaria de Francisco de Araújo en los claustros salmantinos," *CTom* 92 (1965): 203–71; U. Horst, *Papst, Konzil, Unfehlbarkeit*, 252–61; C. O'Brien, "El enigma de Francisco de Araújo," *CTom* 89 (1962): 221–66; 90 (1963): 3–79.

79. Francisco de Araújo, *In Secundam Secundae commentarius* (Salamanca, 1635), a. X, q. 1, a1 dub. II ad 3, no. 14, ed. cit., 113: "quia voluntas Pontificis ex speciali assistentia Spiritus Sancti et auxilio divino determinatur quoad specificationem, ut non possit velle diffinire falsum. Secunda vero quia etiam fides eius, ut caput est Ecclesiae redditur indefectibilis: et similiter tertia, quia pariter eius intellectus ex speciali illustratione divina determinatur ad verum ut ei pro tunc non possit repraesentari falsum sub ratione veri."

80. Ibid., dub. III, nos. 13 and 14, ed. cit., 111–13. Text of *Aeternus ille* in R. Cornely, *Historica et critica introductio in U.T. libros sacros*, vol. 1, *Introductio generalis* (Paris, 1885), 465–74. Cf. P. M. Baumgarten, *Die Vulgata Sixtina von 1590 und ihre Einführungsbulle. Aktenstücke und Untersuchungen*, ATA III, 2 (Münster, 1911), 82–107; F. Amann, *Die Vulgata Sixtina von 1590. Eine quellenmäßige Darstellung ihrer Geschichte* (Freiburg, 1912), 82–107.

81.   See O. Merl, *Theologia Salmanticensis. Untersuchung über Entstehung, Lehrrichtung und Quellen des theologischen Kurses der spanischen Karmeliten* (Regensburg, 1947), esp. 34–46; Enrique del Sagrado Corazón, *Los Salmanticenses. Su vida y su obra. Ensayo histórico y proceso inquisitorial de su doctrina sobre la Inmaculada* (Madrid, 1955); U. Horst, *Die Lehrautorität*, 173–86; idem, "Die Ekklesiologie des 'Cursus Theologicus Salmanticensis,'" *RQ* 69 (1974): 46–67.

82.   Johannes ab Annuntiatione, *Cursus Theologicus Summam Theologicam Angelici Doctoris Thomae complectens*, vol. 11, *Tractatus XVII, De fide, Tractatus XVIII, De spe theologica* (Paris-Brussels, 1878), disp. IV, dub. I, § II, nos. 10 and 11, 253–54: "ergo licet Pontifex *in cathedra* habeat potentiam ad errandum, nulla tamen datur in eo potentia ad errandum *ex cathedra.*"

83.   Ibid.: "Dicendum est . . . Pontificem loquentem ex cathedra habere potentiam et libertatem, ut errare possit in rebus fidei. Hanc assertionem debent amplecti, qui docent Pontificem posse per modum personae particularis errare . . . ut doctrina Pontificis ex cathedra sit infallibiliter vera, *non requiritur impotentia ad errandum absolute, sed sufficit impotentia ad errandum ex cathedra sive impotentia ad conjungendam doctrinam ex cathedra cum errore.*" Ibid., no. 15, 256: "Ultimo dicendum est ad salvandam indefectibilitatem, quam Pontifex habet in docendo ex cathedra res fidei, non requiri aliquam perfectionem habitualem entitativam aut modalem, quae habitualiter determinet Pontificis intellectum, *sed sufficere auxilia ei collata, quando diffinit.*"

84.   Ibid., no. 16, 256 f.: "quoniam sicut ad hoc, quod Pontifici ex cathedra loquenti debeantur praedicta auxilia, non requiritur quod in intellectu Pontificis reperiatur fides (potest enim esse haereticus), ita nec requiritur alia perfectio intrinseca entitativa aut modalis, quae ejus intellectum quasi habitualiter afficiat et determinet tollendo potentiam errandi."

85.   Ibid., 257: "Praesertim quia Pontificem docere ex cathedra magis respicit actum exteriorem quam dispositionem Pontificis; et potest Deus salvare rectitudinem actus exterioris circa Ecclesiam praeter, imo contra quamlibet pravam internam Pontificis dispositionem, ita ut vel volente Pontifice falsum definire Deus hoc malum impediret aut privando Pontificem vita aut pluribus aliis mediis."

86.   Ibid., § III, no. 18, 258: "Pontifici loquenti ex cathedra ea autoritas et indefectibilitas deferri debet, quae necessaria est ad securitatem et infallibilem fidem Ecclesiae Pontifici obedientis: *ad hanc autem sufficit infallibile esse, quod Pontifex ex cathedra loquens non errat.*" No. 20, 259 f.: "Ad hanc autem impotentiam (non errandi) sicut non requiritur, quod Pontifex habeat interius fidem; ita nec requiritur, quod habeat modum aliquem intrinsecum confirmationis, qui excludat potentiam errandi absolute; *sed sufficit, quod Spiritus Sanctus ipsi loquenti ex cathedra subministret auxilia efficacia, ut non erret.*"

87.   The sharpest formulation is that of Gregory of Valencia, *Commentarii Theologici* (Ingolstadt, 1592), disp. I, q. I, *De obiecto fidei*, punct. VII, § 40, in vol. 3, 314: "Itaque studium ac diligentia necessaria est, non ut omnino definiat, atque infallibili sua auctoritate utatur, sed ut convenienter ac recte (hoc est sine peccato), utatur. Sive pontifex in definiendo studium adhibeat sive non adhibeat: modo tamen controversiam definiat, in-

fallibiliter certe definiet atque adeo reipsa utetur auctoritate sibi a Christo concessa. Quod ex promissionibus divinis de veritate per magisterium unius pastoris Ecclesiae satis certissime colligimus." Bellarmine argues as follows in his *Disputationes de controversiis christianae fidei* (Cologne, 1628), *De summo pontifice*, bk. IV, c. 2, 209: "Videntur quidem hi autores aliquo modo inter se dissentire: quia quidam eorum dicunt pontificem non posse errare si mature procedat et consilium audiat aliorum pastorum: alii dicunt pontificem etiam solum nullo modo errare posse; sed revera non dissident inter se. Nam posteriores non volunt negare, quin teneatur pontifex mature procedere et consulere viros doctos; sed solum dicere volunt ipsam infallibilitatem non esse in coetu consiliariorum vel in consilio episcoporum, sed in solo pontifice: sicut e contrario priores non volunt ponere infallibilitatem in consiliariis, sed in solo pontifice; verum explicare volunt pontificem debere facere quod in se est consulendo viros doctos et peritos rei de qua quaeritur." Bellarmine thus makes a mere moral obligation out of the inherently necessary connection between consultation and decision. See W. Klausnitzer, *Das Papstamt im Disput zwischen Lutheranern und Katholiken. Schwerpunkte von der Reformation bis zur Gegenwart*, IThS 20 (Innsbruck, 1987), 299. Cf. also Bellarmine in *Auctarium Bellarminianum. Supplément aux oeuvres du Cardinal Bellarmin*, ed. X.-M. Le Bachelet (Paris, 1913), 521: "Quod summus pontifex non debeat causas graviores definire sine consilio fratrum. Dixi, *non debeat*, non autem, *non possit*, ut significarem eum peccare si definiat causas graviores sine consilio fratrum; non autem rem esse irritam, *quamvis in quibusdam casibus poterit esse irrita.*" See T. Dietrich, *Die Theologie der Kirche bei Robert Bellarmin (1542–1621). Systematische Voraussetzungen des Kontroverstheologen*, KKTS 69 (Paderborn, 1999), 387 ff.

88. Franciscus Suárez, *De summo pontifice*, disp. X, sect. VI, no. 11, *Opera Omnia*, vol. 12 (Paris, 1858), 319. The pope can, as some believe, fall into heresy. However, "Quod licet multi verisimiliter affirment, mihi tamen breviter et magis pium et probabilius videtur, *posse quidem papam ut privatam personam errare ex ignorantia, non tamen ex contumacia.*" Moreover, from *"De Ecclesia et Pontifice.* Introducción y edición de A. Vargas-Machuca," *ATG* 30 (1967): 245–331, here 311: "Quocirca pie satis et probabiliter defendi potest nullum hactenus Pontificem Romanum incidisse in apertam et damnatam haeresim, etiam [ut] personam privatam; ex quo etiam probabile efficitur, quod citati authores volunt: id quod hactenus numquam accidit et spirituali Dei privilegio personae Pontificis concesso, minime posse." Bellarmin, *De summo pontifice*, bk. IV, c. 6, ed. cit., 212: "Probabile est, pieque credi potest, summum Pontificem, non solum ut Pontificem errare non posse, sed etiam ut particularem personam haereticum esse non posse, falsum aliquid contra fidem pertinaciter credendum." For Gregory of Valencia see U. Horst, *Papst, Konzil, Unfehlbarkeit*, 207 f.

89. See P. Stockmeier, "Die causa Honorii und Karl Josef von Hefele," *ThQ* 148 (1968): 405–28; idem, "Der Fall des Papstes Honorius und das Erste Vatikanische Konzil," in *Hundert Jahre nach dem Ersten Vaticanum*, ed. G. Schwaiger (Regensburg, 1970), 109–30; K. Schatz, *Vaticanum I, 1869–1870*, 3 vols. (Paderborn, 1992–94) (index).

90. Cf. U. Horst, "Kardinalerzbischof Filippo Maria Guidi O.P. und das I. Vatikanische Konzil," *AFP* 49 (1979): 429–511.

Bibliography

I. PRIMARY SOURCES

1. Manuscript Sources

Sevilla: Biblioteca de la Universidad, MS 333-53-1
Coimbra: Biblioteca Geral da Universidade, MS 1862
Salamanca: Biblioteca de la Universidad, MS 2206

2. Printed Sources

Abate, G. "Le 'diffinitiones' del capitulo generale di Parigi del 1266," *MiscFranc* 32 (1932): 3–5.
Albertus Magnus. *Super Lucam*, ed. Borgnet, vol. 23 (Paris, 1895).
———. *Super III Sententiarum*, ed. Borgnet, vol. 28 (Paris, 1894).
Alexander de Hales, *Summa Theologica seu "Summa Fratris Alexandri,"* studio et cura PP. Collegii S. Bonaventurae, vol. 4, book 3 (Prologomena) (Quaracchi, 1948).
Araújo, Franciscus de. *In Secundam Secundae commentarius* (Salamanca, 1635).
Báñez, Dominicus. *Scholastica commentaria in Secundam Secundae quibus quae ad fidem spem et caritatem spectant clarissime explicantur* (Duaci, 1615).
Bellarmin, Robert. *Auctarium Bellarminianum. Supplément aux oeuvres du Cardinal Bellarmin*, ed. X.-M. Le Bachelet (Paris, 1913).
———. *Disputationes de controversiis christianae fidei* (Cologne, 1628).
Bernardus Guidonis. *Practica inquisitionis heretice pravitatis*, ed. C. Douais (Paris, 1886).
Bierbaum, M. *Bettelorden und Weltgeistlichkeit an der Universität Paris*, FS.B 2 (Münster, 1920).

Bonaventura. *Apologia pauperum, Opera Omnia*, vol. 8 (Quaracchi, 1898), 233–330.

———. *Epistola de tribus quaestionibus, Opera Omnia*, vol. 8 (Quaracchi, 1898), 331–36.

———. *Expositio super Regulam Fratrum Minorum, Opera Omnia*, vol. 8 (Quaracchi, 1898), 391–437.

———. *Legenda maior S. Francisci, Opera Omnia*, vol. 8 (Quaracchi, 1898), 504–64.

———. *Quaestiones disputatae De perfectione evangelica, Opera Omnia*, vol. 5 (Quaracchi, 1891), 117–98.

———. *Quaestio reportata de mendicitate cum annotationibus Gulielmi de S. Amore*, ed. F. Delorme, in *S. Bonaventurae Collationes in Hexaëmeron* (Quaracchi, 1934).

Brooke, R. B., ed. *Scripta Leonis, Rufini et Angeli, Sociorum S. Francisci: The Writings of Leo, Rufino and Angelo, Companions of St. Francis* (Oxford, 1990).

Bulario de la Universidad de Salamanca (1219–1549), vol. 2, ed. V. Beltrán de Heredia (Salamanca, 1966).

Bullarium Franciscanum, vol. 1, ed. J. H. Sbaralea (Rome, 1759); vol. 5, ed. C. Eubel (Rome, 1898).

Cano, Melchior. *Opera omnia*, ed. H. J. Serry (Bassani, 1746).

Castro, Alfonsus de. *Adversus omnes haereses* (Cologne, 1543).

Concilium universale Chalcedonense, vol. 3, pars altera, Actiones II–VI, ed. E. Schwarz (Berlin-Leipzig, 1936).

Corpus Iuris Canonici, ed. A. Friedberg, 2 vols. (Leipzig, 1879).

Creytens, R. "Les constitutions des frères prêcheurs dans la rédaction de s. Raymond de Peñafort," *AFP* 18 (1948): 5–68.

Delorme, F. M. "Diffinitiones capituli generalis O.F.M. Narbonensis (1260)," *AFH* 3 (1910): 491–504.

———. "Quatre chapitres inédits de Jean de Pecham, O.F.M., sur la perfection religieuse et autres états de perfection," *CFr* 14 (1944): 84–120.

Denifle, H., and Chatelain, E. *Chartularium Universitatis Parisiensis*, 4 vols. (Paris, 1889–97).

———. "Die Constitutionen des Prediger-Ordens vom Jahre 1228," *ALKGMA* 1 (1885): 165–93.

Deza, Diego de. *Novarum defensionum doctrine angelici doctoris beati Thome de Aquino super libris sententiarum questiones profundissime ac utilissime*, 4 vols. (Seville, 1517).

Duval-Arnould, L. "La Constitution 'Cum inter nonnullos' de Jean XXII sur la pauvreté du Christ et des apôtres: Rédaction préparatoire et rédaction définitive," *AFH* 77 (1984): 406–20.

Esser, K., and Grau, E. *Die Opuscula des hl. Franziskus von Assisi. Neue textkritische Edition*, 2d ed., SpicBon 13 (Grottaferrata, 1989).

Faral, E. "Les 'Responsiones' de Guillaume de Saint-Amour," *AHDL* 25–26 (1950/51): 337–94.

Flood, D. *Hugh of Dignes's Rule Commentary*, SpicBon 14 (Grottaferrata, 1979).

Fontes Franciscani, ed. E. Menestò and S. Brufani (Porziuncola, 1995).

Fussenegger, G. "Definitiones Capituli Generalis Argentinae celebrati 1282," *AFH* 26 (1933): 127–40.

Gál, G., and Flood, D., eds. *Nicolaus Minorita: Chronica. Documentation on Pope John XXII, Michael of Cesena and the Poverty of Christ with Summaries in English. A Source Book* (New York, 1996).

Gregory of Valencia. *Commentarii Theologici* (Ingolstadt, 1592).

Grundmann, H. "Die Bulle 'Quo elongati' Papst Gregors IX.," *AFH* 54 (1961): 3–25.

Guido Terreni. *Quaestio de magisterio infallibili Romani pontificis*, ed. B. M. Xiberta, *OTHE.S*, fasc. 2 (Münster, 1926).

Hervaeus Natalis. *Commentaria quibus adiectus est eiusdem auctoris Tractatus de potestate papae* (Paris, 1647).

———. *"De paupertate Christi et apostolorum,"* ed. J. G. Sikes, *AHDL* 12/13 (1937/38): 209–97.

Hofmann, G. "Due discorsi di Giovanni da Torquemada O.P. a Norimberga e Magonza contro il conciliarismo," in *Miscellanea Historiae Pontificiae* II, 2 (Rome, 1940).

Hugo of St. Cher. *Postilla in totam Bibliam. Sexta pars huius operis continens postillam domini Hugonis super quatuor evangelia* (Basil, 1506–8).

Johannes ab Annuntiatione. *Cursus Theologicus Summam Theologicam Angelici Doctoris Thomae complectens*, vol. 11 (Paris-Brussels, 1878).

Johannes de Neapoli. *Quaestiones variae Parisiis*, ed. A. Gravina (Naples, 1618).

Johannes Quidort. *Über königlich und päpstliche Gewalt (De regia potestate et papali)*, ed. F. Bleienstein (Stuttgart, 1969).

Johannes (Stojković) de Ragusio. *Tractatus de Ecclesia*, ed. Fr. Šanjek (Zagreb, 1983).

Johannes Torquemada. *Ioannis a Turrecremata in Gratiani decretorum primam doctissimi commentarii*, vol. 1 (Venice, 1578).

———. *Oratio synodalis de primatu*, ed. E. Candal, Concilium Florentinum documenta et scriptores, Series B, vol. 4, fasc. 2 (Rome, 1954).

———. *Summa de Ecclesia* (Lyon, 1496).

Johannis Pecham. *Fratris Johannis Pecham quondam archiepiscopi Cantuariensis Tractatus tres*, ed. C. L. Kingsford, A. G. Little, and F. Tocco (Aberdeen, 1910).

Jordanus de Saxonia. *Libellus de principiis Ordinis Praedicatorum*, ed. H. C. Scheeben, MOPH 16 (Rome, 1935).

Juan de la Peña. *Eclesiología. Réplica a la Iglesia de Lutero*, ed. R. Hernández, BTE 30 A14 (Salamanca, 1987).

Laurent, M.-H. *Fontes vitae S. Thomae Aquinatis*. Processus canonizationis S. Thomae, Neapoli, Fossae-Novae. De canonizatione S. Thomae Aquinatis (Saint-Maximin, 1937).

Liber de fide trinitatis (anonymous author), in Thomas Aquinas, *Opera Omnia*, ed. Leonina, vol. 40 (Rome, 1969), A109–A157.

Little, A. G. "Definitiones capitulorum generalium Ordinis Fratrum Minorum, 1262–1282," *AFH* 7 (1914): 676–82.

———, ed. *Fratris Thomae vulgo dicti de Eccleston Tractatus de adventu fratrum minorum in Anglia*, 2d ed. (Manchester, 1951).

Miethke, J. "Das Votum *De paupertate Christi et apostolorum* des Durandus von Sancto Porciano im theoretischen Armutsstreit. Eine dominikanische Position in der

Diskussion um die franziskanische Armut (1322/3)," in *Vera Lex Historiae. Studien zu mittelalterlichen Quellen (Festschrift D. Kurze)* (Cologne-Vienna, 1993), 149–96.

Oliger, L. *Expositio quatuor magistrorum super regulam Fratrum Minorum (1241–1242). Accedit eiusdem regulae textus cum fontibus et locis parallelis* (Rome, 1950).

——. "Fr. Bonagratia de Bergamo et eius *Tractatus de Christi et apostolorum paupertate*," *AFH* 22 (1929): 292–335, 487–511.

——. "Die theologische Quaestion des Johannes Pecham über die vollkommene Armut," *FS* 4 (1917): 127–76.

Pedro de Ledesma. *Tractatus de divinae gratiae auxiliis, circa illa verba Esaiae cap. 26 Omnia opera nostra operatus es in nobis Domine: et circa Doctrinam D. Thomae multis in locis* (Salamanca, 1611).

Petrus Ioannis Olivi. *Das Heil der Armen und das Verderben der Reichen. Petrus Johannis Olivi OFM. Die Frage nach der höchsten Armut*, ed. J. Schlageter, FranzFor 34 (Werl, 1989).

——. *Petri Iohannis Olivi Quaestiones de Romano Pontifice*, ed. M. Bartoli, Collectio Oliviana 4 (Grottaferrata, 2002).

——. "Una questione inedita dell'Olivi sull'infallibilità del papa," ed. M. Maccarone, *RSCI* 3 (1949): 309–43.

Petrus de Palude. *Tractatus de potestate papae (Toulouse Bibl. de la Ville, 747)*, ed. P. T. Stella (Zürich, 1966).

Pigge, Albert. *Hierarchiae ecclesiasticae assertio* (Cologne, 1544).

Pou y Martí, J. M. *Visionarios, Beguinos y Fraticelos catalanes siglos XIII–XV* (Vich, 1930).

Pozo, C. "Una teoría en el siglo XVI sobre la relación entre infalibilidad pontificia y conciliar," *ATG* 25 (1962): 257–324.

Raulx, J.-B. *Divi Thomae Aquinatis doctoris angelici sermones et opuscula concinatoria*, vol. 2 (Luxemburg, 1881).

Reichert, B. M., ed. *Acta capituli generalis*, MOPH 3 (Rome, 1898).

Sägmüller, J. B. *Ein Traktat des Bischofs von Feltre und Treviso Teodoro de'Lelli über das Verhältnis von Primat und Kardinalat* (Rome, 1893).

Sarmiento, A. *La eclesiología de Mancio. Introducción y comentario a la 2ª2ᵃᵉ q, 1, a. 10, del ms. 5 de la Catedral de Palencia*, 2 vols. (Pamplona, 1986).

Schwalm, J., ed. *Ludovici appellatio tertia contra processum pontificis*, MGH, Legum sectio IV, *Constitutiones et acta publica imperatorum et regum*, vol. 5 (Hannover and Leipzig, 1909–13), 722–44.

Soto, Dominicus. *Commentarii in Quartum Sententiarum*, 2 vols. (Salamanca, 1557/58 and 1560).

Suárez, Franciscus. "*De ecclesia et pontifice*. Introducción y edición de A. Vargas-Machuca," *ATG* 30 (1967): 245–331.

——. *De summo pontifice, Opera Omnia*, vol. 12 (Paris, 1858).

Tarrant, J., ed. *Extravagantes Iohannis XXII*, MIC.C 6 (Vatican City, 1983).

Thomas, A. H. *De oudste constituties van den Dominicanen. Vorgeschiedenis. Text, bronnen, ontstaan en ontwikkeling (1215–1237) met uitgave van de text*, BRHE 42 (Leuven, 1965).

Thomas Aquinas. *Catena aurea in quatuor evangelia*, 2 vols., ed. A. Guarienti (Torino, 1953).

————. *Contra errores Graecorum, Opera Omnia*, ed. Leonina, vol. 40 (Rome, 1969), A5–A165.

————. *Contra impugnantes Dei cultum et religionem, Opera Omnia*, ed. Leonina, vol. 41 (Rome, 1970), A5–A181.

————. *De potentia, Quaestiones disputatae*, vol. 2, ed. P. Bazzi et al. (Torino, 1949).

————. *Questiones de quolibet*, ed. R. A. Gauthier, *Opera Omnia*, ed. Leonina, vol. 25 (1 et 2) (Rome-Paris, 1996).

————. *Scriptum super sententiis*, ed. M. F. Moos, vol. 4 (Paris, 1947).

————. *Summa Theologiae*, cura et studio Instituti Studiorum Medievalium Ottaviensis, vols. I–V, ed. altera (Ottawa, 1953).

————. *Super evangelium S. Ioannis lectura*, ed. R. Cai (Torino, 1952).

————. *Super evangelium S. Matthaei lectura*, ed. R. Cai (Torino, 1951).

————. *Super Ioannem*, ed. R. Cai (Torino, 1952).

Thomas de Vio Cajetan. *Commentarii S Th II-II*, in *S. Thomae Aquinatis opera omnia cum commentariis Thomae de Vio Cajetani*, ed. Leonina, vol. 10 (Rome, 1899).

————. *De comparatione auctoritatis papae et concilii cum Apologia eiusdem*, ed. V. I. Pollet (Rome, 1936).

Traver, A. *The Opuscula of William of Saint Amour: The Minor Works of 1255–1256*, BGPhMA 63 (Münster, 2003).

Tugwell, S., ed. *Miracula Sancti Dominici mandato magistri Berengarii collecta. Petri Calo legendae Sancti Dominici*, MOPH 26 (Rome, 1997).

Vitoria, Francisco de. *Comentarios a la Secunda Secundae de Santo Tomás*, ed. V. Beltrán de Heredia, 6 vols. (Salamanca, 1932–52).

————. *Vorlesungen I et II (Relectiones). Völkerrecht, Politik, Kirche*, ed. U. Horst, H.-G. Justenhoven, and J. Stüben (Stuttgart, 1995–97).

Walz, A. *Acta canonizationis S. Dominici*, MOPH 16 (Rome, 1935).

William of Tocco. *Ystoria sancti Thome de Aquino de Guillaume de Tocco (1323). Edition critique et notes*, ed. C. le Brun-Gouanvic, STPIMS 127 (Toronto, 1996).

II. Secondary Works

Alcalá, A. *Literatura y ciencia ante la Inquisición Española* (Madrid, 2001).

Alfaro, J. "Supernaturalitas fidei iuxta S. Thomam, II. Functio 'interioris instinctus,'" *Gr* 44 (1963): 731–87.

Amann, F. *Die Vulgata Sixtina von 1590. Eine quellenmäßige Darstellung ihrer Geschichte* (Freiburg, 1912).

Andrés, M. *La teología española en el siglo XVI*, 2 vols. (Madrid, 1976).

Azcona, T. de. "Reforma del episcopado y del clero de España en tiempo de los Reyes Católicos y de Carlos V (1475–1558)," in *La Iglesia en la España de los siglos XV y XVI*, ed. José Luis González Novalín, Historia de la Iglesia de España 3 (Madrid, 1980), 114–210.

————. *Isabel la Católica. Estudio crítico de su vida y reinado*, 3d ed. (Madrid, 1993).

Backes, I. *Die Christologie des hl. Thomas v. Aquin und die griechischen Kirchenväter*, FChLDG 17 (Paderborn, 1931).

Balthasar, K. *Geschichte des Armutsstreites im Fanziskanerorden bis zum Konzil von Vienne*, VRF 6 (Münster, 1911).

Barrientos García, J. "El maestro Pedro de Ledesma y la Universidad de Salamanca," *AD* 5 (1984): 201–61.

Bartoli, M. "Pietro di Giovanni Olivi nella recente storiografia sul tema dell'infallibilità pontificia," *Bulletino dell'Istituto Storico Italiano per il Medio Evo—Archivio muratoriano* 92/2 (1994): 149–200.

Bartoli Langeli. "Il manifesto francescano di Perugia del 1322 alle origini dei Fraticelli 'De opinione,'" *PS* 11 (1974): 204–61.

Bataillon, L.-J. "Saint Thomas et les Pères: de la Catena aurea à la Tertia Pars," in *Ordo sapientiae et amoris, Festschrift J.-P. Torrell* (Fribourg, 1993), 15–36.

———. "Les stigmates de saint François vus par Thomas d'Aquin et quelques autres prédicateurs," *AFH* 90 (1997): 341–47.

Bataillon, M. *Erasmo y España*, 2d ed. (México, 1966).

Bäumer, R. "Die Wiederentdeckung der Honoriusfrage im Abendland," *RQ* 56 (1961): 200–214.

———. "Das Kirchenverständnis Albert Pigges. Ein Beitrag zur Ekklesiologie der vortridentinischen Kontroverstheologie," *Volk Gottes (Festgabe Josef Höfer)* (Freiburg, 1967), 306–22.

Baumgarten, P. M. *Die Vulgata Sixtina von 1590 und ihre Einführungsbulle. Aktenstücke und Untersuchungen*, ATA III, 2 (Münster, 1911).

Bazàn, B. C. "Les questions disputées, principalement dans les facultés de théologie, de droit et de médecine," in *Les questions disputées et les questions quodlibétiques dans les facultés de théologie, de droit et de médecine*, ed. J. W. Wippel, G. Fransen, and D. Jacquart, Typologie des sources du moyen âge occidental, fasc. 44–45 (Turnhout, 1985), 58–70.

Becker, H. J. *Die Appellation vom Papst an ein allgemeines Konzil. Historische Entwicklung und kanonistische Diskussion im späten Mittelalter und in der frühen Neuzeit*, FKRG 17 (Cologne-Vienna, 1988).

Belda Plans, J. "La infalibilidad 'ex cathedra' del Romano Pontífice según Melchor Cano. Estudio de las condiciones de la infalibilidad en cuanto al modo," *ScrTh* 10 (1978): 519–75.

———. "La autoridad del Romano Pontífice según Melchor Cano (en los comentarios inéditos a la II-II, q. 1, a. 10)," *ScrTh* 14 (1982): 59–104.

———. *Los lugares teológicos de Melchor Cano en los comentarios a la Suma* (Pamplona, 1982).

———. *La Escuela de Salamanca y la renovación de la teología en el siglo XVI* (Madrid, 2000).

Beltrán de Heredia, V. "Actuación del maestro Domingo Báñez en la Universidad de Salamanca," *CTom* 25 (1922): 64–78, 208–40; 26 (1922): 63–73, 199–223; 27 (1923): 40–51, 361–74; 28 (1923): 36–47.

————. "Báñez y la inquisición española," *CTom* 37 (1928): 289–309; 38 (1928): 35–58, 171–86.

————. "Vindicando la memoria del maestro fray Domingo Báñez," *CTom* 40 (1929): 312–22; 43 (1931): 193–99.

————. "El tratado del Padre Matías de Paz OP acerca del dominio de los Reyes de España sobre los Indios de América," *AFP* 3 (1933): 133–81.

————. "Colección de documentos inéditos para ilustrar la vida del cardenal Juan de Torquemada O.P.," *AFP* 7 (1937): 210–45.

————. *Francisco de Vitoria* (Barcelona, 1939).

————. *Historia de la reforma de la provincia de España (1450–1550)*, DH 11 (Rome, 1939).

————. *Las corrientes de espiritualidad entre los dominicos de Castilla durante la primera mitad del siglo XVI*, BTE 29 (Salamanca, 1960).

————. *Domingo de Soto. Estudio biográfico documentado*, BTE 20 (Salamanca, 1960).

————. "Noticias y documentos para la biografía del cardenal Juan de Torquemada O.P.," *AFP* 30 (1960): 53–148.

————. *Domingo Báñez y las controversias sobre la gracia. Textos y documentos*, BTE 24 (Salamanca, 1968).

————. "El maestro Juan de la Peña," in *Miscelanea Beltrán de Heredia. Colección de artículos sobre la historia de la teología española*, vol. 2, BTE 26 B6 (Salamanca, 1972), 447–542.

Bentley, J. H. *Humanists and Holy Writ: New Testament Scholarship in the Renaissance* (Princeton, 1983).

Berg, D. *Armut und Wissenschaft. Beiträge zur Geschichte des Studienwesens der Bettelorden* (Düsseldorf, 1977).

————. *Armut und Geschichte. Studien zur Geschichte der Bettelorden im Hohen und Späten Mittelalter*, Saxonia Franciscana 11 (Kevelaer, 2001).

Bernstein, A. "Magisterium and License: Corporate Autonomy against Papal Authority in the Medieval University of Paris," *Viator* 9 (1978): 291–307.

Betti, U. "L'autorità di S. Antonino e la questione dell'infallibilità pontificia al Concilio Vaticano," *MDom* 76 (1959): 173–92.

————. "Assenza dell'autorità di S. Tommaso nel Decreto Vaticano sull'infallibilità pontificia," *Div* 6 (1962): 407–22.

Beuchot, M. "El primer planteamiento teológico-jurídico sobre la conquista de América: John Maior," *CTom* 103 (1976): 213–30.

Bihl, M. "De canonizatione S. Francisci (occasione VII centenarii: 1228–1928)," *AFH* 21 (1928): 468–514.

Binder, K. "Thesis, in passione Domini fidem Ecclesiae in Beatissima Virgine sola remansisse, iuxta doctrinam medii aevi et recentioris aetatis," in *Acta Congressus Mariologici-Mariani in civitate Lourdes anno 1958 celebrati*, vol. 3 (Rome, 1959), 389–488.

————. *Konzilsgedanken bei Kardinal Juan de Torquemada O.P.*, WBTh 49 (Vienna, 1976).

Bischof, F. X. *Theologie und Geschichte. Ignaz von Döllinger (1799–1890) in der zweiten Hälfte seines Lebens. Ein Beitrag zu seiner Biographie*, MKHS 9 (Stuttgart, 1997).

Boureau, A. *La papesse Jeanne* (Paris, 1988).

Boyle, L. E. "The Quodlibets of St. Thomas Aquinas and Pastoral Care," *Thom* 38 (1974): 232–56.

Brady, I. "The Writings of St. Bonaventure Regarding the Franciscan Order," in *San Bonaventura Maestro di vita francescana e di sapienza cristiana a cura di A. Pompei. Atti Congresso Internazionale per il VII centenario di San Bonaventura di Bagnoregio*, vol. 1 (Rome, 1976), 89–112.

Brincken, A.-D. von den. "Johanna, angebl. Päpstin," *LThK*, 3d ed., 5:860.

Brosse, O. de la. *Le pape et le concile. La comparaison de leurs pouvoirs à la veille de la Réforme*, UnSa 58 (Paris, 1965).

Burnham, L. A. "The Visionary Authority of Na Prous Boneta," in *Pierre de Jean Olivi (1248–1298). Pensée scolastique, dissidence spirituelle et société*, ed. A. Boureau and J. Piron (Paris, 1999), 319–39.

Burns, H. "Politia regalis et optima: The Political Ideas of John Maior," *History of Political Thought* 2 (1981): 31–62.

Burr, D. "The Correctorium Controversy and the Origins of the Usus Pauper Controversy," *Spec* 60 (1985): 331–42.

———. *Olivi and Franciscan Poverty: The Origins of the Usus Pauper Controversy* (Philadelphia, 1989).

———. *Olivi's Peaceable Kingdom: A Reading of the Apocalypse Commentary* (Philadelphia, 1993).

———. "Na Prous Boneta and Olivi," *CFr* 67 (1997): 277–300.

———. *The Spiritual Franciscans: From Protest to Persecution in the Century after Saint Francis* (Philadelphia, 2001).

Canetti, L. *L'invenzione della memoria. Il culto e l'immagine di Domenico nella storia dei primi frati Predicatori*, Biblioteca di medioevo latino 19 (Spoleto, 1996).

Castro, M. de. "Fr. Alfonso de Castro, O.F.M. Obs. (1495–1558). Notas bibliográficas," *CFr* 28 (1958): 59–88.

Clasen, S. *Der Hl. Bonaventura und das Mendikantentum. Ein Beitrag zur Ideengeschichte des Pariser Mendikantenstreites (1252–72)* (Werl, 1940).

———. "S. Bonaventura S. Francisci Legendae maioris compilator," *AFH* 54 (1961): 241–72; 55 (1962): 3–58, 289–319.

———. *Franziskus Engel des sechsten Siegels. Sein Leben nach den Schriften des heiligen Bonaventura*, Franziskanische Quellenschriften 7 (Werl, 1962).

———. "Einteilung und Anliegen der Legenda maior S. Francisci Bonaventuras," *FrS* 27 (1967): 115–62.

———. "Bonaventuras Expositio super Regulam Fratrum Minorum," in *S. Bonaventura 1274–1974*, vol. 2 (Grottaferrata, 1973), 531–70.

Congar, Y. "Incidence ecclésiologique d'un thème de dévotion mariale," *MSR* 7 (1950): 277–92.

———. "Aspects ecclésiologiques de la querelle entre mendiants et séculiers dans la seconde moitié du XIIIe siècle et le début du XIVe," *AHDL* 28 (1961): 35–151.

———. "La 'réception' comme réalité ecclésiologique," *RSPhTh* 56 (1972): 369–403.

————. "Saint Thomas Aquinas and the Infallibility of the Papal Magisterium (Summa Theol., II-II, q. 1, a. 10)," *Thom* 38 (1974): 81–105.

————. "Ecclesia Romana," *CrStor* 5 (1984): 225–44.

Conticello, C. "San Tommaso ed i Padri: La Catena aurea super Ioannem," *AHDL* 65 (1990): 31–92.

Cornely, R. *Historica et critica introductio in U.T. libros sacros*, vol. 2, *Introductio generalis* (Paris, 1885).

Courtenay, W. J. "Between Pope and King: The Parisian Letters of Adhesion of 1303," *Spec* 71 (1996): 577–605.

Crowe, M. B. "St. Thomas and the Greeks: Reflections on an Argument in Hans Küng's *Infallible?*," *IThQ* 39 (1972): 253–75.

Dalarun, J. *La malaventure de François d'Assise. Pour un usage historique des légendes hagiographiques* (Paris, 2002).

D'Alverny, M.-T. "Un adversaire de Saint Thomas: Petrus Ioannis Olivi," in *St. Thomas Aquinas 1274–1984. Commemorative Studies*, vol. 2 (Toronto, 1974), 179–218.

D'Amato, A. *I Domenicani e l'università di Bologna* (Bologna, 1988).

Dawson, J. D. "William of Saint Amour and the Apostolic Tradition," *MS* 40 (1978): 223–38.

Delhaye, P. "L'organisation scolaire au XIIᵉ siècle," *Tr* 5 (1947): 211–68.

Dettloff, W. "Die franziskanische Vorentscheidung im theologischen Denken des hl. Bonaventura," *MThZ* 13 (1962): 107–15.

————. "Die Rückkehr zum Evangelium in der Theologie. Franziskanische Grundanliegen bei Bonaventura," *WiWei* 38 (1975): 26–40.

Dietrich, T. *Die Theologie der Kirche bei Robert Bellarmin (1542–1621). Systematische Voraussetzungen des Kontroverstheologen*, KKTS 69 (Paderborn, 1999).

Distelbrink, B. *Bonaventurae scripta. Authentica, dubia vel spuria critice recensita*, SSFr 5 (Rome, 1975).

Döllinger, I. von. *Der Papst und das Konzil* (Leipzig, 1869).

Domínguez Asensio, J. A. "Infalibilidad y 'determinatio de fide' en la polémica antiluterana del Cardenal Cayetano," *ATG* 44 (1981): 5–61.

————. "Infalibilidad y potesdad magisterial en la polémica anticonciliarista de Cayetano," *Communio* (Sevilla) 14 (1981): 205–26.

Domínguez Reboiras, F. *Gaspar de Grajal (1530–1575). Frühneuzeitliche Bibelwissenschaft im Streit mit Universität und Inquisition*, RST 140 (Münster, 1998).

Dondaine, A. "Documents pour servir à l'histoire de la province de France. L'appel au Concile (1303)," *AFP* 22 (1952): 381–439.

————. "La collection des oeuvres de saint Thomas dite de Jean XXII et Jacquet Maci," *Scr* 29 (1975): 127–52.

Dubois, J. "Le travail des moines au moyen âge," in *Le travail au moyen âge. Une approche inter-disciplinaire*, ed. J. Hamesse and C. Muraille-Samarin (Louvain-la-Neuve, 1990), 61–100.

Dufeil, M.-M. *Guillaume de Saint-Amour et la polémique universitaire parisienne 1250–1259* (Paris, 1972).

————. *Saint Thomas et l'histoire* (Aix-en-Provence, 1991).

Dunbabin, J. *A Hound of God: Pierre de la Palud and the Fourteenth-Century Church* (Oxford, 1991).

Duval-Arnould, L. "Les conseils remis à Jean XXII sur le problème de la pauvreté du Christ et des apôtres (Ms. Vat. lat. 3740)," in *Miscellanea Bibliothecae Apostolicae Vaticanae III*, StT 333 (Vatican City, 1989), 121–201.

————. "Elaboration d'un document pontifical: Les travaux préparatoires à la constitution apostolique *Cum inter nonnullos* (12 novembre 1323)," in *Aux origines de l'état moderne: Le fonctionnement administratif de la papauté d'Avignon. Actes de la table ronde. Avignon (23–24 janvier 1988)*, CEFR 138 (Rome, 1990), 385–409.

Ehrle, F. "Petrus Johannis Olivi, sein Leben und seine Schriften," *ALKGMA* 3 (1887): 409–552.

Elizondo, F. "Pontificiae interpretationes regulae franciscanae usque ad annum 1517," *Laur* 1 (1960): 324–58.

————. "Doctrinales regulae franciscanae expositiones usque ad annum 1517," *Laur* 2 (1961): 449–92.

————. "Bullae 'Quo elongati' Gregorii IX et 'Ordinem vestrum' Innocentii IV. De duabus primis regulae franciscanae authenticis declarationibus," *Laur* 3 (1962): 349–94.

————. "Bulla 'Exiit qui seminat' Nicolai III (14 augusti 1279)," *Laur* 4 (1963): 59–117.

Emery, G. "Le photinisme et ses précurseurs chez saint Thomas," *RThom* 95 (1995): 371–89.

————. "La procession du Saint-Esprit a Filio chez saint Thomas d'Aquin," *RThom* 96 (1996): 531–74.

Enrique del Sagrado Corazón. *Los Salmanticenses. Su vida y su obra. Ensayo histórico y proceso inquisitorial de su doctrina sobre la Inmaculada* (Madrid, 1955).

Esser, K. "Die Handarbeit in der Frühgeschichte des Minderbrüderordens," *FS* 40 (1958): 145–66.

Farge, J. K. *Orthodoxy and Reform in Early Reformation France: The Faculty of Theology in Paris, 1500–1543*, SMRT 32 (Leiden, 1985).

Feine, H. E. *Kirchliche Rechtsgeschichte*, vol. 1, *Die katholische Kirche*, 3d ed. (Weimar, 1955).

Ferruolo, C. *The Origins of the University: The Schools of Paris and Their Critics, 1100–1215* (Stanford, 1985).

Figueira, R. C. " 'Legatus apostolicae sedis': The Pope's 'alter ego' According to Thirteenth Century Canon Law," *StudMed* 27 (1986): 527–74.

Flood, D. *Peter Olivi's Rule Commentary: Edition and Presentation*, VIEG 67 (Wiesbaden, 1972).

————. "'John of Wales' 'Commentary on the Franciscan Rule,'" *FrS* 60 (2002): 93–138.

Frank, I. W. "Der Wiener Dominikaner Johannes Werd (†1510) als Verfasser von Thomaskommentaren," in *Thomas von Aquino. Interpretation und Rezeption. Studien und Texte*, ed. W. P. Eckert, WSAMA.P 5 (Mainz, 1974), 609–40.

————. *Franz von Assisi. Frage auf eine Antwort* (Düsseldorf, 1982).

————. "Die Grundlegung des intellektuellen Profils des Predigerordens in seinen Anfängen," *RoJKG* 17 (1998):13–34.

Friedlander, A. *The Hammer of the Inquisitors: Brother Bernard Délicieux and the Struggle against the Inquisition in Fourteenth-Century France*, Cultures, Beliefs and Traditions 9 (Leiden, 2000).

Frugoni, C. *Francesco e l'invenzione delle stimmate. Una storia per parole e immagini fino a Bonaventura e Giotto* (Torino, 1993).

———. *Francis of Assisi: A Life* (London, 1998).

Fuhrmann, H. "Die Fabel von Papst Leo und Bischof Hilarius. Vom Urspung und der Erscheinungsform einer historischen Legende," *AKG* 43 (1961): 125–62.

———. *Einfluß und Verbreitung der pseudoisidorischen Fälschungen. Von ihrem Auftauchen bis in die neuere Zeit*, SMGH 24, I (Stuttgart, 1972).

Ganoczy, A. "Jean Major, exégète gallican," *RSR* 56 (1968): 457–95.

García y García, L. "El primado pontificio y la infalibilidad de la Iglesia en Fray Alfonso de Castro," *LF* 12 (1958): 131–65.

García Miralles. "El cardenalato, de institución divina, y el episcopado en el problema de sucesión apostólica según Juan de Torquemada," in *XVI Semana Española de Teología* (Madrid, 1957), 251–74.

García Oro, J. "Conventualismo y observancia. La reforma de las órdenes religiosas en los siglos XV y XVI," in *La Iglesia en la España de los siglos XV y XVI*, ed. José Luis González Novalín, Historia de la Iglesia de España 3 (Madrid, 1980), 211–349.

———. *La universidad de Alcalá de Henares en la etapa fundacional (1458–1578)* (Santiago de Compostela, 1992).

———. *El cardenal Cisneros. Vida y empresa*, 2 vols. (Madrid, 1992/93).

Gaudemet, J. *Histoire du droit et des institutions de l'Eglise en Occident*, ed. G. Le Bras and J. Gaudemet. Vol. 8, 2, *Le gouvernement de l'Eglise à l'époque classique. II. part. Le gouvernement local*, by J. Gaudemet (Paris, 1979).

———. *Eglise et cité. Histoire du droit canonique* (Paris, 1994).

Gauthier, R.-A. *Somme contre les Gentils* (Paris, 1993).

Geenen, G. "En marge du Concile de Chalcédoine. Les textes du quatrième concile dans les oeuvres de saint Thomas," *Ang* 29 (1952): 43–59.

———. "Doctrinae Concilii Chalcedonensis usus et influxus in theologia S. Thomae Aquinatis," *DT(P)* 56 (1953): 319–42.

Gerulaitis, L. V. "The Canonization of Saint Thomas Aquinas," *Vivarium* 5 (1967): 25–46.

Getino, L. G. A. *El Maestro Francisco de Vitoria. Su vida, su doctrina e influencia*, 2d ed. (Madrid, 1930).

Gierke, O. *Das deutsche Genossenschaftsrecht*, vol. 3, *Die Staats- und Korporationslehre des Alterthums und des Mittelalters und ihre Aufnahme in Deutschland* (Berlin, 1881).

Glorieux, P. "Prélats français contre religieux mendiants," *RHEF* 11 (1925): 309–31, 471–95.

Goñi Gaztambide, J. "Concilio de Pisa y España," *DHEE* (Supl.), 211–19.

Gonzalo de Arriaga. *Historia del Colegio de S. Gregorio de Valladolid, editada, corregida y documentada por M.M. Hoyos*, 3 vols. (Valladolid, 1928–40).

Gössmann, E. *Die "Päpstin Johanna." Der Skandal eines weiblichen Papstes. Eine Rezeptionsgeschichte* (Berlin, 1998).

Grabmann, M. "Der belgische Thomist Johannes Tinctoris (†1469) und die Entstehung des Kommentars zur 'Summa Theologiae' des hl. Thomas von Aquin," in *Studia mediaevalia in honorem A. R. P. Raymundi Josephi Martin O.P.* (Bruges, 1948), 409–36.

Grillmeier, A. "Konzil und Rezeption. Methodische Bemerkungen zu einem Thema der ökumenischen Diskussion der Gegenwart," *ThPh* 45 (1970): 321–52.

Guillemain, B. *La cour pontificale d'Avignon 1309–1379. Etude d'une société* (Paris, 1966).

Guimarães, A. de. "Hervé Noël (†1323). Etude biographique," *AFP* 8 (1938): 5–81.

Hardick, L. "Pecunia et denarii. Untersuchungen zum Geldverbot in den Regeln der Minderbrüder," *FS* 40 (1958): 193–217, 313–28; 41 (1959): 268–90; 43 (1961): 216–44.

Harkins, C. "The Authorship of a Commentary on the Franciscan Rule Published among the Works of St. Bonaventure," *FrS* 29 (1969): 157–248.

Helmrath, J. *Das Basler Konzil 1431–1449. Forschungsstand und Probleme*, KHAbh 32 (Köln, 1987).

Herbers, K. "Die Päpstin Johanna. Ein kritischer Forschungsbericht," *HJ* 108 (1988): 174–94.

Hernández, R. "Actividad universitaria de Francisco de Araújo en los claustros salmantinos," *CTom* 92 (1965): 203–71.

———. *Un español en la ONU. Francisco de Vitoria* (Madrid, 1977).

———. *Francisco de Vitoria. Vida y pensamiento internacionalista* (Madrid, 1995).

Hillenbrand, E. "Kurie und Generalkapitel des Predigerordens unter Johannes XXII. (1316–1334)," in *Adel und Kirche. Gerd Tellenbach zum 65. Geburtstag*, ed. J. Fleckenstein and K. Schmidt (Freiburg, 1968), 499–515.

Hinnebusch, W. A. *The Early English Friars Preachers*, DH 14 (Rome, 1951).

———. *The History of the Dominican Order: Origins and Growth to 1500*, vol. 1 (New York, 1966).

Hödl, L. "Dignität und Qualität der päpstlichen Lehrentscheidung in der Auseinandersetzung zwischen Petrus de Palude (†1342) und Johannes de Polliaco (†1321) über das Pastoralstatut der Mendikantenorden," in *Bonaventura. Studien zu seiner Wirkungsgeschichte*, ed. I. Vanderheyden (Werl, 1976), 136–45.

Höhn, E. "Köln als Ort der ersten Kommentare zur 'Summa Theologiae' des Thomas von Aquin," in *Thomas von Aquino. Interpretation und Rezeption. Studien und Texte*, ed. W. P. Eckert, WSAMA.P 5 (Mainz 1974), 641–55.

Horst, U. "Papst, Bischöfe und Konzil nach Antonin von Florenz," *RThAM* 32 (1965): 76–116.

———. "Die Ekklesiologie des 'Cursus Theologicus Salmanticensis,'" *RQ* 69 (1974): 46–67.

———. *Papst, Konzil, Unfehlbarkeit. Die Ekklesiologie der Summenkommentare von Cajetan bis Billuart*, WSAMA.T 10 (Mainz, 1978).

———. "Kardinalerzbischof Filippo Maria Guidi O.P. und das I. Vatikanische Konzil," *AFP* 49 (1979): 429–511.

———. *Die Diskussion um die Immaculata Conceptio im Dominikanerorden. Ein Beitrag zur Geschichte der theologischen Methode*, VGI 34 (Paderborn, 1987).

———. "Die Loci Theologici Melchior Canos und sein Gutachten zum Catechismo Christiano Bartolomé Carranzas," *FZPhTh* 36 (1989): 47–92.

———. *Autorität und Immunität des Papstes*. *Raphael de Pornassio OP und Julianus Tallada OP in der Auseinandersetzung mit dem Basler Konziliarismus*, VGI 34 (Paderborn, 1991).

———. "Die Lehrautorität des Papstes nach Augustinus von Ancona," *AAug* 53 (1991): 271–303.

———. *Evangelische Armut und Kirche*. *Thomas von Aquin und die Armutskontroversen des 13. und beginnenden 14. Jahrhunderts*, QFGDO n.s. 1 (Berlin, 1992).

———. "Raimundus Bequin und seine Disputation *De paupertate Christi et apostolorum* aus dem Jahr 1322," *AFP* 64 (1994): 101–18.

———. *Evangelische Armut und päpstliches Lehramt*. *Minoritentheologen im Konflikt mit Papst Johannes XXII. (1316–34)*, MKHS 8 (Stuttgart, 1996).

———. "Mendikant und Theologe. Thomas v. Aquin in den Armutsbewegungen seiner Zeit (zu Contra retrahentes c. 15)," *MThZ* 47 (1996): 13–31.

———. "Thomas von Aquin: Professor und Consultor," *MThZ* 48 (1997): 205–18.

———. "Christ, Exemplar Ordinis Fratrum Praedicantium, according to Saint Thomas Aquinas," in *Christ among the Medieval Dominicans: Representations of Christ in the Texts and Images of the Order of Preachers*, ed. K. Emery, Jr., and J. Wawrykow (Notre Dame, 1998), 256–70.

———. "Thomas von Aquin und der Predigerorden," *RoJKG* 17 (1998): 35–52.

———. *Bischöfe und Ordensleute*. *Cura principalis animarum und via perfectionis in der Ekklesiologie des hl. Thomas von Aquin* (Berlin, 1999).

———. "Evangelische Armut und Kirche. Ein Konfliktfeld in der scholastischen Theologie des 13. Jahrhunderts," *MM* 27 (2000): 308–20.

———. "Melchior Cano und Dominicus Báñez über die Autorität der Vulgata. Zur Deutung des Trienter Vulgatadekrets," *MThZ* 51 (2000): 331–51.

———. "Albertus Magnus und Thomas von Aquin zu Matthäus 16, 18f. Ein Beitrag zur Lehre vom päpstlichen Primat," in *Albertus Magnus. Zum Gedenken nach 800 Jahren. Neue Zugänge, Aspekte und Perspektiven*, ed. W. Senner, QFGDO n.s. 10 (Berlin, 2001), 553–71.

———. *Die Gaben des Heiligen Geistes nach Thomas von Aquin*, VGI 46 (Berlin, 2001).

———. "Die Dominikanerschule von Salamanca und das Konzil von Trient," *AHC* 35 (2003): 86–103.

———. *Die Lehrautorität des Papstes und die Dominikanertheologen der Schule von Salamanca*, QFGDO n.s. 11 (Berlin, 2003).

———. "Kardinal Juan de Torquemada und die Lehrautorität des Papstes," *AHC* 36 (2004): 395–428.

Izbicki, T. "Infallibility and the Erring Pope: Guido Terreni and Johannes Turrecremata," in *Law, Church and Society: Essays in Honor of Stephan Kuttner*, ed. K. Pennington and R. Somerville (University Park, PA, 1977), 97–111.

———. *Protector of the Faith: Cardinal Johannes de Turrecremata and the Defense of the Institutional Church* (Washington, DC, 1981).

Jedin, H. *Geschichte des Konzils von Trient*, 4 vols. (Freiburg, 1949–75).

Jericó Bermejo, I. "La definición del Romano Pontífice como regla infalible de fe, según los comentarios escolares de Pedro de Ledesma," *CTom* 125 (1998): 347–400.

———. "Sobre la posible definición de una conclusión teológica. Los comentarios de Pedro de Ledesma (1581)," *Communio* (Sevilla) 32 (1999): 199–226.

———. "Sobre la potestad de la Iglesia postapostólica para decir infaliblemente cuál es la verdadera Sagrada Escritura, y si lo es en concreto la edición Vulgata. Los comentarios de Pedro de Ledesma (1581)," *ScrTh* 31 (1999): 413–35.

Jotischky, A. *The Carmelites and Antiquity: Mendicants and Their Pasts in the Middle Ages* (Oxford, 2002).

Kaeppeli, T. "Vie du frère Martin Donadieu de Carcassonne OP (1299). Ecrite par Bernard et Pierre Gui," *AFP* 26 (1956): 276–90.

———. *Scriptores Ordinis Praedicatorum Medii Aevi*, 4 vols. (Rome, 1970–93).

Kemp, E. W. *Canonization and Authority in the West* (Oxford, 1948).

Klauser, R. "Zur Entwicklung des Heiligsprechungsverfahrens bis zum 13. Jahrhundert," *ZRGKA* 60 (1954): 85–101.

Klausnitzer, W. *Das Papstamt im Disput zwischen Lutheranern und Katholiken. Schwerpunkte von der Reformation bis zur Gegenwart*, IThS 20 (Innsbruck, 1987).

Koch, J. "Der Prozess gegen Magister Johannes de Polliaco und seine Vorgeschichte (1312–1321)," *RThAM* 5 (1933): 391–422.

Körner, B. *Melchior Cano De locis theologicis. Ein Beitrag zur theologischen Erkenntnislehre* (Graz, 1994).

Kreuzer, G. *Die Honoriusfrage im Mittelalter und in der Neuzeit*, PuP 8 (Stuttgart, 1975).

———. "Honorius I," *LThK*, 5:265–66.

Kriechbaum, M. *Actio, ius und dominium in den Rechtslehren des 13. und 14. Jahrhunderts*, Münchener Universitätsschriften. Abhandlungen zur Rechtswissenschaftlichen Grundlagenforschung 77 (Ebelsbach, 1996).

Küng, H. *Unfehlbar? Eine Anfrage* (Zürich-Cologne, 1970).

Kuttner, S. "La réserve papale du droit de canonisation," *Revue historique du droit français et étranger* 17 (1938): 172–228.

Ladero Quesada, M. A. *La España de los Reyes Católicos* (Madrid, 1999).

Lambert, M. D. "The Franciscan Crisis under John XXII," *FrS* 32 (1972): 123–43.

———. *Franciscan Poverty: The Doctrine of the Absolute Poverty of Christ and the Apostles in the Franciscan Order, 1210–1323*, rev. ed. (New York, 1998).

Landgraf, A. M. "Das Axiom 'facienti quod est in se Deus non denegat gratiam,'" *Dogmengeschichte der Frühscholastik*, Part 1, vol. 1 (Regensburg, 1952), 249–64.

Landi, A. *Concilio e papato nel Rinascimento (1449–1516). Un problema irrisolto* (Torino, 1997).

Lang, A. *Die Loci Theologici des Melchior Cano und die Methode des dogmatischen Beweises*, MSHTh 6 (Munich, 1925).

Langholm, O. *Economics in the Medieval Schools: Wealth, Exchange, Value, Money and Usury according to the Paris Theological Tradition, 1200–1350*, STGMA 29 (Leiden, 1992).

Leclerc, J. "'Pars corporis pape.' Le sacré collège dans l'ecclésiologie médiévale," in *L'homme devant Dieu. Mélanges offerts au Père Henri de Lubac*, vol. 2 (Paris, 1964), 183–98.

Lederer, S. *Der spanische Kardinal Johann von Torquemada. Sein Leben und seine Schriften* (Freiburg, 1879).

Leff, G. *Heresy in the Later Middle Ages: The Relation of Heterodoxy to Dissent c. 1250–1450*, 2 vols. (Manchester, 1967).

Le Goff, J. "Arbeit (Mittelalter)," *TRE* 3:626–35.

Leturia, P. "Maior y Vitoria ante la Conquista de América," *EE* 11 (1932): 44–82.

Levillain, P. "Jean XXII," *Dictionnaire de la papauté* (Paris 1994), 943–47.

Lewry, O. "Papal Ideas and the University of Paris, 1170–1303," in *The Religious Role of the Papacy: Ideals and Realities, 1150–1300*, ed. C. Ryan (Toronto, 1989), 363–88.

Little, A. G. *The Grey Friars in Oxford*, Oxford Historical Society 20 (Oxford, 1892).

Lowe, E. *The Contested Theological Authority of Thomas Aquinas: The Controversies between Hervaeus Natalis and Durandus of St. Pourçain*, Medieval History and Culture 17 (New York, 2003).

Lückerath, C. A. "Johannes XXII," *TRE* 17:109–12.

Madrigal Terrazas, J. S. *La eclesiología de Juan de Ragusa O.P. (1390/1443). Estudio e interpretación de su Tractatus de Ecclesia* (Madrid, 1995).

Maggiani, V. "De relatione scriptorum quorundam S. Bonaventurae ad Bullam 'Exiit' Nicolai III (1279)," *AFH* 5 (1912): 3–21.

Maier, A. "Annotazioni autografe di Giovanni XXII in codici vaticani," *RSCI* 6 (1952): 317–32.

———. "Zur Textüberlieferung einiger Gutachten des Johannes de Neapoli," *AFP* 40 (1970): 5–27.

Mäkinen, V. *Property Rights in the Late Medieval Discussion on Franciscan Poverty*, RThAM, Bibliotheca 3 (Leuven, 2001).

Maleczek, W. "Das Papsttum und die Anfänge der Universität im Mittelalter," *RöHM* 27 (1985): 85–143.

Mandonnet, P. "La canonisation de Saint Thomas d'Aquin 1317–1323," *Mélanges Thomistes*, BiblThom 3 (Le Saulchoir, 1923), 1–48.

Manselli, R. *Spirituali e Beghini in Provenza*, Studi Storici 31–34 (Rome, 1959).

———. "Bernard Gui face aux Spirituels et aux Apostoliques," in *Bernard Gui et son monde*, CFan 16 (Toulouse, 1981), 265–78.

Massi, P. *Magistero infallibile del papa nella teologia di Giovanni da Torquemada*, Scrin-Theol 8 (Torino, 1957).

Mathes, F. A. "The Poverty Movement and the Augustinian Hermits," *AAug* 31 (1968): 5–154; 32 (1969): 5–116.

May, W. H. "The Confession of Prous Boneta. Heretic and Heresiarch," in *Essays in Medieval Life and Thought Presented in Honor of Austin Patterson Evans*, ed. J. H. Mundy, R. M. Emery, and B. N. Nelson (New York, 1955), 3–30.

McIntyre, J. "Aquinas, Gratian and the Mendicant Controversy," in *Proceedings of the Ninth Congress of Medieval Canon Law, Munich, 13–18 July 1992*, ed. P. Landau and J. Müller (Vatican City, 1997), 1101–35.

McKeon, P. R. "The Status of the University of Paris as *Parens Scientiarum*: An Episode in the Development of Its Autonomy," *Spec* 39 (1964): 651–75.

Merl, O. *Theologia Salmanticensis. Untersuchung über Entstehung, Lehrrichtung und Quellen des theologischen Kurses der spanischen Karmeliten* (Regensburg, 1947).

Miccoli, G. *Francesco d'Assisi. Realtà e memoria di un'esperienza cristiana* (Torino, 1991).

———. "Considerazione sulle stimmate," in *Franciscana I (Bolletino della Società internazionale di studi francescani)* (Spoleto, 1999), 101–21.

Michaud-Quantin, A. "Le droit universitaire dans le conflit parisien de 1252–1257," *StGra* 8 (1962): 577–99.

———. *Universitas. Expressions du mouvement communautaire dans le moyen âge latin*, L'église et l'état au moyen âge 13 (Paris, 1970).

Minnich, N. "The Healing of the Pisan Schisma (1511–13)," *AHC* 16 (1984): 59–192.

Moorman, J. R. *The Grey Friars in Cambridge* (Cambridge, 1938).

———. *A History of the Franciscan Order from Its Origins to the Year 1517* (1968; repr. Oxford, 1998).

Morard, M. "Une source de Saint Thomas d'Aquin: Le deuxième Concile de Constantinople (553)," *RSPTh* 81 (1995): 371–89.

———. "Thomas d'Aquin lecteur des conciles," *AFH* 98 (2005): 211–365.

Morris, E. S. "The Infallibility of the Apostolic See in Juan de Torquemada," *Thom* 46 (1982): 242–66.

Moynihan, J. A. *Papal Immunity and Liability in the Writings of the Medieval Canonists*, AnGr 120 (Rome, 1961).

Mulchahey, M. M. *"First the Bow is Bent in Study . . .": Dominican Education before 1350*, STPIMS 132 (Toronto, 1998).

Nieto, J. C. *El renacimiento y la otra España. Visión cultural socioespiritual*, Travaux d'humanisme et Renaissance 315 (Geneva, 1997).

Nimmo, D. *Reform and Division in the Medieval Franciscan Order: From Saint Francis to the Foundations of the Capuchins*, BSC 33 (Rome, 1987).

Nold, P. *Pope John XXII and His Franciscan Cardinal: Bernard de la Tour and the Apostolic Poverty Controversy* (Oxford, 2003).

Noreña, C. G. *Studies in Spanish Renaissance Thought* (The Hague, 1975).

Oakley, F. "Almain and Major: Conciliar Theory on the Eve of the Reformation," *AHR* 70 (1964/65): 673–90.

———. *The Conciliarist Tradition: Constitutionalism in the Catholic Church 1300–1870* (Oxford, 2003).

Oberman, H. A. *"Facientibus quod in se est Deus non denegat gratiam.* Robert Holcot OP and the Beginning of Luther's Theology," *HThR* 55 (1962): 317–42.

O'Brien, C. "El enigma de Francisco de Araújo," *CTom* 89 (1962): 221–66; 90 (1963): 3–79.

Oeyen, C. "Döllinger und die pseudo-kyrillischen Fälschungen," in *Geschichtlichkeit und Glaube. Zum 100. Todestag Johann Joseph Ignaz von Döllingers (1799–1890)*, ed. G. Denzler and E. L. Grasmück (Munich, 1990), 341–90.

Paciocco, R. *"Sublimia negotia." Le canonizzationi dei santi nella curia papale e il nuovo Ordine dei Frati Minori* (Padova, 1996).

Paravicini-Bagliani, A. *Il trono di Pietro. L'universalità del papato da Alessandro III a Bonifacio VIII* (Rome, 1996).

Pástor, E. "S. Bonaventura: biografo di S. Francesco? Contributo alla 'questione frances-cana,'" *Doctor Seraphicus* 27 (1980): 83–107.

Pennington, K. *Pope and Bishops: The Papal Monarchy in the Twelfth and Thirteenth Centuries* (Philadelphia, 1984).

Pérez, J. *Isabelle et Ferdinand. Rois Catholiques d'Espagne* (Paris, 1988).

———. *Histoire de L'Espagne* (Paris, 1996).

Peuchmaurd, M. "Le prêtre ministre de la parole dans la théologie du XIIᵉ siècle (Cano-nistes, moines et chanoines)," *RThAM* 29 (1962): 52–76.

———. "Mission canonique et prédication. Le prêtre ministre de la parole dans la que-relle entre mendiants et séculiers au XIIIᵉ siècle," *RThAM* 30 (1963): 122–44, 251–76.

Plöchl, W. *Geschichte des Kirchenrechts*, 5 vols. (Vienna-Munich, 1953–67).

Post, G. "Alexander III, the *Licentia docendi* and the Rise of the Universities," in *C. H. Haskins Anniversary Essays in Medieval History*, ed. C. H. Taylor and J. L. La Monte (Boston, 1929), 255–77.

———. "Parisian Masters as a Corporation, 1200–1246," *Spec* 9 (1934): 421–45.

Prügl, T. *Die Ekklesiologie Heinrich Kalteisens OP in der Auseinandersetzung mit dem Basler Konziliarismus*, VGI 40 (Paderborn, 1991).

———. *Antonio da Canara: De potestate pape supra Concilium Generale contra errores Basiliensium*, VGI 41 (Paderborn, 1996).

———. "Der häretische Papst und seine Immunität im Mittelalter," *MThZ* 47 (1996): 197–215.

———. "Patristische Fundamente der Ekklesiologie des Thomas von Aquin," in *Väter der Kirche. Ekklesiales Denken von den Anfängen bis in die Neuzeit (Festgabe H. J. Sieben)*, ed. J. Arnold, R. Berndt, and M. W. Stammberger (Paderborn, 2004), 745–69.

Ratzinger, J. "Zum Einfluß des Bettelordensstreites auf die Entwicklung der Primats-lehre," in J. Ratzinger, *Das neue Volk Gottes. Entwürfe zur Ekklesiologie* (Düsseldorf, 1969), 49–71.

Reinhardt, K. *Bibelkommentare spanischer Autoren (1500–1700)*, vol. 1 (Madrid, 1990).

Reusch, F. H. *Die Fälschungen in dem Traktat des Thomas von Aquin gegen die Griechen Opus-culum contra errores Graecorum ad Urbanum IV.*, Bayerische Akademie der Wissen-schaften/Historische Klasse: Abhandlungen, vol. 18, 8 (Munich, 1889), 676–742.

Rieden, O. von. "De S. Francisci Assisiensis stigmatum susceptione. Disquisitio historico-critica luce testimoniorum saec. XIII," *CFr* 33 (1963): 210–66, 392–422; 34 (1964): 5–62, 241–338.

Ries, M. "Heiligenverehrung und Heiligsprechung in der Alten Kirche und im Mittel-alter. Zur Entwicklung des Kanonisationsverfahrens," in *Bischof Ulrich von Augsburg, 890–973. Seine Zeit—sein Leben—seine Verehrung. Festschrift aus Anlaß des tausendjähri-gen Jubiläums seiner Kanonisation im Jahre 993*, ed. M. Weitlauff (Weissenhorn, 1993), 143–67.

Ríos Fernández, M. "El primado del romano pontífice en el pensamiento de Huguccio de Pisa decretista," *Comp* 6 (1961): 42–97.

———. "El primado del romano pontífice en el pensamiento de Huguccio de Pisa de-cretista," *Comp* 11 (1966): 29–67.

Rodríguez, P. "'Infallibilis'? La respuesta de Santo Tomás de Aquino. (Estudio de la termi-nología 'infallibilis-infallibiliter-infallibilitas' en sus tratados 'de fide,'" *ScrTh* 7 (1975): 51–123.

Sägmüller, J. B. *Die Thätigkeit und Stellung der Cardinäle bis Bonifaz VIII historisch-canonistisch untersucht und dargestellt* (Freiburg, 1896).

Schatz, K. "Papsttum und partikularkirchliche Gewalt bei Innozenz III. (1198–1216)," *AHP* 8 (1970): 61–111.

———. *Vaticanum I, 1869–1870*, 3 vols. (Paderborn, 1992–94).

Schenk, M. *Die Unfehlbarkeit des Papstes in der Heiligsprechung*, ThomStud 9 (Freiburg/ Schw., 1965).

Schlageter, J. "Die Kirchenkritik des Petrus Johannis Olivi und ihre ekklesiologische und soziale Relevanz," *FS* 65 (1983): 19–34.

———. "Die Entwicklung der Kirchenkritik des Petrus Johannis Olivi von der 'Quaestio de altissima paupertate' bis zur 'Lectura super Apocalypsim,'" *WiWei* 47 (1984): 99–131.

Schleyer, K. *Anfänge des Gallikanismus im 13. Jahrhundert. Der Widerstand des französischen Klerus gegen die Privilegierung der Bettelorden*, HS 314 (Berlin, 1937).

Schlosser, M. *Lucerna in caligonoso loco. Aspekte des Prophetie-Begriffes in der scholastischen Theologie*, VGI 43 (Paderborn, 2000).

Schmitt, C. "Fraticelles," *DHGE* 18:1063–1108.

———. "Fraticelli," *DIP* 4:807–21.

Scholz, R. *Die Publizistik zur Zeit Philipps des Schönen und Bonifaz' VIII.* (Stuttgart, 1903).

Seckler, M. *Instinkt und Glaubenswille nach Thomas von Aquin* (Mainz, 1961).

Sheehan, M. W. "The Religious Orders, 1220–1370," in *The History of the University of Ox-ford*, vol. 1, *The Early Oxford Schools*, ed. J. I. Catto (Oxford, 1984), 192–221.

Sieben, H. J. "Lateran IV," *TRE* 20:481–89 (Lateran I–IV).

———. *Die Konzilsidee der Alten Kirche* (Paderborn, 1979).

———. *Die Konzilsidee des lateinischen Mittelalters (847–1378)* (Paderborn, 1984).

Sommer-Seckendorff, E. M. F. *Studies in the Life of Robert Kilwardby O.P.*, DH 8 (Rome, 1937).

Stickler, A. M. "Alanus Anglicus als Verteidiger des monarchischen Papsttums," *Sa* 21 (1959): 346–406.

Stieber, J. W. *Pope Eugenius IV, The Council of Basel, and the Secular and Ecclesiastical Au-thorities in the Empire: The Conflict over Supreme Power in the Church*, SHCT 13 (Leiden, 1978).

Stockmeier, P. "Die causa Honorii und Karl Josef von Hefele," *ThQ* 148 (1968): 405–28.

———. "Der Fall des Papstes Honorius und das Erste Vatikanische Konzil," in *Hundert Jahre nach dem Ersten Vaticanum*, ed. G. Schwaiger (Regensburg, 1970), 109–30.

Strika, Z. *Johannes von Ragusa (†1443). Kirchen- und Konzilsbegriff in der Auseianandersetzung mit den Hussiten und Eugen IV.* (Augsburg, 1998).

Tapia, J. "La vida y la obra de Melchor Cano, marco de su reflexión eclesiológica," *AnAn* 36 (1988): 11–76.

Tarello, G. "Profili giuridici della questione della povertà nel francescanesimo prima di Ockham," in *Università degli studi di Genova. Annali della facoltà di giurisprudenza*, vol. 3 (Milan, 1964), 338–448.

Teeuwen, M. *The Vocabulary of Intellectual Life in the Middle Ages* (Turnhout, 2003).

Tellechea Idígoras, J. I. *El arzobispo Carranza y su tiempo*, 2 vols. (Madrid, 1968).

———. "El proceso del arzobispo Carranza," in *Historia de la Inquisición en España y América*, ed. J. Pérez Villanueva and B. Escandell Bonet, vol. 1 (Madrid, 1984), 556–98.

Thomas, W. *La represión del protestantismo en España, 1517–1648* (Leuven, 2001).

———. *Los protestantes y la Inquisición en España en tiempos de la Reforma y Contrarreforma* (Leuven, 2001).

Tierney, B. *Foundations of the Conciliar Theory: The Contribution of the Medieval Canonists from Gratian to the Great Schism* (Cambridge, 1968).

———. *Origins of Papal Infallibility, 1150–1350: A Study on the Concepts of Infallibility, Sovereignty and Tradition in the Middle Ages*, SHCT 6 (Leiden, 1972).

———. "A Scriptural Text in the Decretales and in St. Thomas: Canonistic Exegesis of Luke 22:32," *StGra* 20 (1976): 361–78.

———. "'Only the Truth Has Authority': The Problem of 'Reception' in the Decretists and in Johannes Turrecremata," in *Law, Church, and Society: Essays in Honor of Stephan Kuttner*, ed. K. Pennington and R. Somerville (University Park, PA, 1977), 69–96.

Torrell, J.-P. *Initiation à saint Thomas d'Aquin* (Fribourg-Paris, 1993).

Traver, A. G. "Rewriting History? The Parisian Secular Masters' *Apologia* of 1254," *History of Universities* 15 (1997/99): 9–45.

———. "Thomas of York's Role in the Conflict between Mendicants and Seculars at Paris," *FrS* 57 (1999): 179–202.

Tugwell, S. "The Evolution of Dominican Structures of Government. I. The First and Last Abbott," *AFP* 69 (1999): 5–60.

———. "The Evolution of Dominican Structures of Government. II. The First Dominican Provinces," *AFP* 70 (2000): 5–109.

———. "The Evolution of Dominican Structures of Government. III. The Early Development of the Second Distinction of the Constitutions," *AFP* 71 (2001): 5–182.

———. "The Evolution of Dominican Structures of Government. IV. Election, Confirmation and 'Absolution' of Superiors," *AFP* 72 (2002): 27–159.

Turley, T. P. "Infallibilists in the Curia of Pope John XXII," *Journal of Medieval History* 1 (1975): 71–101.

———. "The Ecclesiology of Guido Terreni" (diss., Cornell University, 1978).

Uribe, F. *Introduzione alle fonti agiografiche di san Francesco e santa Chiara d'Assisi (secc. XIII–XIV)* (Assisi, 2002).

Vallin, P. "Travail," *DS* 15:1208–37.

Valois, N. "Jacques Duèse, pape sous le nom de Jean XXII," in *Histoire littéraire de la France*, vol. 34 (Paris, 1914), 391–630.

Vauchez, A. *La sainteté en Occident aux derniers siècles du moyen âge d'après les procès de canonisation et les documents hagiographiques*, BEFAR 241 (Rome, 1988).

————. "Autour de la stigmatisation de saint François," *RMab* 5 (1994): 270–74.

Villoslada, R. G. *La Universidad de Paris durante los estudios de Francisco de Vitoria O.P. (1507–1522)*, AnGr 14 (Rome, 1938).

Walz, A. "Von Cajetans Gedanken über Kirche und Papst," in *Volk Gottes (Festgabe J. Höfer)* (Freiburg, 1967), 336–60.

————. "Papst Johannes XXII. und Thomas von Aquin. Zur Geschichte der Heiligsprechung des Aquinaten," in *St. Thomas Aquinas, 1274–1974: Commemorative Studies*, vol. 1 (Toronto, 1974), 29–47.

Watt, J. A. "The Early Medieval Canonists and the Formation of Conciliar Theory," *IThQ* 24 (1957): 13–31.

————. "The Theory of Papal Monarchy in the Thirteenth Century," *Tr* 20 (1964): 179–317.

————. "The Constitutional Law of the College of Cardinals: Hostiensis to Johannes Andreae," *MS* 33 (1971): 127–57.

Weakland, J. E. "John XXII before His Pontificate, 1244–1316: Jacques Duèse and His Family," *AHP* 10 (1972): 161–85.

Weijers, O. *Terminologie des universités au XIIIᵉ siècle* (Rome, 1987).

————. *Le maniement du savoir. Pratiques intellectuelles à l'époque des premières universités (XIIIᵉ–XIVᵉ siècles)* (Turnhout, 1996).

Weitz, T. A. *Der Traktat des Antonio Roselli "De conciliis ac synodis generalibus." Historisch-kanonistische Darstellung und Bewertung* (Paderborn, 2002).

Wilms, H. *Der Kölner Universitätsprofessor Konrad Köllin*, QFGDO o.s. 39 (Cologne, 1941).

Wittneben, L. E. *Bonagratia von Bergamo. Franziskanerjurist und Wortführer seines Ordens im Streit mit Papst Johannes XXII*, SMRT 90 (Leiden, 2003).

Wittreck, F. *Geld als Instrument der Gerechtigkeit. Die Geldrechtslehre des Hl. Thomas von Aquin in ihrem interkulturellen Kontext* (Paderborn, 2002).

Zerbi, P. "L' 'ultimo sigillo' (Par. XI, 107). Tendenze della recente storiografia italiana sul tema delle stigmate di S. Francesco. A proposito di un libro recente," *RSCI* 48 (1994): 7–42.

Zeyer, R. *Die theologische Disputation des Johannes de Polliaco zur kirchlichen Verfassung* (Bern, 1976).

Zimara, C. "Einblicke in die Unterrichtsweise des Franz de Vitoria O.P.," *DT(Fr)* 24 (1946): 429–46; 25 (1947): 192–224, 255–89.

Xiberta, B. M. *De scriptoribus scholasticis saeculi XIV ex ordine Carmelitarum* (Louvain, 1931).

————. *Guiu Terrena, Carmelita de Perpinya* (Barcelona, 1932).

Index of Names

Abate, G., 71n50
Alanus Anglicus, 77n87
Albert the Great, 16, 75n70, 78n90
Alexander IV, Pope, 10
Alexius, Saint, 70n46
Alfaro, J., 74n66
Almain, Jacques, 44
Amann, F., 103n80
Andrés, M., 94n2
Antoninus of Florence, Saint, 32, 86n49
Araújo, Francisco de, 55–56, 103n79
Azcona, T. de, 94n2

Backes, I., 76n82
Balthasar, K., 80n6
Báñez, Dominicus, 53–55, 57, 102n68, 102n71
Barrientos García, J., 103n74
Bartoli, M., 85n40
Bartoli Langeli, A., 84n31
Bataillon, L.-J., 70n45, 73n58, 74n67, 98n40
Bataillon, M., 94n4
Bäumer, R., 98n37, 101n64
Baumgarten, P. M., 103n80

Bazàn, C., 78n89
Becker, H. J., 85n39
Belda Plans, J., 97n32, 98n39, 99n48, 102n67, 103n74
Bellarmine, Robert, Saint, 57, 105nn87–88
Beltrán de Heredia, V., 90n75, 94n1, 94n3, 95n6, 97n26, 97n32, 100n56, 102n67, 103n76
Benedict XI, Pope, 33
Benedict of Nursia, Saint, 70n46
Bentley, J. H., 94n4, 98n40
Berengar of Landora, 4
Berg, D., 69n35
Bernard Gui, 27, 82nn24–25
Bernstein, A., 69n39
Betti, U., 79n98, 86n50
Beuchot, M., 95n15
Bihl, M., 73n61
Binder, K., 90n75, 101n62
Bischof, F. X., 75n74
Bonagratia of Bergamo, 28–29
Bonagrazia of St. John in Persiceto, 26
Bonaventure, 6, 7, 11–14, 20, 25–27, 70n46, 71n49, 71n51, 72n56, 79n1, 81n11

Ulrich Horst, O.P., is emeritus senior professor and director of the Grabmann Institute at the University of Munich. He is the author of a number of books, including *Papst, Konzil, Unfehlbarkeit* and *Unfehlbarkeit und Geschichte*.